International Perspectives on James Joyce

edited by

Gottlieb Gaiser

The Whitston Publishing Company
Troy, New York
1986

Copyright 1986
Gottlieb Gaiser

Library of Congress Catalog Card Number 85-51201

ISBN 0-87875-312-5

Printed in the United States of America

International Perspectives on James Joyce

Acknowledgments

Some essays in this book appeared originally in journals. Grateful appreciation of permissions granted to republish the revised essays is hereby acknowledged.

Peter Egri, "A Portrait of the Artist as a Caricaturist: Picasso, Joyce, Britten," in: *Comparative Literature Studies* 19 (1982), No. 2, pp. 97-120.

Sonja Bašić, "Joyce's Fire and Ice: The Reader of 'Ulysses' between Involvement and Distanciation," in: *Studies Romanica et Anglica Zagrabiensia* 26 (1981), No. 1/2, pp. 367-395.

Contents

Preface

When I attended my first James Joyce Symposium in Dublin in 1977, I was a student in my third year at a university, with a reader-response background and an immense love of a book I first had read only a year before: *Ulysses.* Then I wanted to meet all those famous professors who had written all those famous books on Joyce: "Joyceans," as they chose to call themselves. After that week at Trinity College I knew for sure that I'd never, never be a Joycean. Scholars had I expected, fans I met. They all loved Joyce, patting the backs of his books, caressing every single page, every line, every curve of every letter, French if the Master willed. For He was there. With a hundred little ants—or earwigs?—piling up a dungheap to preserve the letter, burying the message. Shauns and Shems in a univocal adoration of their guru, polishing the halo they had forged in the smithy of their woeful, wilful exile. "Methodology" was crushed to a four-letter word, any approach beyond close reading and biographical criticism caused a shudder like the sacrilegious act of a ghoul.

Seven years later, at the Frankfurt symposium, the scene had changed. They were still there, our old new critics and our cheerleaders, with superb and blunt readings and biographical background information straight from the horse's mouth. But they were no longer pre-dominant. They were figures in a carpet which displayed the whole range of possible approaches to literature, both traditional and post-traditional. And Joyce's works shifted from the undisputed centre of the literary world to the more appropriate place of an outstanding paradigm of modern literature, which deserved special attention from all points of view, opening up the Joyce universe to more universal contexts—an idea which must be incomprehensible to a "real" Joycean.

But I had already been reconciled with the Joyce community a few years before, away from the big symposia, in a place with nothing specially "Joycean" about it, in a setting as picturesque as a guide book may want it to be: a fortress rising on a rock, amidst pine-woods and palm trees, flowering hibiscus and agaves, lemon trees and scenting myrtle; and beyond a steep creek the ancient city of Dubrovnik, with the saint and the canon keeping their anachronistic guard. This is the view from the Inter-University Centre of Postgraduate Studies, a unique insitition which allows academics from East and West to establish contacts and discuss all kinds of issues from their different backgrounds. It was here that Morton Levitt and Ivo Vidan organized a Joyce seminar from 11th to 29th May 1981. The Dubrovnik "Joyce Studies" proved extremely rewarding for all its thirty participants (from eleven countries) because, unlike the symposia, the small scale of this seminar favoured a very casual and spontaneous relationship between resource persons and students, which were about equal in number. As a consequence, the presentations were supplemented with lively, often essential discussions in which the students took an active part.

It is from this seminar that the volume in hand originates. All its contributors participated in the Dubrovnik "Joyce Studies," as lecturers or students. Many of the papers collected here have been presented in a more or less elaborated version, but they all have been considerably revised or rewritten in the light of the subsequent discussions or new insights. Unfortunately, we had to reject almost as many papers as we finally could accept.

The division of this volume in two parts, in a way, reflects the difference in the approaches of Eastern and Western scholars at this seminar. Most Eastern research persons presented papers on comparative subjects, and the presentations that dealt with Joyce's texts as such showed a preference for analogy, context, and overall views, always connected with a clear sense of history. The Western lecturers, on the other hand, paid special attention to textual detail and mostly focused on certain aspects or chapters of Joyce's texts. But as both kinds of approaches are complementary, their encounter proved to be most fruitful. The most controversial subject of these "Joyce Studies," however, did not find its way into this volume: the problem of a(?) narrator in *Ulysses*. The opposing views of Franz Stanzel and Morton Levitt had triggered off a discussion in which all participants, vehemently at times, had engaged from the first to the last night. But a number of books on narration in

Ulysses have appeared since, so that this discussion, unlike the contributions contained in this volume, isn't as much up to date now as it was a few years ago.

Finally, I'd like to acknowledge the share of Carl Eichelberger in this book, who had started as my co-editor, but was forced to withdraw from this project due to other commitments. Steve Gilles from Konstanz helped me to polish up the English of some of the essays, and Bernard Benstock never got tired of encouraging me and offering his assistance. My greatest thanks, however, are addressed to the contributors of this volume, who have diligently met an early deadline and never got impatient, when the publication of their essays was delayed again and again.

Konstanz, August 1985   Gottlieb Gaiser

Abbreviations

References to Joyce's works are cited parenthetically within the body of the paper, using the following abbreviations:

CW   *The Critical Writings of James Joyce,* ed. Ellsworth Mason and Richard Ellmann, (New York: Viking Press, 1959).

D   James Joyce, *Dubliners,* ed. Robert Scholes [cons. Richard Ellmann.] (New York: Viking Press, 1967).

FW   James Joyce, *Finnegans Wake,* (London: Faber & Faber, 1939).

Letters   *Letters of James Joyce,* vol, I, ed. Stuart Gilbert, (New
I, II, III York: Viking Press, 1965), vols, II, III, ed. Richard Ellmann, (New York: Viking Press, 1966).

Portrait James Joyce, *A Portrait of the Artist as a Young Man,* (Harmondsworth: Penguin Books, 1960).

SH   James Joyce, *Stephen Hero,* ed. John J. Slocum and Herbert Cahoon, (New York: New Directions, 1963).

U   James Joyce, *Ulysses,* (New York: Random House, 1961).

TEXTUAL ANALYSES

Through a Cracked Looking-glass: Sex-role Stereotypes in *Dubliners*

Suzette A. Henke
Binghamton, New York U.S.A.

At the time he was composing *Dubliners,* Joyce was fond of envisaging himself as an "Irish Zola" (*Letters* II, 137). In a 1904 letter to Constantine Curran, he declared that his short-story collection would "betray the soul of that hemiplegia or paralysis which many consider a city" (*Letters* I, 55). It would hold up to his fellow citizens a "nicely polished looking-glass" of moral opprobrium and offer a caustic, multi-dimensional mimesis of sex-role stereotypes in Ireland.[1] Throughout *Dubliners,* Joyce satirizes an authoritarian power structure defended by blustering and impotent males. Women provide a translucent screen on which men act out melodramatic scripts or engage in bizarre, narcissistic behavior. Like so many of Joyce's works, *Dubliners* reiterates the theme of patriarchal futility. The men of Dublin struggle to defend the law and the word; they desperately adhere to logocentric principles, though reason and logic founder in a haze of inebriate confusion.[2]

The women of *Dubliners,* even more than the men, are clearly depicted as societal victims. Only three of the tales in Joyce's collection—"Eveline," "Clay," and "A Mother"—have women as protagonists. In most of the stories, female characters are identified as the wives, sisters, mothers, or lovers of men. They are condemned to involuntary celibacy by their own timidity and fear, or to loveless marriages and altruistic motherhood. Subservient to fathers and patriarchal husbands, women are doomed to vent personal frustration through shrewish and manipulative behavior.

In *Dubliners,* as in life, it is all too easy to "blame the victim." Critics have shown a disturbing tendency to relegate the women in Joyce's short-story collection to stereotyped categories of female behavior, be it passive or predatory. They sometimes fail to take into account Joyce's subtle and elusive sense of irony, as well as his pervasive disdain for soul-destroying Irish institutions. All too often, the women of *Dubliners* have been maligned, misapprehended, or simply ignored. In the past several years, however, feminist interpretation has encouraged a radical reconsideration of Joyce's fictional creations. His female characters appear in a more compassionate and sympathetic light when situated within the context of Irish social and historical forces. In all the tales in this collection, Joyce portrays the lesser reality of female life faithfully and with broadly satirical strokes.

I.   *Childhood and Initiation*

The beginning of *Dubliners* is oddly sterile and womanless. Joyce depicts a dessicated Garden of Eden inhabited by a fallen race whose maternal center has been erased, lost to memory, and eradicated from the mind of the child-narrator who appears in the text as a self-generating character. Maternal separation is the background of his emerging consciousness, the wound or scar that "unmans" him even before he has developed a sense of individuation. The perpetual gap in the narrative is the unnamed loss of a mother never mentioned—a symbolic absence àt the heart of a barren world.

Joyce's inaugural story, "The Sisters," is dominated by the shadow of an unseen partriarch, a phallic lawgiver whose physical deterioration and mental paralysis were abruptly terminated by a fatal stroke. The boy in the tale has apparently been captivated by the mesmerizing name of the Father. His "impressionable" mind resembles an Aristotelian *tabula rasa,* an unformed wad of clay to be molded in the hands of a slightly demented and spiritually impotent patriarch.

Barred by paternal authority from self-defining utterance, the child writhes in a world of silence and isolation. He does not speak but curiously ponders the contradictory "grown-up" voices that have appropriated the powers of language. The boy tries to sublimate passion in futile, animal gestures: "I crammed my mouth with stirabout for fear I might give utterance to my anger" (*D* 11). Because he is incapable of naming the father who has died and betrayed him, he reverts to a semiotic system of bodily maneuvers. He is left alone to ponder the impenetrable ellipses of adult discourse that obscure the identity of a Father-God that failed.[3]

In quest of a paternal surrogate, the orphaned boy has submitted to rigorous training in the kind of casuistry that destroyed his tutor. Yet it is he who functions as "confessor" to the drooling prelate in a dream that forbodes a reversal of power. As a paralyzed spectre, the dead priest confesses his sins of agnosticism, hypocrisy, and "simony" to the terrified child. For the first time, the old man is identified as a simoniac guilty of foisting a canon of outmoded ecclesiastical principles onto his impressionable charge. He has sinned against his disciple by luring him into a trap of Jansenist scrupulosity. Though the priest can mimic the most august of Church Fathers, he has evidently lost faith in the dogma that he preaches. His stance is hypocritical, his tutelage a game. The chalice he dropped apparently symbolized the terrifying gap between belief and clerical duty. With his faith in sacramental absolution shattered, Father Flynn could no longer "atone for" the haunting doubts that finally drove him mad.

As in traditional myth, the impotent patriarch must be killed in order that the young—and the simple—may survive. Joyce calls attention to Father Flynn's sisters in the title of the story, despite their seemingly peripheral role in the narrative. Nannie and Eliza are ignorant and ill-educated, naive, and somewhat fatuous. They employ malapropisms, talk about "rheumatic wheels" and the *Freeman's General,* and superstitiously proclaim that James's "life was, you might say, crossed" (*D* 17). The women, however, feel sympathy for their brother, whom they tried to shield from the assaults of a hostile world: "We wouldn't see him want anything while he was in it" (*D* 16). The first version of "The Sisters" is more explicit about Father Flynn's arrogance: "He had an egoistic contempt for all women-folk and suffered all their services to him in polite silence" (*D* 247).

When women in the story attempt to speak, their words are reduced to vacuous gibberish. Deprived of power and logocentric control, they cannot master the language of the dominant society and must function as servants to the cultural imperatives that circumscribe their lives. Female utterances belong to the little language of social banter and "polite" conversation—a discourse that tends to be euphemistic and evasive.

Poor deaf Nannie is "wore out" from catering to her brother's idiosyncrasies and from serving as a female drudge. Like a classical fate or a figure out of Dante, this wizened, battered old woman points upwards and repeatedly beckons to the terrified child. Her "mutterings" and elocutionary failures so distract the boy that he almost forgets to notice the silent corpse laid out before him.

It is significant that the child's aunt cannot bring herself to utter the word "die" and cloaks the act in dramatic mystery: "Did he . . . peacefully?" she asks. Death is obscured by euphemistic language until the reality fades into a static verbal icon.   The vocabulary of prettiness and tidiness reduces the priest to an aesthetic object, a decorous and decorative artifact. "No one would think he'd make such a beautiful corpse" (*D* 15). If we recall St. Thomas Aquinas' definition of beauty as "that which is pleasing to the sight," we begin to understand the sisters' unconscious sentiment of pleasure and relief at their brother's demise.   Freed from the intrusions of patriarchal authority, the survivors celebrate a wake that releases them from deep-seated hostility and allows them to admire the priest safely crystallized in a non-threatening, photographic tableau.

If Nannie and Eliza are contemporary versions of the New Testament figures Martha and Mary, their brother is portrayed as a parodic Lazarus with little potential for resurrection. The moribund Father Flynn could hardly be aroused from his sedentary torpor and, in the last years of his life, seemed only to respond to the pleasurable stimulus of *High Toast* snuff. Death comes as a climax to protracted paralysis—a condition that may, ironically, have been symptomatic of tertiary syphilis.[4]

It is clear that the sisters project their own sense of spiritual liberation onto Father Flynn's death. "He's gone to a better world," chirps Eliza, mouthing consoling clichés. "He had a beautiful death, God be praised" (*D* 15). Released from nurturant obligations imposed by family ties, the sisters unconsciously exult in their newfound independence. They ludicrously describe the dead man as a "beautiful corpse" and see in his pallid visage a figure of repose: "he looked that peaceful and resigned" (*D* 15).

Though obviously mocking sentimental religious rhetoric, Joyce shows us two women whose simple faith and charity protect them from authoritarian engulfment. Oblivious of the

Draconian complexities that tormented their brother, Nannie
and Eliza minister to his needs without succumbing to dementia.
They respond to the priest's truculence with beef-tea and conversation; and they survive, like Anna Livia in *Finnegans Wake,*
to serve the "communion" of sherry and crackers at his wake.

If Father Flynn's life was "crossed" and "disappointed,"
it is largely because of the self-defeating nature of his "orgulous"
vocation. The logocentric pursuit of authority is bound to be
disappointing, simply because one can never learn enough to
penetrate the mysteries of ecclesiastical discourse—a language
which is deliberately obscure, hermetic, and impenetrable.
The patient's frustrated desire for power and discipleship makes
him a Luciferian figure, portrayed in the oblique light of Blake's
Urizen rather than the comforting penumbra of the "Daedalian"
artist.

The "queer old josser" of "An Encounter" casts still
another shadow of the failed patriarch who tries to lure an
adolescent to religious or physical perversion. Fired by a
"cowboy and Indian" notion of heroic prowess, the boy and
his friend Mahony go off to seek adventure at the mysterious
Dublin Pigeon House. Their initiation into manhood is frustrated
by a disturbing encounter with a pederast. Circling around
fetishes of "white hands" and "beautiful soft hair," the tramp
conjures up hypnotic images of virginal nymphettes, then rises,
apparently to masturbate. The romantic heroines of Wild West
tales and American detective stories are suddenly revealed in
their pornographic potential. The titillating *machismo* of male
aggression and female vulnerability degenerates into homoerotic
perversion, as the "wild sensations" of youth become the
obsessions of senility. At some level, both the narrator and
his companion recognize, but never fully acknowledge, that an
aggressive code of male prowess can degenerate into sexual
dementia.

In "Araby," the protagonist, grown slightly older, turns
from homoerotic to heterosexual preoccupations. Perched precariously on the brink of erotic expression, he sublimates
burgeoning physical desire beneath sentimental fantasies of
an ideal, chivalric love. The boy's *inamorata,* simply identified
as "Mangan's sister," is portrayed as a perfect romantic heroine.
Shadowy and elusive, she plays the role of seductive temptress,
with swinging dress and a "soft rope" of hair suggestive of
fetishistic entrapment. Her appearance inspires Wordsworthian

rapture, though she is little more than the shadow of a dream—a "brown figure" stalked each morning in a gesture of ritual pursuit. The young woman becomes a goddess shrouded in mystery; her adored icon is detached from the real world and kept safe from mundane defilement. It soon becomes clear that the narrator is enamored not of Mangan's sister, but of her sanctified image, which he cherishes untainted in his heart. In the tradition of courtly love, this modern-day knight has been entranced by an older woman, an eroticized virgin who becomes the focal point of sacerdotal obeisance. Like Sir Galahad, he bears his chalice of devotion "safely through a throng of foes" (*D* 31).

In all the ardor and confusion of adolescent obsession, the narrator fails to recognize the intense sexuality sublimated by ritual homage. Shyly, he admits: "my body was like a harp and her words and gestures were like fingers running upon the wires" (*D* 31). The musical simile, borrowed from Coleridge's "Aeolian Harp," represses a strong desire for tactile stimulation—for the "wires" of the boy's newly-awakened phallic consciousness to be fondled by the delicate white hands of his beloved. The protagonist longs for sensuous contact, and his language is saturated with Freudian *double entendre* when he imagines "fine incessant needles" of rain impinging on the earth's sodden labial beds (*D* 31). Like a monk struggling for self-control, he finds solace in a litany of ejaculations, repeatedly murmuring: *"O love! O love!"* (*D* 31).

When the distant object of his affection finally speaks to him, the boy is understandably disoriented. Mangan's sister twists a silver bracelet "round and round her wrist," unconsciously engaged in a ritual of hypnotic seduction. Trained in the body language of flirtation, she unwittingly tempts and taunts her suitor. The boy, in turn, focuses not on her face but on fetishistic projections of her figure—the "white curve of her neck," her illumined hair, a hand clutching the spike of the railing, and the "white border of a petticoat" (*D* 32). Luxuriating in Eastern enchantment, the narrator promises, like a knight of old, to bring back a "trophy" for his lady from the bazaar. As the adolescent girl vanishes from sight, she fades into the shadows, a wistful "brown-clad figure" of the boy's imagination (*D* 33).

When the protagonist finally reaches the "Chapel Perilous" of his chivalric quest, he discovers a deserted gallery bereft of oriental splendor. The stall attendant flirting with two English "gentlemen" exposes the vulgar side of eroticism, and the boy is forced to acknowledge the profane reality of his own infatuation: "I saw myself as a creature driven and derided by vanity; and my eyes burned with anguish and anger" (D 35). Earlier, he had envisaged himself as an heroic priest of love, secretly bearing the chalice of Platonic devotion through a vulgar, commercialized world. Now he realizes that he, too, is one of the vulgar. Try as he might, he cannot detach himself from the human comedy of sexual experience, and he chafes at the powerful illusions perpetuated in the name of romantic love.

Eveline Hill similarly dreams of escape and salvation through love, though her fantasies are imbued with all the exotic trappings of a late nineteenth-century ladies' magazine. She sees Frank as a modern-day Prince Charming who offers the promise of redemption and a life of marital bliss. Paradoxically, Eveline's suitor proves unable to rouse his sleeping beauty from her life-long trance of Dublin paralysis. Caught up in the excitement of "having a fellow," Eveline only begins to *like* Frank as an afterthought. This Dublin Desdemona floats on illusion and seeks emotional refuge in amorous dream. In her rife imagination, the "kind, manly, open-hearted Frank" takes on mythic stature. Absorbing the figures of Odysseus and Sir Galahad, he becomes just as unreal as the tales of the "terrible Patagonians" with which he amuses his betrothed.

If Eveline is bewitched by Frank's stories of adventure, she feels equally moved by "the pitiful vision of her mother's life," a vision that lays its "spell on the very quick of her being" (D 40). In contemplating her parent's battered servitude, Eveline has terrible premonitions of her own future. Those haunting words, "Derevaun Seraun!" (D 40), uttered in meaningless madness, call Eveline to a vocation of spectral dissolution. Self-sacrifice to the point of dementia will be the ghost's sole benefice. Wresting a promise of filial duty from her docile daughter, the dying mother seals Eveline in bonds of incestuous entrapment. The young girl, torn between the pledge of duty and the promise of happiness, conducts both sides of a mental debate whose outcome has been predetermined. The motif of "home" resounds like a metronome throughout the story, suggesting the compulsions that hypnotize consciousness and preclude the possibility of change. In this trial of the soul, Eveline serves as both prosecutor and defendant. She pits emotion and fantasy against the judgmental voice of conscience, a force that proves more powerful than arguments for personal freedom.

Thoroughly programmed in a life of altruism and self-effacement, Eveline lets her mind switch to "automatic pilot" by the end of the story. As she prays to God to show her "her duty," she reverts to the rhetoric of docility and allows the terms of her invocation to determine her course.[5] Resolute in her impotence, Eveline stares vacantly at her departing suitor. Nausea and bodily distress indicate mounting sexual anxiety. Elopement with Frank would mean, in realistic terms, a commitment to the kind of physical union that has never come within the purview of her disembodied dreams. In a moment of Freudian panic, Eveline imagines drowning in the "seas of the world," an oceanic symbol that displaces erotic terror. Conflating Frank with the father who "would drown her," she holds her ground "like a helpless animal" against her seducer (*D* 41).

Finally, Eveline is victimized not only by church and family, but by her own diminished self-esteem. Bound from childhood to a negative self-image, she can never extricate herself from the web of words woven around the sacrosanct Irish family. In this incestuous world of psychic imprisonment, the docile girl becomes surrogate spouse to a tyrannical "Da" and is sacrificed on the altar of filial devotion. Clearly, Eveline is destined to repeat the sado-masochistic patterns of her mother's life—"that life of commonplace sacrifices closing in final craziness" (*D* 40).

II.   *Courtship and Marriage*

"Two Gallants," "The Boarding House," and "A Little Cloud" form a courtship and marriage trilogy in which Joyce deals with various stages of adult sexual repression. In several of these stories, the frustrated Dubliner turns his own failure or pent-up rage against those who are even more oppressed, socially and economically, than he. The sexes are pitted against one another in an adversary relationship, with each trying to take advantage of the other's weakness and vulnerability. All of life is a sexual competition, and neither gender has a market on sex-role exploitation.

The woman of "Two Gallants" is thinly-sketched, but none-theless pitiable in her gullible naiveté.[6] A country lass who, like Nora Barnacle, came to the city to work as a "slavey," the young girl is buxom and ingenuous to the point of caricature. "Frank rude health glowed in her face, on her fat red cheeks and in her unabashed blue eyes. Her features were blunt. She had broad nostrils, a straggling mouth which lay open in a contented leer, and two projecting front teeth" (D 55-56). The girl's porcine nostrils and "contented leer" suggest simple-mindedness, if not stupidity. In contrast to the rude dairyman who once courted this country lass, the sweat-laden Corley cuts a fine figure and appears to have "a bit of class," despite his "large, globular and oily" head. Impressed by this "gay lothario," the young woman agrees to sexual abasement. She brings Corley cigarettes and fine cigars, eagerly provides him with Sunday sex and, at the end of the evening, "pays" a sovereign to retain his favor.

Corley is portrayed as a pedestrian Don Juan, bragging of his exploits as the bold conqueror of servant girls. He despises those middle-class women "off the South Circular" who demand entertainment and refuse to "pan out." The only one he re-members with fondness was predictably driven to "the turf" of prostitution. All women, he implies, resemble race-horses, whom males bet on to win or lose. And in most of Dublin society, women are definitely the losers. Even the lowest man on the Dublin totem pole can at least give thanks that he was not created female.

Lenehan, for his part, derives voyeuristic satisfaction from Corley's adventures, as he mentally re-enacts the amorous scene while downing a plate of peas. Substituting food for sex, he takes keen pleasure in a homoerotic reconstruction of his friend's sexual conquest. Lenehan alleviates the depression of "his own poverty of purse and spirit" through "Cinderfella" fantasies of redemption by a rich woman: "He might yet be able to settle down in some snug corner and live happily if he could only come across some good simple-minded girl with a little of the ready" (D 58).

The title of the story is painfully ironic. Of Joyce's two "gallants," one triumphs in fantasy, the other in actuality, over an ignorant, licentious, lower-class female. The woman is obviously Corley's social and sexual victim, enthralled by her lover's urban sophistication.   Exploited by every stratum of Dublin society, this country lass looks forward to a bleaker future than either of her predators—especially if she should be caught by the "master" in the act of filching sovereigns.[7]

In "The Boarding House," as in "Two Gallants," Joyce exposes Dublin courtship as little more than organized prostitution.   Romance is a ritual debased by greed, and both sexes are guilty of invidious moral simony.   Predatory roles are reversed in this tale, as two women connive in the conquest of an ingenuous male.   Mrs. Mooney, *The Madam,* is hardly more attractive than Corley.   A calculating and determined woman, she deals with moral problems "as a cleaver deals with meat" (*D* 63).   Imagery of meat, execution, and sacrifice pervades the chapter.   Mrs. Mooney, the butcher's daughter, is on the prowl for a "staggering bob" or young calf to sacrifice on the altar of matrimony.   Doran is led like a lamb to the slaughter, despite an instinct that "urged him to remain free. . . . Once you are married you are done for, it said" (*D* 66).

Pretty Polly, a little "perverse Madonna," is left in her "wise innocence" to fend for herself.   Scheming to trap a gullible mate, she enjoys the sanction of her mother's approval.   But Polly, like Doran, is a victim of limited circumstances.   She knows she must choose between an ill-paid career as a typist and the comforts of middle-class marriage.   Her future is contingent on a random selection of down-and-out boarders, only one of whom appears eligible and gullible enough to be "caught."   Joyce satirically portrays cages within cages of constraint and unhappiness.   Polly chooses between Doran and a life of clerical drudgery.   In the game of chance that determines her future, the young girl's sole playing card is her body.   Claims of despoiled virginity and possible pregnancy are the trumps she uses to capture Doran in the sexual sweepstakes.

The timorous Doran is far too weak and pusillanimous to challenge the "weight of social opinion."   Tormented by guilt, and cowed by moral platitudes, Doran feels he must "make reparation" for his sexual misdemeanors.   He meekly yields to the threat of Dublin gossip and ecclesiastical censure.   Having struggled so hard for middle-class respectability, Doran resents his betrothed for her bad grammar, loose reputation, and lower-class origins.   "But what would grammar matter if he really loved her?" (*D* 66).   The irony, of course, is that Bob does *not* love Polly, or even like her.   He feels that he has been seduced by a virginal vamp, wrenched from the security of monkish celibacy, and forced to endure an ignominious liaison in punishment for a few moments of erotic delirium. "He had a notion that he was being had" (D 66).

Like so many of Joyce's Dubliners, Doran suffers from a limited imagination. He willfully colludes in his own victimization and, like Eveline before him, refuses to extricate himself from a situation of entrapment. Doran is finally vanquished by a deep-seated need for bourgeois respectability. He becomes the victim of his own puritanical sensibility, mentally yielding to the same moral sanctions that Mrs. Mooney plans to invoke in dissembled outrage. Bound to the strictures of Victorian propriety, Doran cannot envisage autonomous action. Fearful and passive, he takes refuge in implausible fantasies of literal flight: "He longed to ascend through the roof and fly away to another country where he would never hear again of his trouble" (D 67-68).

The hunting of Doran unfolds with such ritual regularity that Pretty Polly, doffing her mask of distress, almost forgets to "wait for" Bob's marriage proposal. All have acted their parts in a nineteenth-century melodrama of wounded honor and virginal violation. Mrs. Mooney succeeds in getting her daughter "off her hands" with a dowry of threats and coercion. Paradoxically, she never realizes that she is condemning her daughter to the same cycle of anxiety and frustration that characterized her own disastrous marriage. And Polly chooses a gullible mate in the image of dear old Dad. As we learn in *Ulysses,* Doran will be a henpecked, irascible, alcoholic spouse. On June 16, 1904, he is portrayed on a "periodical" binge of drinking and whoring in an effort to escape connubial dreariness. Through guileful seduction, Polly wins the "prize" of a timid, resentful groom. Under the direction of a stern, conniving matriarch, she manipulates herself and Doran into the trap of a life-long misalliance. Who is to say which will be unhappier, predator or victim? Once again, Joyce depicts a domestic cage housing luckless moral counterparts.[8]

"A Little Cloud" goes on to portray the kind of conjugal frustration that proves emotionally stultifying for both partners. Little Chandler is an Irish Walter Mitty, a diminutive figure who "gave one the idea of being a little man" (D 70). Chandler plays the role of henpecked husband, trapped in a submissive relationship to an aggressive, domineering spouse. There is more than a touch of self-indulgence about Chandler's romantic and "melancholic" temperament. Ignatius Gallaher and Lord Byron both serve as alter-egos in the dreams of this Irish poetaster. The effete and dandified Chandler resembles a transvestite Gerty MacDowell: "His hands were white and small his frame was fragile, his voice was quiet and his manners refined. He took the greatest care of his fair silken hair and moustache and used perfume discreetly on his handkerchief" (*D* 70). As in "Nausicaa," Joyce employs what Hugh Kenner describes as the "Uncle Charles Principle," whereby the "normally neutral narrative vocabulary" of the author is "pervaded by a little cloud of idioms which a character might use if he were managing the narrative."[9] Chandler's experiences are filtered through the cloying, unselfconscious tropes that clutter the mind of a would-be aesthete.

Chandler envisages himself as the kind of Irish poet that Joyce deliberately refused to be—a melancholic Celtic bard who transforms a dessicated Ireland into a land of fairy dreams. Despite his metaphorical mind and sporadic epiphanies, Chandler will never be able to extricate himself from sticky, romantic clichés. He lacks the clear, "unclouded" aesthetic eye that focuses on the realities of human experience. Lost in a haze of narcissism and self-deception, he will pipe the Celtic note in exaggerated, purple prose crafted to impress a British audience.

Chandler proves all the more fatuous in his sychophantic admiration of Gallaher, a second-rate journalist who defines "manly" prowess largely as a function of drinking, smoking, and womanizing. Monogamy, he claims, is a stale meal, and wedlock a "black sack" that precedes the hangman's noose. Gallaher treats women as morsels to be tasted and devoured or victims to be exploited in gigolo liaisons.

As Chandler returns to the prison-house of his marriage, he is tormented by feelings of envy and self-pity. But from Annie's point of view, this dreamy poet must seem a thoughtless and wayward spouse. He is late for tea and forgets to bring her package of coffee. What must life be like for Annie Chandler, whose consciousness the story never penetrates? The young wife is left alone at home with a demanding infant. She is relieved of child care only two hours a day and has no amicable contacts apart from her sister Monica. Annie is even more trapped than her husband. Chandler can drink whiskey and smoke with the boys, foster dreams of poetic eminence, and luxuriate in reveries of Celtic melancholy. But Annie must stay indoors, cook, clean and tend her baby. She has little adult company and no social outlet. All her concerns are focused on an over-protected son, her sole source of emotional gratification.

Because the story is told from Chandler's point of view, Annie is perceived entirely through her husband's "clouded" perspective. Coldly staring at his wife's photograph, he imagines piercing, defiant eyes that irritate and repel him. He searches for the rapture that might be found in the "dark Oriental eyes" of the Jewesses lauded by Gallaher. Chandler longs for the glamor of Eastern enchantment, but his demands on reality clearly exceed the possibilities of his character and situation. Inept and impractical, he is totally dependent on his wife's care, even if the life she has arranged is a "prim and pretty" model of middle-class respectability.

Chandler is tied to Annie in a pathological relationship of Oedipal dependency. Childlike and helpless, this "little man" agrees to play the role of son-husband to an authoritarian spouse—a *magna mater* who offers both domestic security and emotional bondage. Having bartered personal freedom for maternal solicitude, he inevitably feels resentment and sibling rivalry toward the child entrusted to his care. His newborn son has usurped its father's place and title in Annie's affections. Characteristically, Chandler tries to ignore the baby, whom he identifies solely in terms of the objective pronoun "it"—never "him" or "my son." In a moment of terror, he imagines what would happen "if it died" (*D* 84); but his anxiety is founded more on a fear of his wife's wrath than on the potential loss of the child.

Chandler has sought the security of a bourgeois household, complete with furniture purchased on the hire system and a screaming baby. Having created a domestic nest that turns out to be a prison, he now balks with envy at Gallaher's bachelor freedom. "Was it too late for him to try to live bravely like Gallaher?" he wonders (*D* 83). Ironically, it has *always* been too late for Chandler to escape the paralysis of Ireland. He is ill-equipped to deal with the real world and can only take refuge in romantic fantasies of Oriental adventure. Reading Byron's lyric "On the Death of a Young Lady," he apparently identifies with the grief-stricken poet mourning a woman's untimely death. Chandler would clearly prefer a maudlin corpse to a living spouse: reduced to a lump of lifeless clay, Annie would cease to threaten his virility. Unconsciously, he desires to defuse his wife's power by invoking the "narrow cell" of death. But the doleful cell merely reminds him of his own incarceration in a marriage that has made him a "prisoner for life."

And what about Annie? Is she no less a prisoner? Does her competence and realistic adaptation shelter her from emotional pain? The hatred in her eyes may, in fact, be a reflection of angry disillusionment with the impotent man she has married. Bound to a helpless, ineffectual dreamer, she transfers both spousal and maternal love to the "little mannie" she worships as a miniature Christ, "Mamma's little lamb of the world" (D 85). Marital frustration erupts in shrewish bullying, and romantic love gives way to a mother's idolization of her infant son.[10]

III. *Maturity and Adulthood*

In "Counterparts," Joyce peripherally depicts a Dublin marriage at a later stage of entrapment, when conjugal co-existence has ossified into a mutual reign of terror. Ada Farrington is described as "a little, sharp-faced woman who bullied her husband when he was sober and was bullied by him when he was drunk" (D 97). And from the evidence of the story, we may assume that Farrington is drunk most of the time. Caught in a dead-end job as a copy-clerk, a kind of human xerox machine, Farrington buries his anger in alcoholism and domestic violence.

If Chandler feels frustrated by the inequities of life, Farrington is moved to fantasies of atavistic brutality: "He felt strong enough to clear out the whole office singlehanded. His body ached to do something, to rush out and revel in violence" (D 90). When subjected to a tirade of abuse by his employer Mr. Alleyne, Farrington cannot resist making a fool of this "manikin" in the presence of Miss Delacour, "a stout amiable person" who responds with a smile of amusement. Farrington knows, however, that he will pay dearly for his impertinence. He is left feeling "savage and thirsty and revengeful, annoyed with himself and with everyone else" (D 92).

Women form an important part of the background of
Farrington's compulsive need to assert masculine prowess.
Drinking the dregs of his earnings from a pawned watch, he
stares lasciviously at a woman in the bar—a voluptuous and
exotic music-hall *artiste* dressed in peacock-blue muslin. He
imagines that she notices him and answers his gaze, but feels
disappointed when she leaves without a parting glance. Even
this faint erotic snub is sufficient to move Farrington to flex
his biceps before the company. An arm-wrestling contest with
the British "stripling" Weathers ends in further humiliation.
Having failed on all counts to "prove his manhood," the defeated
clerk returns home "full of smouldering anger and
revengefulness" (D 96). The pitiable final scene offers a classic
example of aggression-frustration displacement. All the rage
and disappointments of the day are paid for by Farrington's
son Tom, the only person that the furious man can control.

If marriage has its pitfalls in *Dubliners,* celibacy seems
to offer a more dangerous trap of physical and spiritual isolation.
"Clay" and "A Painful Case" give us portraits of a contented
spinster and a tormented bachelor, respectively. Maria's
ostensible self-sufficiency is clearly bred of illusion and
psychological repression. As Charles Peake observes, "Maria
is the only central character in *Dubliners* who appears satisfied
with her lot. Yet this is mere appearance: her insistence that
everything is 'nice' hides fundamental frustration."[11]

When Joyce finally allows us to explore the consciousness
of a woman, he exposes a sensibility oppressed by loneliness
but eager to adapt to diminished circumstances. From the
"Uncle Charles Principle," we might surmise that Maria is a
bit child-like and simple-minded—or perhaps infantilized by
her subservient position in the *Dublin by Lamplight* laundry.
Small and wizened, Maria is described in the language of folklore or fairytale. She "was a very, very small person indeed
but she had a very long nose and a very long chin" (D 99),
possibly suggestive of witch-like characteristics.[12]

Maria apparently "nursed" the two brothers, Joe and
Alphy, while they were growing up. Joe used to remark:
"Mamma is mamma but Maria is my proper mother" (D 100).
Having prematurely assumed domestic responsibilities, she
served as maternal surrogate well into her prime. By the time
her charges were ready to quit the nest, she found herself un-

marriageable. Rather than depending on those who had once depended on her, Maria accepts a position in a home for reformed prostitutes. As Joyce declared in a letter to Stanislaus, the shelter "is a wicked place full of wicked and lost women whom a kindly committee gathers together for the good work of washing my dirty shirts" (*Letters* II, 192). The institution resembles a prison where Maria is veritably incarcerated; she must beg permission even to spend an evening out. Though she assures herself that she likes her work, Maria has few sources of emotional gratification—a word of praise from the "genteel" matron and occasional opportunities to play "maiden aunt" to Joe's children. Insisting that "she didn't want any ring or man either," the lady protests too much to conceal her "disappointed shyness" (*D* 101).

Maria proves just as ineffectual as Little Chandler in dealing with the outer world. Like Joyce's earlier protagonist, she suffers from inveterate timidity. Shopping for plumcake becomes a major expedition, and she must summon all her energies to traverse the labyrinthine metropolis. Maria is so unused to contact with the opposite sex that casual remarks by a drunken gentleman in the tram throw her into complete confusion. Befuddled by his address, she leaves her cake behind in a gesture that evokes "shame and vexation and disappointment" (*D* 103-104).

Trained in a life of self-effacement, this "very small" person tries to diminish herself even further in social situations, though she is characteristically naive and bumbling in her child-like efforts to please. Maria joins the Hallows Eve communion with a certain amount of reluctance. She manages to make herself unwelcome at the festivities by putting in a good word for the estranged Alphy, then offers profuse apologies for arousing Joe's displeasure. The peacemaker finds herself helpless and intrusive. Significantly, Maria is the only adult to participate in the children's Halloween game. The clay she touches may be a portent of her death—or of the death-in-life that characterizes her service in the Protestant workhouse, where she is trapped in life-denying celibacy without the consolations of religious commitment.

Maria's aspirations are more amorous and worldly than she cares to admit. Blushing with modesty, she celebrates in song the aristocratic life of feudal elegance for which she secretly pines. Art gives her the nobility that life denies. Maria escapes into fantasies of "marble halls" where she lays claim to a double inheritance of wealth and love. It is no wonder that Maria forgets the second verse of Balfe's lyric.[13] Her own fate is so unlike that of Arline, the "Bohemian girl," that she cannot bring herself to imagine a medley of suitors and knights on bended knee. Does her Freudian slip suggest the repression of a long-lost love? Or is she merely too timid and demure to envision erotic bliss?

Whatever the motive, Maria forgets to sing the second verse and repeats the lyrics of the first. Her omission seems a tacit acknowledgment of future isolation. This Irish Cinderella will never be seduced by a Dublin Prince Charming. No suitors will seek the spinster's trembling hand; no knight will attempt to storm the fortified castle of her maiden heart. No one—not even Joe or Alphy—will "love her still the same" as they did when they were children. Dreaming of marble halls and ancient palaces, Maria is destined to return to the steam-laden halls of her own institutional vassalage.

If Maria is humble in her celibacy, James Duffy arrogantly clings to Nietzschean exile. "A Painful Case" presents a woman trapped in a stultified marriage and a man insistent on self-imposed alienation. Emily Sinico is one of the more sympathetic females portrayed in *Dubliners*. In her first meeting with Duffy, her dark blue eyes reveal "a temperament of great sensibility" and her astrakham jacket strikes a "note of defiance" against bourgeois propriety (*D* 109-110). Passionate and proud, Emily might well be expected to question the puritanical mores of "dear dirty Dublin."

It is remarkable that this sensitive matron is able to penetrate the carapace of Duffy's bachelor reserve and to touch a man so resolutely disdainful of communion with others. "He had neither companions nor friends, church nor creed" (*D* 109). Mrs. Sinico becomes mother and confessor to Duffy, who gradually bares his saturnine soul to her. Under her nurturance, his personality blossoms. "Her companionship was like a warm soil about an exotic. . . . This union exalted him, wore away the rough edges of his character, emotionalised his mental life" (*D* 111). Duffy, however, represses the emotional dimension of their liaison. He wants a muse rather than a lover and cannot accept Emily as a warm-blooded woman with erotic needs of her own. When she clutches his hand and passionately presses it to her cheek, she inadvertently destroys the illusion of detachment. Duffy, who lives "at a little distance from his body," is shocked by her effusive gesture. Convinced of his "soul's incurable loneliness," he insists that they break off their intercourse. "Every bond, he said, is a bond to sorrow" (D 112). Mrs. Sinico implicitly demands of Duffy warmth, compassion, and amorous fulfillment. But the bachelor is so frightened of physical intimacy that he denies his friend's emotional appeal and retreats into prudish propriety. A would-be superman, he chooses an austere, moralistic world of Nietzschean isolation, where he finds comfort in reading *The Gay Science* and *Thus Spake Zarathustra.*

Duffy reacts to the "painful case" of Emily's death with ludicrous self-righteousness, at first accusing the deceased woman of degrading him by her vulgar end: "He saw the squalid tract of her vice, miserable and malodorous. . . . Evidently she had been unfit to live" (D 115). Reversing roles with his one-time confessor, he plays the part of judgmental patriarch, refusing absolution to Emily's ghost. Only gradually does the lonely man begin to acknowledge responsibility for his friend's death. He has driven Emily to drink and despair, and he has driven himself to an empty, meaningless existence. "Why had he withheld life from her? Why had he sentenced her to death?. . . One human being had seemed to love him and he had denied her life and happiness: he had sentenced her to ignominy, a death of shame" (D 117).

Has Duffy experienced a genuine epiphany—a revelation of his wretchedness and the cruelty of his behavior? Or is this attitude of exaggerated self-abasement, in which he imagines himself a failed savior and virtual executioner, simply another mode of self-indulgence? As he moves from cold detachment to sentimentality and self-pity, he never seems to escape an invidious circle of narcissism.

Like an abandoned child, Duffy complains that "No one wanted him; he was an outcast from life's feast" (D 117). Having resolutely refused communion with others, he now discovers that Nietzsche's "feast of pure reason" provides the soul with carrion comfort. Gnawing on the bone of his own rectitude, he envies the "venal and furtive" lovers who celebrate the joys of erotic union. Duffy ends by acknowledging his chronic emotional starvation: "He felt that he was alone" (D 117). Stripped of pompous rhetoric and purple prose, he at last confronts the reality of existential isolation. His words have the force of both revelation and painful prophecy.[14]

IV. *Public Life*

In Joyce's three tales of "public life," women are conspicuous either for their absence or for their powerlessness in
relation to the dominant society.   They are excluded from
participation in the stagnant political life of Ireland, a world
of apathy and corruption satirically exposed in "Ivy Day in
the Committee Room."   Irish nationalism has obviously gone
to seed, and Dublin politics is little more than an excuse for
male camaraderie, idle talk, and endless rounds of stout.   Now
that Parnell is "dead and gone," the men feel free to sanctify
his memory through sentimental legends and nostalgic elegies.
They welcome a visit from King Edward VII, whose patronage
will mean an influx of money, though he is recognized as "a
bit of a rake" (*D* 132).   They apparently forget that Parnell,
the uncrowned king of Ireland, was deposed by a "fell gang
of modern hypocrites" for his liaison with Kitty O'Shea.   Only
Mr. Lyons points out the discrepancy, later reiterated in Joe
Hynes's saccharine verses at the end of the story.   Though
puerile and ingenuous, the elegy constitutes a moving tribute
to Parnell, whose ideals are presently betrayed by the senti-
mentalists bantering in the committee room.
It is clear from "Grace" that no woman need apply to
the deity for commercial salvation, either in this life or in the
next.   Mrs. Kernan is described as an "active, practical woman"
who "believed steadily in the Sacred Heart . . . but, if she was
put to it, she could believe also in the banshee and in the Holy
Ghost" (*D* 158).   For the Irish housewife, religion is a mixture
of domestic faith and fairy superstition.   She has evidently
been excluded from the male coterie that wields ecclesiastical
power and from an institution that celebrates the strategies
of mercantile success.
At the retreat sermon, Father Purdon betrays the spiritual
ideals of Catholicism when he describes the deity as a great
accountant in the sky and exhorts his listeners to be "straight
and manly with God" (*D* 174).   Jesus, he insists, was a compromising businessman eager to bargain with the "mammon of
iniquity."   Paradoxically, Catholicism becomes an affair of male

bonding, and religious observance has little to do with Christian humility or compassion. Cunningham proclaims that "our religion is *the* religion, the old, original faith" (*D* 166). And the Dubliners bitterly indict the convert Harford "as an Irish jew and an illiterate," even though "he had never embraced more than the Jewish ethical code" (*D* 159). The Church emerges as an exclusive men's club, a social organization that covertly sanctions bigotry and self-righteousness.

Perhaps the most pathetic example of a woman trying to break into a male-dominated power structure occurs in "A Mother." Mrs. Kearney, the protagonist of the tale, is a stubborn, self-willed matriarch who tries to live vicariously through her daughter Kathleen. As a young woman, she remained chilly and aloof, repressing her "romantic desires by eating a great deal of Turkish Delight in secret" (*D* 136-137). On the brink of spinsterhood, she chose to marry a bootmaker, whose humble and steady qualities would "wear better than a romantic person" (*D* 137). Mrs. Kearney has displaced her secret "romantic" ideas onto the lives of her daughters. She sends Kathleen to the Academy and employs an Irish tutor at home. A shrewd opportunist, she determines to take advantage of her daughter's Celtic name by encouraging association with the nascent Irish Revival.

The scheme succeeds when Kathleen is invited to accompany a series of concerts organized by the *Eire Abu* society. Mrs. Kearney ingratiates herself with Hoppy Holohan, the inept and scatterbrained secretary in charge of the program. But her facade of graciousness and lady-like gentility quickly erodes the moment she suspects that Kathleen might be cheated of her salary. Stubbornly defending her daughter's contractual rights, she insists that Kathleen refuse to perform without payment in advance. The Society, she is convinced, is trying to take advantage of Kathleen's social vulnerability: "They wouldn't have dared to have treated her like that if she had been a man" (*D* 148).

As an autocratic Irish matron, Mrs. Kearney mistakenly assumes that the tactics of stubborn manipulation she uses to control her family will prove effective in the larger world of Dublin society. She cannot see the value of tact, cooperation, or the kind of "team spirit" that sometimes demands compromise. Schooled exclusively in the art of domestic willfulness, Mrs. Kearney has never been a member of a male-dominated group. When she lapses into shrewish invective, her conduct becomes bizarre and inappropriate. Paradoxically, her staunch defense of Kathleen's financial rights may prove disastrous to the girl's future in the Irish cultural renaissance. Mrs. Kearney unwittingly condemns her daughter to the same repressions that she herself experienced in adolescence. As O'Madden Burke grimly predicts, the "scandalous exhibition" will put an end to "Miss Kathleen Kearney's musical career . . . in Dublin" (D 147).

Hoppy Holohan's final "put-down" is delivered in a tone of male condescension: "I thought you were a lady" (D 149), he says reproachfully. How dare Mrs. Kearney violate the public role of feminine docility expected of a married woman? Almost all the men present censure her irrational outburst as decidedly "unladylike." Her bold attempt to challenge the musical establishment proves short-sighted and futile. The petit-bourgeois impresario she assaults has the power to reject both Kathleen and her mother, and he has the backing of a large array of male cronies. "I'm done with you" (D 149), says Holohan triumphantly. His retort seems to imply that the Irish Revival has done with the hapless Kathleen, as well.

V. *"The Dead"—An Epilogue*

In his portrait of Gretta Conroy in "The Dead," Joyce fashioned the image of a passionate, nurturant, and life-giving female. For the first time, he celebrated in his fiction the rich, intuitive life of a woman modeled on Nora Barnacle. "The Dead," Richard Ellmann tells us, comprises "one of Joyce's several tributes to his wife's artless integrity. Nora Barnacle, in spite of her defects of education, was independent, unself-conscious, instinctively right. Gabriel acknowledges the same coherence in his own wife, and he recognizes in the west of Ireland, in Michael Furey, a passion he has himself always lacked" (JJ 249).

Gabriel Conroy is, at least in part, a figure of the arrogant Irish pedant Joyce might have become had he remained in his native country. A writer of book reviews and after-dinner speeches, Gabriel prides himself on his continental perspective and feels a bit ashamed of his Galway wife, whom his mother once described as "country cute." He compulsively protects his family from the hazards of nature by insistent recourse to galoshes, green shades, dumb bells, and stirabout. A minion of modern civilization, he betrays a deep-seated fear of exposure to the perilous fluidity of life, symbolized by the ruggedness of a western Irish terrain "beyond the pale" of urban amenities.

Gabriel hides in a psychological shelter of purple prose, a world of words that hinges on sentimentality and self-righteousness. Cut off from the unconscious, he successfully represses both instinct and passion, love and hate. Like T. S. Eliot's Sweeney, he can relate neither to heroic violence nor to erotic obsession. With a mixture of nostalgia and condescension, he contemplates two pictures of "the balcony scene in *Romeo and Juliet*" and of the "murdered princes in the Tower which Aunt Julia had worked in red, blue and brown wools when she was a girl" (*D* 186). The embroideries transform Renaissance tragedy into a "casual comedy" of the nineteenth-century drawing room. Sanitized, and robbed of cathartic effect, the scenes become part of a static memorial to Shakespearean drama. Though contemptuous of his aunts' Victorian life-style, Gabriel proves just as guilty as they of consigning both heroism and passion to the frame of aesthetic stasis.

Throughout the Christmas party, Gabriel is intent on constructing a viable shelter for his highly self-conscious and vulnerable ego. He carefully erects a scaffold of remarks and social banter that will enhance his fragile self-esteem. Despite erudition, civility, and intellectual sophistication, Gabriel considers every personal encounter a contest for psychological domination and, like the classic narcissist, harbors an ideal self-image that he obsessively imposes on society. He compulsively courts recognition and approval, and his after-dinner speech is a model of exhibitionism. Caught between arrogance and insecurity, Gabriel panders to an audience whom he secretly disdains for a "grade of culture" that "differed from his" (*D* 179). He worries about "airing his superior education" and quoting an esoteric allusion to Browning. Will his rhetoric be effective? How can he court the admiration of family and friends without alienating their doltish sensibilities?

All the world becomes a stage for Gabriel's narcissism. He perpetually bolsters his ego by denigrating other people, especially his wife, who "takes three mortal hours to dress herself" (*D* 177). Similarly, he tries to relegate Lily the serving-maid to diminutive female roles by treating her as a school-girl, a courting adolescent, or a pre-married woman. "We'll be going to your wedding one of these fine days" (*D* 178) he observes. Caught off guard by Lily's sarcastic retort that "the men that is now is only all palaver and what they can get out of you" (*D* 178), he attempts to make amends by offering the girl a compensatory coin of male patronage.

Though habitually condescending toward women, Gabriel is nonetheless sensitive to female opinion. Despite his annoyance with the nationalist Miss Ivors, he dares not "risk a grandiose phrase" with her. He never openly expresses his agitation, but indulges instead in mental exercises of self-vindication: "Of course the girl or woman, or whatever she was, was an enthusiast but there was a time for all things. Perhaps he ought not to have answered her like that. But she had no right to call him a West Briton before people, even in joke. She had tried to make him ridiculous before people, heckling him and staring at him with her rabbit's eyes" (*D* 190). In this tacit appeal to male privilege, Gabriel dismisses Miss Ivors as a childish female whose brashness has so "unsexed" her that she seems to belong to a third, un-namable gender. The rabid patriot is rhetorically transformed into a heckling rabbit, hopping about in irrational frenzy.

Gabriel, like a petulant child, saves his final thrust for last. In his pompous postprandial speech, he implicitly condemns Miss Ivors as a member of the "new and very serious and hyper-educated generation" that betrays traditional Irish hospitality (*D* 192). "Very good," he thinks, "that was one for Miss Ivors. What did he care that his aunts were only two ignorant old women?" (*D* 192). Gabriel will "put down" one woman by elevating two others who serve as pawns to balance the scales of his male indignation. He delights in traducing his enemy as "discourteous" and "hypereducated." Ironically, his indictment of a sceptical and thought-tormented age is largely an act of projection: Gabriel is obviously the most self-conscious figure in the story. Although he mourns the loss of a more "spacious" age "gone beyond recall," he is ill prepared to cherish the memory of an Irishman whose fame his wife Gretta cannot "willingly let die" (*D* 203).

Like Torvald Helmer in Ibsen's *A Doll's House,* Gabriel

sees his wife not as an individual with feelings and needs of
her own but as a static symbol feeling his creative imagination
"He asked himself what is a woman standing on the stairs in
the shadow, listening to distant music, a symbol of. If he were
a painter he would paint her in that attitude. . . . *Distant Music*
he would call the picture" (*D* 210). Shrouded in "grace and
mystery," Gretta becomes a model of feminine tranquility,
an impressionistic image of blue and bronze, blurred in a setting
of vague nostalgia. Gabriel refuses to acknowledge the world
of memory and desire stirred by Gretta's response to the Irish
folk song. Though *The Lass of Aughrim* clearly has auditory
impact on his wife, he translates her mood into a vapid visual
impression. Through his Whistleresque fantasy, he
characteristically distances himself from the emotive qualities
of the music and from its primitive, Celtic associations. Like
Stephen Dedalus, he freezes the moment and imposes the
"spiritual-heroic refrigerating apparatus" of art onto Gretta's
experience.

En route to the Gresham Hotel, Gabriel lavishes on his
spouse the masculine protection earlier refused by Miss Ivors.
Like Ibsen's Helmer, he luxuriates in dreams of romantic desire
summoning their "wild and radiant hearts to a new adventure"
(*D* 215). On the brink of erotic frenzy, Gabriel feels an overwhelming urge to seize, "crush," and "overmaster" Gretta in
a gesture of conjugal appropriation. His thoughts circle
neurotically around images of male dominance and female
submission, as he relishes the sweet victory of sexual conquest.
Gretta, however, is lost in a separate, inaccessible world of
amorous reverie. Her thoughts focus on Michael Furey, a boy
whose meteoric passion took the form of tragic self-sacrifice.
The Irish suitor who "died of love" offered the ultimate gift
of himself. In giving his life for the sake of a woman, Furey
became a Christ of love, taking permanent possession of Gretta's
heart.

For the first time, Gabriel is forced to recognize the
complex "otherness" of his wife's subjectivity. He feels shocked
to encounter an inaccessible past that flows into the present
and makes the dream of conjugal possession an impotent male
fantasy. Cuckolded by a dead man, Gabriel feels rage, then
pitiable confusion. As he is stripped of the bulwark of male
assumptions that has always sustained him, he begins to
acknowledge the narrowness and pettiness of his self-centered

vision: "A shameful consciousness of his own person assailed him. He saw himself as a ludicrous figure, acting as a pennyboy for his aunts, a nervous, well-meaning sentimentalist, orating to vulgarians and idealising his own clownish lusts" (D 219-20).

Humiliated by the ashes of burnt-out lust, Gabriel is shocked to confront the memory of a man whose passion flared with consummate ecstasy. Gretta once knew true "romance": "a man had died for her sake" (D 222). "Better pass boldly into that other world, in the full glory of some passion, than fade and wither dismally with age" (D 223). Touched by the living presence of Michael Furey, Gabriel begins to cast off his shell of egotistical self-absorption. He feels his identity "fading out into a grey impalpable world; the solid world itself . . . was dissolving. . . . The time had come for him to set out on his journey westward" (D 223).

The ending of Joyce's tale is finely ambiguous.[15] At the conclusion of "The Dead," the logocentric consciousness of the male swoons into a will-less world of semiotic process where birth and growth are balanced by their polar opposites, decay and death. Gabriel begins his "journey westward" and sinks into the primitive, repressed world of the unconscious. He goes to encounter a buried life heretofore denied by a willful and narcissistic ego.

Like Anna Livia Plurabelle, Gretta Conroy miraculously resurrects the shade of a dead man as a living, potent spirit. And like Molly Bloom, she draws the past into the present in the mode of impassioned memory. Revitalizing the ghost of her long-dead lover, Gretta gives mythic, poetic stature to a man whose life ended in tragic consummation. In contrast to the casual comedy enacted by the Dubliners, Gretta succeeds in endowing Ireland with heroic grandeur. In so doing, she makes possible the spiritual redemption of Gabriel, whose aesthetic pretensions have degenerated into the fatuities of l'homme moyen sensuel. Gretta proves to be the true "artist" of the tale, a woman whose imagination regenerates the past and gives birth to a romantic legend that inspires the final epiphany of the story. Gretta has captured the heroic world of love and violence "domesticated" by her aunts and "refrigerated" by her husband.[16]

By offering a vivid myth of salutary passion, Gretta resuscitates the moribund spirit of her husband, who will "announce" the message of life-in-death at the conclusion of

Dubliners. As mother and lover to both Michael and Gabriel, Gretta emerges as the first of Joyce's contemporary heroines— a woman whose naturalness and emotional vitality will later inform the female portraits of *Exiles, Ulysses,* and *Finnegans Wake.* In touch with the fluid rhythms of life and exposed to the primitive world of the unconscious, Gretta reveals an artistic potential that looks forward to the lyrical triumphs of Bertha Rowan, Molly Bloom, and Anna Livia Plurabelle.

Notes

[1] Engaged in controversy with Grant Richards over the publication of *Dubliners,* Joyce explained: "My intention was to write a chapter of the moral history of my country and I chose Dublin for the scene because that city seemed to me the centre of paralysis. I have tried to present it to the indifferent public under four of its aspects: childhood, adolescence, maturity and public life. The stories are arranged in this order. I have written it for the most part in a style of scrupulous meanness" (*Letters* II, 134). "It is not my fault that the odour of ashpits and old weeds and offal hangs around my stories. I seriously believe that you will retard the course of civilisation in Ireland by preventing the Irish people from having one good look at themselves in my nicely polished looking-glass" (*Letters* I, 63-64).

[2] In "*Dubliners*: Women in Irish Society," Florence Walzl examines Joyce's female characters within the context of Dublin culture and analyzes gender attributions operative in late nineteenth-century Ireland. She concludes that "when Joyce pits men against women in his tales, it can be proved that drastic economic and social pressures actually forced Dubliners into such situations of frustration, deprivation, and hostility. He spares neither sex. . . . That Joyce felt sympathy for women caught in restrictive social conditions is clear, but it is a sympathy often tempered by ironic dissection of feminine weakness or hypocrisy or sometimes biased by male ambivalence" (*Women in Joyce,* ed., Suzette Henke and Elaine Unkeless [Urbana: University of Illinois Press, 1982], p. 53).

[3] Phillip Herring, in "Structure and Meaning in Joyce's 'The Sisters,'" successfully anatomizes the "gnomonic nature of the story's language"—a

language filled with ellipses, hiatuses, silences, malapropisms, and empty, ritualistic dialogue. Ellipsis in *Dubliners*, he concludes, "has the effect of enlisting a reader as co-creator in the production of meanings that are in harmony with the author's political intentions" (*The Seventh of Joyce*, ed., Bernard Benstock [Bloomington: Indiana University Press, 1982], p. 135). According to Jean-Michel Rabaté in "Silence in *Dubliners*," the incomplete figure of the dead or absent father is inscribed in the text of *Dubliners*, "until finally everything will appear hinged on the silent name of the capitalised Father" (*James Joyce: New Perspectives*, ed., Colin MacCabe [Bloomington: Indiana University Press, 1982], p. 48).

[4]See Burton A. Waisbren and Florence L. Walzl, "Paresis and the Priest: James Joyce's Symbolic Use of Syphilis in 'The Sisters,' " *Annals of Internal Medicine*, 80 (June 1974), 758-62; J. B. Lyons, *James Joyce and Medicine* (New York: Humanities Press, 1974), pp. 84-91; and Zack Bowen, "Joyce's Prophylactic Paralysis: Exposure in *Dubliners*," *James Joyce Quarterly*, 19, No. 3 (Spring 1982), 257-273. Hugh Kenner emphasized the association of Nannie and Eliza Flynn with the biblical sisters Martha and Mary in his talk entitled "Signs on a White field," Eighth International James Joyce Symposium, Dublin, Ireland, June 17, 1982.

[5]John Paul Riquelme notes that "early in the story we have the impression of Eveline in meditation and of her process of mind as a logical, orderly procedure, though not a sophisticated one." As the tale progresses, however, narrative styles begin to shift erratically and gradually build toward "a climactic state of frenzy." Almost as "an admission that Eveline's state of mind is beyond the reach of referential language, the act of shifting styles *itself* represents that state of mind which cannot be rendered adequately through psycho-narration, quoted monologue, and narrated monologue" (*Teller and Tale in Joyce's Fiction* [Baltimore: The Johns Hopkins University Press, 1983], pp. 110-11).

[6]Florence Walzl observes that the girl in "Two Gallants" evokes "Christian and nationalistic types. She wears blue, the Virgin's colors, but as a slavey in a rich man's house, she recalls the legendary Cathleen ni Houlihan, the figure of Ireland, serving her English conquerors and betrayers. She is associated with a harp, the emblem of Ireland, on which patriotic tunes are played, but significantly it is a harp whose 'coverings' have 'fallen'" ("A Book of Signs and Symbols," *The Seventh of Joyce*, pp. 120-21).

[7]In response to the printer's objection to "Two Gallants," Joyce asked in a letter to Grant Richards: "Is it the small gold coin . . . or the code of honour which the two gallants live by which shocks him? . . . I would strongly recommend to him the chapters wherein Ferrero examines the moral code of the soldier and (incidentally) of the gallant" (*Letters* II,

132-33). In *Joyce's Politics* Dominic Manganiello explains that in Guglielmo Ferrero's book *L'Europa giovane* "the moral code of the soldier consists in arousing men's 'inert brutality.' Ferrero associates this militaristic activity, which he considered typical of the Germanic races, with the art of gallantry" (London: Routledge & Kegan Paul, 1980), p. 50. Manganiello makes a convincing case for attributing many of Joyce's early political enthusiasms to the work of authors such as Ferrero.

[8] As Florence Walzl explains, "the frustration of Dublin's women—a consequence of their dull, empty rounds of existence—results in a circular plot in which the evils of the first generation are visited upon the second." In both "Eveline" and "The Boarding House," "each girl makes a life choice that insures her a repetition of her mother's life." Walzl concludes: "As mothers, so daughters. It is clear in these stories that the situation of the first generation becomes the condition of the second and that mothers tend to transform their daughters into replicas of themselves" ("*Dubliners:* Women in Irish Society," pp. 47-49).

[9] Hugh Kenner, *Joyce's Voices* (Berkeley: University of California Press, 1978), p. 17.

[10] As Philip Slater points out in *The Glory of Hera,* in a household that is mother-dominant and father-avoidant, the woman tends to treat her son as a substitute husband. At times, she may relate to him as an idealized spouse; but such maternal devotion is often characterized by a "deeply narcissistic ambivalence." The mother "does not respond to the child as a separate person, but as both an expression of and a cure for her narcissistic wounds. Her need for self-expansion and vindication requires her both to exalt and to belittle her son, to feed on and to destroy him." Such a pattern of socialization results in a vicious cycle: "A society which derogates women produces envious mothers who produce narcissistic males who are prone to derogate women" ([1968; rpt. Boston: Beacon Press, 1971], pp. 33, 45). Clearly, this kind of male is evident in Joyce's *Dubliners.* Reacting against a formidable matriarchal figure, boys develop an unstable self-image that demands continual validation in the outer world. (Consider Jimmy Doyle, Ignatius Gallaher, Little Chandler, and Farrington). As adults, Irish males tend to flee the prison of a matrifocal household for the sanctuary of the pub and homoerotic companionship.

[11] C. H. Peake, p. 32.

[12] Florence Walzl, analyzing Maria as a typal paradigm, remarks that "the narrative modulates between Maria as a Virgin Mary figure—a 'peacemaker' and loving 'mother' to those she works with—and the figure of a Celtic witch in her physical appearance and troublemaking" ("A Book of Signs and Symbols," p. 120). Mary Reynolds believes that "the witchlike appearance of Maria . . . clearly owes something to the presence of another

virgin in *Inferno* 20, the prophetess Manto" ("The Dantean Design of Joyce's *Dubliners*, p. 125).

[13]Maria omits the following verse from Balfe's *Bohemian Girl*:

> I dream'd that suitors besought my hand,
>   That knights upon bended knee,
> And with vows no maiden heart could withstand
>   That they pledged their faith to me.
> And I dream'd that one of this noble host
>   Came forth my hand to claim;
> Yet I also dream'd, which charmed me most,
>   That you loved me still the same.

[14]In "'A Painful Case': The Movement of a Story through a Shift in Voice," Suzanne Katz Hyman offers an excellent analysis of the way in which Duffy uses language as a mode of logocentric control. He eschews emotional involvement "by structuring his world through rigorous linguistic means." A "walking embodiment of the Cartesian split," Duffy has recourse to the use of aphorism, cliché, and self-irony to achieve intellectual detachment and to force experience "into a prearranged mold." He manipulates language "to color and control experience so as to make it manageable." Finally, at the end of the story, "language gives way to silence." The tale culminates in two nonverbal images of venal lovers and a sinister, worm-like train. (*James Joyce Quarterly*, 19, No. 2 [Winter 1982], III, 115, 117-18).

[15]Richard Ellmann argues that Gabriel has achieved a sense of maturity and connection with all the living and the dead, a redemptive understanding of "interrelationship" and union (*JJ* 262). Similarly, Florence Walzl sees the story as a journey of development "from insularity and egotism to humanitarianism and love" ("Gabriel and Michael: The Conclusion of 'The Dead,'" *James Joyce Quarterly*, 4, No. 1 [Fall 1966] 17-31). Edward Brandabur, in contrast, diagnoses Gabriel as a neurotic victim of "compulsive sadomasochism" whose hostility towards his wife finds "an effective mythic and psychological structure in the story of Michael Furey" (*A Scrupulous Meanness* [Urbana: University of Illinois Press, 1971], p. 122). And Charles Peake, in less vehement terms, interprets the books's culminating paragraph as a "critical evocation of resignation to spiritual death" (p. 53). Mary Reynolds shares this assessment when she compares the "vision of a frozen Ireland" at the end of "The Dead" to Dante's evocation of a frozen world in the final canto of the *Inferno*. "The closing sentence of 'The Dead' recalls frozen Cocytus, Dante's last image of despair" ("The Dantean Design of Joyce's *Dubliners*," p. 124).

[16]In "What Is a Woman . . . a Symbol of?," Tilly Eggers discusses Gretta Conroy as "a composite portrait of woman in *Dubliners*" and an archetypal "symbol of all women." Gretta's "past and Michael Furey are alive in her. The woman implies that memory of her 'girlself' (*E* 122) renews her woman self and that expression of independence affirms a connection." "Joyce indicates individuality, presence, and completeness by expressing commonality, absence, and partiality; one term calls forth its opposite, for their meanings are interdependent" (*James Joyce Quarterly*, 18, No. 4 [Summer 1981], 389, 392-93).

The Mysteries of *Ulysses*

Bernard Benstock
Tulsa, U.S.A.

As Leopold Bloom spends his twilight hour along Sandymount Strand, he observes a casual stroller on an evening walk,
and is tempted to turn the observation into a work of literature: *"The Mystery Man on the Beach,* prize titbit story by Mr
Leopold Bloom" (*U* 376)*. Title and author are fixed, but the
titular hero goes unnamed, because Bloom never gets far enough
in his creative impulse to decide on a fictional name and because
he does not know the stroller's actual name. "Here's this nobleman passed before" (*U* 375), he had commented, attaching
a mock designation for the gentleman as he continues to
speculate on his post-prandial constitutionals, his eating capacity,
and even his bank balance (all fictions within a fiction). A
relative stranger to the Sandymount area, Bloom has been sufficiently observant to spot the mystery man/nobleman coming
and going. Gerty MacDowell, a resident of the region, has seen
him before, as has her friend Cissy Caffrey. Although "wrapt in
thought" (*U* 354) when he passes—and therefore not quite as
observant—Gerty "scarce saw or heard" (*U* 354) either her
companions or the stroller, yet she knows him well enough to
know that he is no mysterious figure (much less a nobleman).
Her subliminal thoughts assure us that she is acquainted generally
with where he lives ("the gentleman off Sandymount green" (*U*
354), and that he bears a certain resemblance to her own father
("that Cissy Caffrey called the man that was so like himself"
U 354). In her comparison with Mr. MacDowell, his daughter
seems to know that our mystery man is a sober citizen: "You

---

*All quotations from James Joyce, *Ulysses*, New York: Random
House, 1961.

never saw him anyway screwed but still and for all that she would not like him for a father . . . or his carbuncly nose with the pimples on it and his sandy moustache a bit white under his nose" (*U* 354). Gerty creates her "fiction" out of what are presumably observable facts, yet despite the closeness of her depiction it is apparent that she too does not know his name.

He passes by twice observed and then vanishes into hypothesis, only to resurface in the most fictional of fictions as an emanation in "Circe," one of at least four-score of pursuers after Bloom, collectively known as THE HUE AND CRY, at the tailend of the pursuit and listed as *the mystery man on the beach* among the substantial minority of the unnamed, along with such "mystery men" as *The Nameless One, The Citizen, Whatdoyoucallhim, Strangeface, et al.* The absence of a named identity alone provides dozens of mysteries in James Joyce's *Ulysses,* many of them necessarily unsolvable. Paramount, of course, is the misnamed "M'Intosh," since he presumably appears more than once, and also because the attachment of a false identity compounds the mystery several times over. Bloom makes the immediate association of one mysterious figure with another when he parallels his "nobleman" with "that fellow today at the graveside in the brown macintosh" (*U* 376). This mysterious personage has been labeled "The Man in the Macintosh" by critical convention and has attracted a great deal of speculation since *Ulysses* became the fascinating puzzle of the professors. He has been "identified" in terms of Joyce's previous fictions (the James Duffy of "A Painful Case"), as Joyce himself, symbolically as Death, the number 13, the Christ of the Last Supper, metaphorically as the poet James Clarence Mangan, mystically as the personification of invisibility (akin to Turko the Terrible), and spiritually as the Dear Departed, the Walking Dead. Although we may not have a close-up of him, carbuncles and pimples and all, quite a dossier has been collected from internal evidence, as he is tracked through the Ulyssean day. What we can be most certain about Mr. M'Intosh is that his name is not M'Intosh—but with somewhat less certainty than that the name of the boy in "An Encounter" is not Smith.

Bloom himself expounds on the mysteriousness of this quintessential mystery man at the first encounter:

> Now who is that lankylooking galoot over there in the macintosh? Now who is he I'd like to know? Now, I'd

give a trifle to know who he is. Always someone turns
up you never dreamt of. (*U* 109)

Except for his unusual garb *M* (let *M* stand for the Mystery Man
M'Intosh) is characterized only by Bloom's choice of descriptive
epithets, a *lankylooking galoot.* Yet Joe Hynes, the journalist
who will create the fiction-out-of-facts, does nothing constructive
to augment the dossier when he asks, "do you know that fellow
in the, fellow was over there in the. . ." (*U* 102)—by presenting
the blank space for Bloom to fill in, Hynes only obfuscates the
mystery. *M* immediately vanishes from the gravesite—indeed has
already vanished, as Hynes's *"was* over there" indicates, and
Bloom makes as much of the missing *M* as he did of his
mysterious appearance:

Where has he disappeared to? Not a sign. Well of all
the. Has anyone here seen? Kay ee double ell. Become
invisible. Good Lord, what became of him? (*U* 102)

Except that, as in the case of the nobleman, there are *two* eye-
witnesses, one might even doubt the existence of the mysterious
stranger.
    Appearance/disappearance/reappearance: at the end of
the Wandering Rocks *M* materializes as one more such pedestrian
in the busy city, not just one of thirteen, but one out of the
entire population of the city of Dublin ("In Lower Mount
street a pedestrian in a brown macintosh, eating dry bread,
passed swiftly and unscathed across the viceroy's path" (*U 254*).
Now we know that the macintosh is *brown* (later corroborated
by Bloom), and although no further description of the man
himself is given, facets of his circumstances can be recuperated
from the narrative account. The state of his finances and the
state of his mind come into serious question: the way he feeds
himself and the unheeding dodging in front of the horses lead
us to assume that we have encountered one of life's unfortunates,
a poor looney (Bloom will eventually reveal that what he fears in
old age is becoming an "aged impotent disenfranchised rate-
supported moribund lunatic pauper," *U* 725). *M*'s presence at
the grave of someone he may not even have known (if he is
unknown to two of Dignam's acquaintances, what chance is there
that he was well-acquainted with Dignam?) suggests a certain
aimlessness to his wanderings through Dublin. *M* conveniently

falls into the classification of a demented vagabond.

In "Sirens" Bloom corroborates that *M*'s macintosh at Glasnevin was brown, and also seems to assume that the man was feebleminded. Thinking about the croppy boy and the British officer disguised as a priest ("All the same he must have been a bit of a natural not to see it was a yeoman cap. Muffled up," *U* 290), he shifts his thought to: "Wonder who was that chap at the grave in the brown mackin" (*U* 290). Is it the association with *muffled up* or with *a bit of a natural* that leads Bloom's thoughts to *M*?

When *M* makes his third and final appearance (in the flesh), he is the subject of discussion among several of the drinkers at Burke's pub, and it can be assumed that he passed or paused by the open door within sight of Bloom and the others. The confusion of conversations—ten of them went from the hospital to the pub, and there are several conversations going on simultaneously when *M* is commented on—consists of the following:

> Golly, whatten tunket's yon guy in the mackintosh? Dusty Rhodes. Peep at his wearables. By mighty! What's he got? Jubilee mutton. Bovril, by James. Wants it real bad. D'ye ken bare socks? Seedy cuss in the Richmond? Rawthere! Thought he had a deposit of lead in his penis. Trumpery insanity. Bartle the Bread we calls him. That, sir, was once a prosperous cit. Man all tattered and torn that married a maiden all forlorn. Slung her hook, she did. Here see lost love. Walking Mackintosh of lonely canyon. Tuck and turn in. Schedule time. Nix for the hornies. Pardon? See him today at a runefal? (*U* 427)

The last sentence responds to Bloom's identification of this particular vagrant as the one he saw at Dignam's funeral, and this is only the second time during the day that he has spotted *M*. Is there sufficient reason, however, to assume that Bloom can now make a positive identification, or does the chance glimpse of a brown macintosh and the attendant talk of the man as a lunatic cause Bloom to draw an approximate—but not necessarily exact—conclusion?

The nature of the cross-purpose conversation(s) is enough for the basic identification of the brown macintosh and presumably other peculiar garments, yet neither Bloom nor Hynes, who saw him in broad daylight, ever commented on any other aspect of his "wearables." The undernourished look of the tramp (Dusty Rhodes) causes comment among the medical students, and if he is indeed a known looney whom they have named Bartle the Bread, the association with the eater of dry bread in Wandering Rocks appears safe. The medicals, however, are talking about someone they know from their work at the Richmond Asylum, either this particular person or someone that he reminds them of. In any case they are sure of their diagnosis: sexual frustration and grief due to the death of the man's wife, and a consequent decline from once having been a prosperous citizen. An anticipation of this condition can be found in the "love list" offered as a side-commentary to the narrative of Cyclops: "The man in the brown macintosh loves a lady who is dead" (*U* 333). A composite portrait of a case history has taken sufficient shape through these appearances and references to *M* to serve as prima facie evidence.

M's "afterlife" in *Ulysses* consists of three variations: in Circe he is conjured up as an aspect of psychological fantasy, performing for Bloom in characteristic fashion by appearing quite suddenly (unmiraculously *"through a trapdoor,"* *U* 485) and as suddenly disappearing (shot out of a cannon)—a circus performer! And since Bloom has inadvertently been guilty of misnaming him, he turns the tables and doubly denounces him: "Don't you believe a word he says. That man is Leopold M'Intosh, the notorious fireraiser. His real name is Higgins" (*U* 485). And in Eumaeus he has his own permanent mis-attribution, having his name as M'Intosh appear in the pink edition of the *Telegraph*. Finally, in Ithaca, Bloom is seen to be still involved with his "selfinvolved enigma" (*U* 729) of "Who was M'Intosh"—the very wording of the sentence itself a patent error.

Even the medical students who presumably observed *M* in the Richmond Asylum are not forthcoming with a real name, and without that name not only are we never sure of his identity, we are also not sure that there is only *one* man-in-the-macintosh passing through *Ulysses*. The major burden of proof is with Bloom, who cannot be trusted to have identified accurately the same person in the dark doorway of the pub after a lapse of over ten hours, when the sole item of identification is the brown macintosh. Such a piece of clothing is, on the one hand, overly common in Dublin, but on the other, somewhat rare on a sunny day in June during a period of drought. (Malachi Mulligan and Alec Bannon have had their good clothes drenched that evening for want of a macintosh, since like most sane Dubliners they brought along no protection from the rain, while a parallel looney, Cashel Boyle O'Connor Fitzmaurice Tisdall Farrell, has tramped the city streets with dustcoat and umbrella). For Bloom the basic question still remains, Who was the Man in the Macintosh, since his preoccupation is with the figure he saw at the grave, but for the rest of us the question might well be, Who are the *Men* in the Macintosh? Despite the rather neat overlap of bits of evidence, there is no certainty that in a city that contains Farrell and Breen, two or three vagabonds wearing brown macintoshes may not be on the loose.

Bloom is unusually fascinated by "mystery men" (Joe Hynes considers Bloom a "bloody dark horse himself," *U* 335), yet one particular mysterious event fails to excite him: determining the author of the "U.P.: up" postcard sent to Denis Breen. With all of Dublin to choose from (at least all of the adult male population likely to perpetrate the offense), Bloom immediately narrows down the possibilities to a mere two: "I'll take my oath that's Alf Bergan or Richie Goulding. Wrote it for a lark in the Scotch house" (*U* 160). Bloom's method of elimination could hardly satisfy a scientific detective like Sherlock Holmes—when Bloom scrutinizes W. B. Murphy he is quite intense in "Sherlockholmesing him up" (*U* 636)—but the problem that is of earthshaking importance to Breen is negligible to Bloom. It is not the particular *individual* in this case that concerns him, but the *type*, that typical prankster who spends most of his time in pubs and is capable of just so trivial a lark. Bloom has ample opportunity during the afternoon to engage in "Sherlockholmesing" both Bergan and Goulding, and the latter during their meal at the Ormond seems totally oblivious of either Breen or the postcard, while the former at Barney Kiernan's laughs himself silly over the incident. Bloom never pronounces a verdict, but during his imaginary encounter with Mrs. Breen in Nighttown, Bergan intrudes, dogging Denis Breen's steps and ejaculating "U.P.: Up" (*U* 446), followed by Goulding—who is again oblivious to Breen. We can assume that as far as Leopold Bloom is concerned the case is closed—a very minor mystery at best. (Molly Bloom is even less concerned: although Bloom has told her about the postcard, she is much more intent on Breen's habit of getting into bed with his muddy boots on).

The postcard itself remains something of an enigma, all the more so since nowhere in *Ulysses* is its message ever explicated, and no one seems the least concerned with speculating about its "meaning." The assumption is that all those involved (sender, receiver, receiver's wife, and others who have been vouchsafed a glimpse of the card or orally presented with its wording) are confident that the letters and words in their particular semantic construction are universally understood, and that Breen has every reason—even if he were "reasonable"—to be offended. Yet only once is the reader present when the card is openly displayed: Mrs. Breen shows it to Bloom, whose "reading" of it produces an interrogative "U.P.?" (*U* 158). The conventions of printed texts conceal as well as reveal, and Mrs. Breen's rejoinder to Bloom's question is simply, "U.P.:up she said," (*U* 158). Is her "up" a supplemental explication, or is Bloom's "U.P." a condensed form, vocally avoiding the repetition contained in the message? All subsequent versions of the concise text have the duplication, either because all four letters are actually there on the card or because the formula for reading-cum-explicating expands the two letters into four. In a conventional mystery-thriller the text might visually provide a facsimile of the original message, but Joyce's narrative method in *Ulysses* subsumes the postcard into the fabric of the verbal discourse between characters. As all subsequent transmissions in *Ulysses* duplicate Mrs. Breen's four-letter version (with some minor variations—and even the variations in the Joyce manuscripts and the numerous editions of the book are inconsequential), the accepted reading seems to be: You Pee Up! The convention determined by Joyce for Molly's night thoughts, innocent of punctuation, causes still a final variation in an overly simplified "up up"—so that we might well wonder what sort of communication took place between tired Bloom and sleepy Molly when he orally informed her of the contents of the postcard. Her "version" denudes the message of any scatalogical implications, and she may possibly be underplaying its potent significance because of faulty comprehension. What to Breen a cataclysmic offense, and to Mrs. Breen "a great shame" (*U* 158), and to Bergan a sidesplitting lark, is to Bloom only a minor mystery, and to Molly apparently no mystery at all.

Stephen Dedalus, himself the sender of a cryptic message to Mulligan on this day (having been brought back to Dublin by a telegram, he now sends one as a substitute for his presence at The Ship), allows for a mental manipulation of isolated letters of the alphabet into a message: remembering his debt to George Russell (it was "one guinea" when he recalls it in Proteus (*U* 31), but has been reduced to "that pound he lent you" by Scylla and Charybdis, *U* 189), he strings out the five vowels into "A.E.I.O.U." The prime vowel for Stephen is "I"—the first-person singular designating himself—and he has compounded aspects of himself in time into a trinity of selves, past and present, child and adult, totalling a unity:

> But I, entelechy, form of forms, am I by memory
> because under changing forms.
> I that sinned and prayed and fasted.
> A child Conmee saved from pandies.
> I, I and I. I.
> A. E. I. O. U. (*U* 189-90)

(It is no orthographic accident that in *Ulysses* George Russell's pen name invariably appears as the initials A.E. and never as the digraph AE, so that Bloom makes an incorrect mystery of his "names": "A. E.: what does that mean? Initials perhaps. Albert Edward, Arthur Edmund, Alphonsus Eb Ed El Esquire," *U* 165).

Stephen had earlier jotted down on the bottom part of a page of Deasy's letter to the Press a quatrain of poetry that he composed while on Sandymount Strand—another document never presented to the reader of *Ulysses* in facsimile, but incorporated into the text of the Aeolus chapter, where Stephen recalls it rather than reads it. His presence on the strand that morning make Stephen also a Mystery Man on the Beach (and fit subject for a titbit), and for a brief instant he leaves his mark on its transitory sands: "He stood suddenly, his feet beginning to sink slowly in the quaking soil. Turn back. / Turning, he scanned the south shore, his feet sinking again slowly in new sockets" (*U* 45). Had those footprints remained for any length of time, they might have served as a personal message, as in *Robinson Crusoe,* but the implication in Proteus of the "quaking soil" leaves little doubt that no message would be left for the next stroller on the strand to read. Ten hours later Leopold Bloom rests for a long while on Sandymount Strand, hardly aware of any residual presence of the young man who at that place had thought, "Signatures of all things I am here to read" (*U* 37). Bloom also muses on a variant of the "limits of the diaphane" as he recalls the mnemonic device of an anagram he had been taught in the High School for the colors of the rainbow: "Roygbiv Vance taught us: red, orange, yellow, green, blue, indigo, violet" (*U* 376). And in his turn he begins to record his message to Gerty MacDowell, unfortunately having only the "quaking soil" for a slate:

> Mr Bloom with his stick gently vexed the thick sand at his foot. Write a message for her. Might remain. What?
>   I.
> Some flatfoot tramp on it in the morning. Useless. Washed away. Tide comes here a pool near her foot. . . .
>   AM. A.
> No room. Let it go.
> Mr Bloom effaced the letters with his slow boot.
>   (*U* 381)

That incomplete message stands as a paradigm of *Ulysses*, a novel of such intimate revelations that delves deep inside the thinking processes of the main characters and yet leaves some of their most important thoughts unrecorded and unrecoverable. In a book in which we know the precise birthday of Molly Bloom (8 September), and Milly Bloom (15 June), and even the dead Rudy Bloom (29 December), no birthday is ever given for Leopold Bloom by an author for whom birthdays were important. And, although we known when Bloom's father died (26 June 1887) and where he is buried (Ennis, County Clare), we are never informed when his mother died—except that her death preceded her husband's, but by how many days? months? years?—or where she is buried. Bloom at Prospect Cemetery in Glasnevin thinks of his own eventual interment: "Mine over there towards Finglas, the plot I bought. Mamma poor mamma, and little Rudy" (*U* 111). Is Mrs. Bloom buried there in Glasnevin, or is her son only thinking of his dead mother and son as *dead,* not necessarily located "over there towards Finglas?" Since his father died when Leopold Bloom was only twenty-one, and his mother some time prior, it is hardly likely that Bloom would have bought a family plot at the time of her death, when he himself was probably but a teenager. The mysteries of *Ulysses* persist in the lacunae created by the narrative.

And the mysteries would be solved were we equipped with the isolated pieces necessary to fill in the blank spaces. "I am a. . ." the message begins, and Joycean cryptologists have been hard at work to complete the simple sentence by supplying the word Joyce never wrote (assuming that it is merely a single word that will make all the difference). A drunken and distraught Stephen asks the ghost of May Dedalus, "Tell me the word, mother, if you know now. The word known to all men" (*U* 581), but Mrs. Dedalus is as unresponsive to his urgent need as is the *Ulysses* text. Most commentators on the mysterious word left untranscribed in the Sandymount sands transmute the question into an overwhelming one, assuming that alone under the stars at a transcendental moment in his life, Bloom would uncover the essence of his existence, the depths of his soul, the word known to all men—if they but knew it. Consequently, the sentence is conjecturally completed to *define* Leopold Bloom, in universal terms, or in terms of his vital masculinity (I am a Man/man), or in terms of his much-overlaid racial heritage (I am a Jew), or—assuming that the ultimate letter given is not the indefinite article, but the first letter of the final word—in terms of his state of isolation (I am alone). One can even suppose that this is a statement of his recent humiliation (I am a cuckold) or a confession of guilt for his masturbation (I am ashamed), which returns the consideration back to the literal situation, Leopold Bloom addressing Gerty MacDowell. If his intention, at least momentarily, is to leave a message for her that she could read and act upon, a thoroughly ordinary and even practical communication, he might be arranging for a future tryst (I am at. . .). But what could he possibly add, his Westland Row postal address? In which case the message reads, *I am anonymous*—a non-message impermanently implanted in shifting sand so that not even the flat feet of a Stephen Dedalus could tramp on it the next morning.

In *Ulysses* mysterious messages on occasion answer themselves (all questions contain their own answers; texts that provide puzzles supply the answers upsidedown in diminished print on a far-subsequent page). When Buck Mulligan atop the Martello Tower gave "a low whistle of call" (*U* 3), he eventually was rewarded when "Two strong shrill whistles answered through the calm." (If he had not expected them, he nonetheless took the coincidental responses in stride, with thanks, but then again he may have been sufficiently familiar with the timing of the mailboat to anticipate a response). "Circe," a chapter that recapitulates with a vengeance the Ulyssean day and captures the basic mystique of the book, mysteriously begins with *"Whistles call and answer:"*

> THE CALLS
> Wait, my love, and I'll be with you.
> THE ANSWERS
> Round behind the stable.
>
> (*U* 429)

And although Bloom may once have "marked a florin . . . and tendered it in payment . . . for possible, circuitous or direct, return" (*U* 696), only to have to admit that after almost six years the coin has not returned, certain mysterious elements of *Ulysses* have their circuitous—and even elliptical—returns. Having abandoned his statement of self in the sand, Bloom "flung his wooden pen away. The stick fell in silted sand, stuck. Now if you were trying to do that for a week on end you couldn't. Chance" (*U* 382). Bloom may accidentally have made his own "signature of all things" in the sand.

The sexually charged "Nausicaa" chapter has as its climax the coincidental occurrence of Bloom's ejaculation and the bursting forth in the sky of a Roman candle during the fireworks display: "and it was like a sigh of O! and everyone cried O! O! in raptures and it gushed out of it a stream of rain gold hair threads and they shed and ah! they were all greeny dewy stars falling with golden, O so lively! O so soft, sweet, soft" (*U* 366-67). The pyrotechnic shaft serves here as a totem of Bloom's sexual potency, which in his later stage of detumescence he refers to prosaically as "My fireworks. Up like a rocket, down like a stick" (*U* 371). The wooden pen that he then flings aside turns him symbolically to a new state of tumescence, a cycle beginning with erection and returning to ressurection. Yet Molly in her Circean manifestation reduces the symbolic significance to the most mundane interpretation: "O Poldy, Poldy, you are a poor old stick in the mud!" (*U* 440). Once again for Molly there is no mystery to uncover: as mystery-man-on-the-beach Leopold Bloom has his magnificent moment, but for Molly the blank is easily filled in with a simple "stick-in-the-mud."

The traditional requirements of the mystery novel dictate that not only must the major enigma be satisfactorily (and even logically) resolved, but that all attendant minor mysteries as well—all loose ends neatly tied up. Such texts exist within a locked room in a snow-bound manor house inside a closed universe, what Michael Innes likens to a "submerged submarine." *Ulysses,* on the other hand, exists in an open universe of a Dublin city containing thousands and accessible to the outside world. The mysteries of *Ulysses* are those of an ordinary day in an extraordinary universe, and are only mysteries because they contain and present unsolved and unresolved dilemmas and possibilities. The "nobleman" passes into the eternity of Friday morning with his anonymity preserved, and even Gerty's surname remains unknown to Leopold Bloom. The man in the macintosh is slated to appear and reappear both as himself and as a duplication of himself, as other men in macintoshes, and Alf Bergan remains at liberty, neither arrested nor exonerated, while a weary traveler, an unraveler of mysteries that remain mysteries, transformed for the nonce from Leopold Bloom to Sinbad the Sailor, persists as an aposiopesis, a perfect _____.

"An actuality of the possible as possible": Reflections on the theme of history in 'Nestor'

Ulrich Schneider
Erlangen, F.R.G.

In his plans for *Ulysses* Joyce listed history as the "art" of the 'Nestor' episode, and from the frequent references to historical topics, beginning with the school history lesson, it is not hard to see why. 'Nestor' is only the focus for the topic of history, however, it has already cropped up in the first chapter and will play an important role in the later course of the novel. In the first episode Stephen and Haines have a conversation which touches on a historical subject. Stephen characterizes himself as a servant of two masters, of the "imperial British state" and the "holy Roman Catholic and Apostolic Church" (20). Haines, an Englishman, finds it a bit awkward that Stephen should bring up such a touchy subject as that of English rule in Ireland with him, but he answers the way a well-brought-up Englishman should, that is to say "calmly": "We feel in England that we have treated you rather unfairly. It seems history is to blame" (20). Stephen does not answer this remark of Haines' directly; instead he begins to think of the origins of that second empire of which he feels himself a subject, of the origins of the Roman Catholic Church, which as a "church militant" (21) has defended its unity and might against all heretics. Thus Haines' words are left dangling in the air, until one begins to see the entire second chapter as a series of reflections on the question of just what this "history" that Haines mentions actually is. Of course, 'Nestor' does not offer an explicit answer, and still less a precise definition of the term "history," but it does contain a number of different perspectives and interpretations which might stimulate the reader to think about the questions raised.

While Stephen's own ideas on the subject of history are in a state of flux, Mr. Deasy has all the answers; the headmaster is full of unshakable convictions. For him "All history moves towards one great goal, the manifestation of God" (34). Mr. Deasy's belief in a divine plan of history stands, as Richard Ellmann has observed, in opposition to Haines' view of history as "some demonic force," that is to say, the work of the devil instead of God.[1] But whether history is thus regarded as "divinely" or "infernally" inspired, these two attitudes have one thing in common—and this is a point which Ellmann does not deal with—namely, for both, Haines and Deasy, history is a process in which everything is determined, a process which in the last analysis cannot be affected by human action. If, however, history is understood to be a chain of necessary and predetermined events, a process which follows its own laws, then every rebellion against the status quo appears senseless, and the conditions which prevail at any particular time and place are inevitable. Such a concept can be reduced to Alexander Pope's statement in *An Essay on Man:* "Whatever is, is right." Seen in this light, even the British Empire is merely an unavoidable development in the course of history, and everything about it which may appear to be unjust can be assumed to serve a higher purpose in the end. Thus even for Haines history is not really "diabolical," since he, too, is convinced that English rule over Ireland merely demonstrates and confirms the law of evolution as a development through lower to higher forms of life and civilization. To be sure, Haines is interested in the revival of the Irish language and Irish culture, but he pursues it in the manner of an anthropologist studying the customs of a primitive people, without serious doubt that English rule in Ireland represents the victory of reason and evolution. The revival of Irish culture is one thing for him, and British rule in Ireland another.

Since Haines sees history as responsible for everything that happens in the world, the question of human guilt and responsibility does not even arise; he accepts the world as it is. Thus, his belief in history as a powerful independent force, a belief which was especially popular in the last quarter of the nineteenth century, can be interpreted as an apology for the existing order. This type of historicism was sharply criticized by Karl Marx, who observed that the ruling order is always also the order of the rulers. It was also attacked by Friedrich Nietzsche, who referred to it as the mythology of the seemingly enlightened man in his *Unzeitgemäße Betrach-*

tungen. Nietzsche recognized perceptively that the "religion of the historical power . . . over and over again turns into a naked admiration of success, and leads to idolatry of the actual."[2]

What has been said about Haines is also valid for Deasy, but with the addition of a new factor. If both Haines and Deasy, in their reverence for the force of history, tend to accept the existing order of things, or even to "idolize the actual" in Nietzsche's words, then when Joyce has Deasy speak about the past, he is showing how precarious our grip on this "actuality" can be. History may be a world force, but it is also what human beings remember, and the human memory is often extremely selective. In his conversation with Stephen Deasy mentions numerous events in the history of Ireland as proof for the correctness of his views, but in most cases, as R. M. Adams has shown in a painstaking study, Mr. Deasy mixes truth and falsehood to produce a highly eccentric historical hodgepodge.[3]   He proudly claims to have a better memory than his adversaries, a claim to which Stephen silently responds, "glorious, pious, and immortal memory" (31).[4]   With this phrase, which sounds so positive, Stephen is actually being sarcastic, for the words were used as a toast to the victory of William of Orange, a Protestant, in Ireland by the Northern Irish Orange Lodges. With this toast they celebrate their loyalty to Protestantism and the union with England.   This memory, Mr. Deasy's memory, Stephen is saying to himself, is anything but objective; no matter how many facts Mr. Deasy can cite, his version of the history remains ideologically colored, dyed in the colors of the "black north and true blue Bible" (31), as Stephen reflects.

All the details which Stephen notes in Mr. Deasy's study while he waits for him to finish the letter reveal Deasy's orientation towards England: Over the fireplace hangs a portrait of the present King as Prince of Wales, and the walls are hung with pictures of famous English racehorses (32). This may be taken as an indication that he attaches importance to success and victory, in horseracing as well as history. An outsider like "Throwaway" would have no chance with Mr. Deasy.

The whole atmosphere of the study has something of the past, of a museum about it. Deasy is the born collector; in addition to his racing prints he has a collection of coins, shells, and of spoons with the twelve apostles on them. Each of these details helps to characterize him. The Stuart coins bear witness to his Protestant and pro-English convictions, since the coins which the Stuart kings circulated in Ireland were of inferior metal and thus offer proof of Stuart corruption, which was fortunately ended by the victory of William of Orange. The twelve apostles on the spoons suggest an extreme case of the trivialization of what was once a powerful and living force in religion. And the shells point to the incrustation and withdrawal which are more typical of Deasy's old age than true wisdom. The shells represent something stony and hard, a kind of armor which protects from the outside world, but which keeps it at a distance as well. They, too, like the spoons, suggest the transformation of a substance which was once alive into something dead, of a living experience gone dead and rigid, exactly like history. In the following episode the reader will meet with the precise opposite of this process, namely the dissolution of everything solid, the Protean metamorphosis of supposedly so solid matter.

But to return to the parallels between Haines' view of history and Mr. Deasy's, one is struck by their need to find historical scapegoats. Both are convinced that the Jews are to blame for what, in their eyes, is the decline of England. Although Deasy remarks to Stephen that, for human understanding, God moves in mysterious ways (34), nonetheless he appears to possess inside information on God's intentions. He knows exactly who the heroes and villains of history are, and if anything goes wrong, then either the Jews or women are responsible: A woman—was she a Jewish woman?—was to blame for the first sin in the Garden of Eden; the Trojan War was fought for ten years over a woman; the English conquered Ireland because of a woman, and Parnell's career was destroyed by a woman as well (34-35). Unlike Stephen, Deasy has no doubts about his views; "There can be no two opinions on the matter," (32) he claims, and with a triumphant "That's why," (36) he makes his exit.

Stephen asks himself, "Is this old wisdom?" (34) and refuses, understandably, to be impressed. Worlds separate Stephen and Mr. Deasy, and the distance is nowhere better reflected than in their attitudes towards history. Deasy's view of history as a gradual revelation of divine will stands in great contrast to Stephen's despairing pessimism, whereby Mr. Deasy belongs to the nineteenth century and Stephen strikes us as far more modern. For to him history appears as a nightmare from which he is trying to awake (34). When we look at how Irish history has continued up to the present day, it is hard not to agree with him. Stephen does not see history as a rational form of progress towards a particular goal, but rather as something chaotic and senseless. If there is any law at all behind historical events, then it is at best merely that "history repeats itself," particularly its worst errors. In Mr. Deasy's study the words of the Creed occur to Stephen ironically: "As it was in the beginning, is now, . . . and ever shall be" (29).

This idea of a meaningless cycle of repetition is perhaps one of the reasons why Joyce is at pains to draw parallels between events and figures of different historical epochs throughout the novel, although, of course, there are other important reasons as well. By means of these parallels he underlines the notion that certain constellations repeat themselves, without in any way suggesting that the world has moved nearer to the fulfillment of a divine plan. In the 'Nestor' episode, so early on in the novel, none of these parallels becomes fully clear, of course; Joyce's plan is conceived on a large scale, and many of the allusions which fall in this chapter do not have the full significance which they will acquire later. It is significant, however, that the mention of the Greek general Pyrrhus is followed by allusions to Moses Maimonides and Averroes, the Jewish and Arabian philosophers, who were so important in the rediscovery of Aristotle in medieval philosophy, and finally by reference to the Irish rebel leader Parnell, for these three strands of history—Greek, Jewish, and Irish—are the most important of those which Joyce tries to bring into connection with each other. In the later 'Aeolus' episode the theme of disappointment shortly before the attainment of a goal is repeated in many intricate variations, and here the general Pyrrhus appears again, as a figure parallel both to Moses, who does not live to enter the Promised Land, and to Parnell, who failed to free Ireland from English rule (133-134). This theme of failure and disappointment fills the joke Stephen makes in 'Nestor' on the word "pier" with additional meaning. When one of the pupils can associate nothing with the name of Pyrrhus except the word "pier," Stephen takes up the humorous tone and asks the boys what a pier is. The answer is: "a disappointed bridge" (25). In the later episode Joyce makes it clearer that the lives of all three figures—Moses, Pyrrhus, and Parnell—remained incomplete in one way or another; they were all disappointed bridges."

At the very beginning of the 'Nestor' episode, while Stephen is mechanically quizzing his pupils on the dates of the battles which Pyrrhus fought against the Romans, he is occupied by the thought of history as something unreal, or dream-like. This theme is taken up again later when Stephen calls history a nightmare; here the association of "fable" occurs to him, and in this connection a phrase of William Blake's springs to his mind. Stephen thinks of history as the art "fabled by the daughters of memory" (24). The significance of this quotation, we may assume for Joyce as well as for Stephen, is that Blake contrasted these "daughters of memory" with the true muses, whom he called the "daughters of inspiration." The "daughters of memory" represent an inferior sort of muse to Blake, and thus he condemns in the preface to his poem "Milton" those poets who follow them.[5] By this Blake means several things: to follow the daughters of memory means to imitate the classical poets, and to adhere to academic rules of poetic composition, and Blake appeals to future artists to free themselves from the tyranny of traditional, academic art and to follow the Bible and their own inspiration alone. But he also, significantly, rejects the epics of Homer and Virgil in this passage, because they glorify war and military "virtues" instead of peace and charity towards one's enemies, as the New Testament preaches. Stephen, by applying the phrase "daughters of memory" to history, reveals that the conflict occupying him is the relative merits of history and poetry, whereby history is assigned the inferior position.

The quotation from Blake which occurs to Stephen is so short as to appear cryptic in the context, and it is therefore of some interest that 'Nestor' is not the first occasion on which Joyce used it. In 1902, writing on the Irish poet James Clarence Mangan, Joyce observed:

> Poetry . . . is always a revolt against artifice, a revolt, in a sense, against actuality. It speaks of what seems fantastic and unreal to those who have lost the simple intuitions which are the test of reality; and as it is often

found at war with its age, so it makes no account of
history, which is fabled by the daughters of memory
. . . History or the denial of reality, for they are two
names for the same thing, may be said to be that which
deceives the whole world.[6]

Poetry, Joyce writes, is a "revolt against actuality" and history
a "denial of reality." We can take, perhaps, these phrases as a
key to Stephen's brief and cryptic reflections at the beginning
of 'Nestor'. And what they amount to, in the end, is a defence
of poetry against the claims of history to deal with the truth,
with life as it really is. History does not convey "reality" to
us, Joyce is having Stephen say; on the contrary, history denies
it. And conversely, while poetry appears fantastic, while it
revolts against the actual, it achieves what history cannot; it
leads us towards a grasp of the complexity of truth and reality.

Why is history a "denial of reality?" Joyce attempts to
show us this in the entire 'Nestor' episode, and indeed, throughout the novel. To begin with, history denies reality because it
is occupied exclusively with the past and must necessarily withdraw its attention from the present and from living experience.
Haines, who favors the artificial re-introduction of the Irish
language, while at the same time refusing to take any notice
of the current political problems of the country, appeared in
the first chapter as a prime example of this attitude. The history
lesson which Stephen gives at school is also devoted to events
long past, events which appear to have no connection at all
with the lives and interests of the schoolboys who must learn
them; for them they are merely names and dates to be mem-
orized. Stephen himself is no exception; even he must refer
to the textbook in order to recall the obscure dates. This reduction of history to the "bare bones" of facts frustrates the
boys' imagination, and they beg to be told a ghost story instead, since Roman history is so dull. Armstrong's nonsensical
association—or so it appears at the time—of the name "Pyrrhus"
with the word "pier" represents a desperate and comical attempt
to establish some connection between the seemingly meaningless
facts they are expected to learn and the boys' own world.

The school history lesson contains another example of
how history can be called a denial of reality, since it illustrates
beautifully how selectively historical memory operates. In this
it parallels Mr. Deasy's conversation later in the episode. All that

remains of a series of complex events and intertwined human lives is a list of battles and a few phrases that famous men are supposed to have spoken, "that phrase the world has remembered" (24), as Stephen says of Pyrrhus. A history which limits itself to recounting the deeds of great generals and their military careers leaves out so much of life that the words "denial of reality" do indeed seem apposite. Since women are ignored or merely used as scapegoats in this type of history, some English-speaking feminists have even stopped using the word, and prefer to study "herstory" instead. Something else which history often leaves out is the point of view of the losing side in the battles; the losers don't write the history books. As Bertolt Brecht put it in *Das Verhör des Lukullus*:

> It is always
> The victor who writes the history of the vanquished.
> The man with the club
> Disfigures his victim. The weak
> Vanish from the world, what remains
> Is a lie.[7]

Or, to take an example from the other subject occupying Stephen's thoughts, namely the Catholic Church: An English historian recently wrote that the Middle Ages may merely appear to be the "Age of Faith," "because nearly all the evidence which survives was written by monks and priests."[8] Heretics, obviously, were not encouraged to spread their opinions.

Stephen, as an Irishman living under English rule and working for the pro-English Mr. Deasy, has an instinctive sympathy with the underdogs and losers of history. It is certainly no accident that the history lesson concerns Pyrrhus, one of the most famous losers in history. Stephen's allusion to Averroes and Moses Maimonides is another case in point. Deasy blames the Jews for having "sinned against the light" (34), and Stephen, too, associates Christianity with light and the non-Christian philosophers with darkness ("dark men in mien and movement," 28). But by parodying the beginning of St. John's Gospel he suggests that the "light" did not illumine the Christians enough to understand the "dark" philosophy of Averroes and Maimonides, "a darkness shining in brightness which brightness could not comprehend" (28). Nor, as one might add, did it illumine them to understand and tolerate

Jews in general. Looking at today's situation in the Near East it is hard to believe that there was a time when Jews and Arabs got along with each other, but such a time did exist in the Caliphat of Cordoba, a civilization, which has been called "the most advanced . . . between the decline of Rome and the Renaissance" and the "Golden Age" of the history of Judaism.[9] Persecution of the Jews set in with the end of the Caliphat and with the Christian reconquest of Spain. Bloom, who understandably identifies "force, hatred, history, all that" (333), draws his own conclusion from these events: "History . . . proves up to the hilt Spain decayed when the Inquisition hounded the jews out . . ." (644). Deasy, of course, would not agree.

Similarly, Stephen in his thoughts spontaneously comes to the defence of the other group which Deasy made responsible for all the evil in the world, namely women. The unprepossessing pupil Sargent, who is "scraggy," "weak," "dull and bloodless" (27), makes Stephen think of the woman who must love him anyway, his mother, and he reflects on mother love as perhaps the only real force opposed to the egotism and will to power of the world: "Was that then real? The only true thing in life?" (27).

The history lessons which Stephen must teach to his pupils, with their lists of famous generals and battles, appear to him so stereotyped that they run together in his mind to a single, composite image: "From a hill above a corpestrewn plain a general speaking to his officers, leaned upon his spear. Any general to any officers" (24). Stephen cannot accept this as reality any more than his pupils can; what he is able to do, however, is to recognize a connection between the history lessons and the boys' lives. The boys leave the classroom to play hockey; to them the two things have nothing to do with each other. Stephen, however, listening to the noise of their game, associates it mentally with the noise of a battle: "Jousts, slush and uproar of battles, the frozen deathspew of the slain, a shout of spear spikes baited with men's bloodied guts" (32). The boys are playing a game, but Stephen's association makes it appear as a kind of practice for real combat. This sort of training will prepare them to be good soldiers, or, as the famous phrase has it: "The battle of Waterloo was won on the playing fields of Eton," or, as Bloom in another situation puts it: "Or children playing battle. Whole earnest" (379). The history the boys are learning matches this athletic activity very well; the children are merely not aware of it, whereas the children in the chorus of Brecht's *Verhör des Lukullus* sing:

> In our schoolbooks (they chant)
> Are written the names of the great generals.
> Learn their battles by heart,
> Memorize their wonderful lives,
> Whoever would follow in their footsteps.
> To follow their lead
> To stand out among the crowd
> That is our duty.[10]

In this manner history lessons, combined with sports, may serve to teach that "might is right," that struggle and war are the content of the heroic life.

Stephen Dedalus' discomfort during the history lessons arises not primarily from his concern with politics and pacifism, however, but from his concerns as an artist. However much he may dislike Mr. Deasy's pro-British attitudes and conservative ideology, the quotation from William Blake about the "daughters of memory" shows that Stephen's main preoccupation is with the relationship between history and imaginative literature, and their respective claims to hold the key to the truth of human existence. If Stephen is reminded of William Blake at the beginning of the episode, it is because he sees in Blake a spiritual ally, another artist who rebelled against the tyranny of traditional norms, against the omnipotence of "facts." Blake was certainly one of the great visionaries of English poetry, indeed of world literature. His poetic visions transcend the empirical world and therefore correspond to Stephen's ideas of poetry; in this they are a "revolt against actuality." In Blake's apocalyptic visions such as "A Vision of the Last Judgment," he is striving to liberate the imagination from the bonds of time and space and to render visible a higher reality, a reality in which the inferior poetry inspired by the "daughters of memory" is forgotten. Stephen, too, has an apocalyptic vision in which the categories of space and time, within which empirical evidence is restricted, are destroyed: "I hear the ruin of all space, shattered glass and toppling masonry, and time one livid final flame" (24).

Unlike Blake, however, Stephen with a certain anxiety

poses the question of what remains if the world of empirical
evidence is destroyed: "What's left us then?" (24). At the
opening of 'Nestor' Stephen's question is immediately interrupted by the continuing history lesson, and the reader is not
provided with any more information to flesh out Stephen's
reservations about Blake as an artist. The question implies
such reservations, however, and for help in understanding
Stephen's train of thought we can turn to another of Joyce's
essays, this time the essay on Blake from the year 1912. There
we find the sentence:

> Blake killed the dragon of experience and natural wis-
> dom, and, by minimizing space and time and denying
> the existence of memory and the senses, he tried to paint
> his works on the void of the divine bosom.[11]

Stephen, like Joyce, sees a certain danger in Blake's "other-
worldliness"; art cannot be created in a void, after all, but only
out of human experience and the evidence of our senses. For
just this reason Stephen resolves later in the novel, in the scene
in the library, to "hold to the now, the here," and not, like the
theosophical poets of the Irish revival, who are strongly influenced by Blake, to "creepycrawl after Blake's buttocks into
eternity" (186). To put it in simpler terms, both Stephen and
Joyce admire Blake's rebellion against a prosaic and superficial
understanding of "reality" which places too much emphasis on
"hard facts," but they see in Blake's wish to transcend all sensual experience the risk of going to the other extreme.

After reflecting on the visionary poet Blake, Stephen's
thoughts turn to Aristotle, as he continues to mull over the topic
of history. Stephen, like Joyce, had read Aristotle's works in the
National Library in Paris. Stephen now remembers the Aristotelian definition of movement as "an actuality of the possible as
possible" (25),[12] and applies it, as he had applied the Blake
quotation before, to historical events. According to Aristotle,
the essence of a phenomenon consists of the sum of possibilities inherent in it; these possibilities are revealed as one of
them is realized or actualized. Thus, without movement or
change the essential nature of things would remain hidden.
Applied to history, this idea means that there exist at any moment in time numerous possibilities, of which only one is
realized; each historical event is a choice which cannot be un-

done. Stephen must be thinking along these lines when he observes that events such as the early death of Pyrrhus or the murder of Julius Caesar "are not to be thought away" (25). In the
words of Agathon quoted approvingly by Aristotle:

> For this alone is lacking even to God,
> To make undone things that have once been done.[13]

In a certain sense, however, the poet possesses this power
which Aristotle denies even to God. The poet is capable of
imagining away a historical event, of imagining that something
entirely different had happened. History must deal with the
one event which occurred, while poetry is in the better position
of being able to deal with the entire range of suppressed possibilities. In Aristotelian terms these merely imagined possibilities partake equally of the nature or essence of the event,
and are thus—paradoxically—no less "real." Stephen and Joyce,
can be called Aristotelians to the extent that Aristotle offers
a philosophical justification for considering poetry the higher
art.
There is a passage in Aristotle which confirms this interpretation quite succinctly, although it is not in the works to
which most scholars have turned for clarification of Stephen's
meditations. The quotation which actually occurs in 'Nestor',
the definition of movement as "an actuality of the possible as
possible," comes from Aristotle's works on physics and metaphysics. But since Stephen brings this quotation into association with his reflections on history, there is good reason for
turning to the passage in the *Poetics* in which Aristotle mentions history, and specifically the difference between history
and poetry. The word which leaps out of the page at us in
this passage is the word "possible." Here it seems that the
bridge between Aristotle's theory of metaphysics and the
subject occupying Stephen, namely history, has been found.
In a passage which has often been used since as an apology
for poetry, Aristotle writes:

> . . . The poet's function is to describe not the thing that
> has happened, but a kind of thing that might happen,
> i. e. what is possible as being probable or necessary. The
> distinction between historian and poet is not in the one
> writing prose and the other verse . . . it consists really

> in this, that the one describes the thing that has been, and the other a kind of thing that might be. Hence poetry is something more philosophic and of graver import than history, since its statements are of the nature rather of universals, whereas those of history are singulars.[14]

The realm of history is thus the factual, the unique, whereas the realm of poetry is the possible, the typical. This provides a background before which we must see Joyce's definition of poetry as a "revolt against actuality." We have seen how easily history is cited to excuse this actuality in *Ulysses,* no matter how bad it may be. Haines' remarks in chapter one are a good case in point. But poetry can put the necessity of this reality in doubt, by dissolving it, reforming its boundaries, projecting alternatives to what exists. While the historian limits himself to the area of known facts and attempts to explain why certain events had of necessity to follow others, aesthetic reflection is characterized by a stronger sense of contingency, that is to say, by an awareness that events might take or might have taken an entirely different course. Historical processes require the selection of one possibility among many, while the artist can reverse this procedure, and place the one possibility which became fact back in its original place as merely one among many alternatives.

Grammatically speaking, one might say that the mood of the historian is the indicative, whereas the mood of the creative writer is the subjunctive. The nature of poetry itself contains a large element of the utopian; particularly in the modern period an important function of literature has been to remind us of the possibilities, desires, or visions which have not been actualized, which have not become historical fact up to now. The quality of the creative artist who writes down or otherwise produces these visions was called "the sense of possibility" by the Austrian writer Robert Musil. In his novel *The Man Without Qualities* Musil described this sense as follows:

> Whoever possesses it does not say, for example: here this or that happened, will happen, must happen, but rather he invents: Here something could, ought to, should happen; and if someone tells him about any thing that is, as it is, then he thinks: Well, it could probably be other-

wise, too. And so the sense of possibility could be defined as precisely the ability to think of everything that just as well might be, and as the ability not to take whatever is more seriously than whatever is not.[15]

There can be no doubt that James Joyce possessed this sense in the highest degree. The task of bringing to light the enormous potential which is contained in one single day in the life of a so-called "ordinary" citizen of Dublin, this task took Joyce approximately 800 pages in *Ulysses* to achieve. And it helps to explain the innumerable quotations and references in the novel; with their aid it becomes clear that Leopold Bloom is a potential Moses, a potential Shakespeare, or a potential Christ. Bloom calls the barrister O'Molloy, who in spite of his great gifts has not succeeded in his career, a "mighthave been" (125), and the fate of most Dubliners in *Ulysses*, being crippled in the development of their potentiality by that general disease "paralysis," could thus be succinctly summed up. One of the many questions the novel raises is whether or not this is necessarily part of the human condition, "and ever shall be."

Notes

[1] Richard Ellmann, *Ulysses on the Liffey* (London: Faber & Faber, 1972), 20-21.

[2] " . . . jene Bewunderung vor der 'Macht der Geschichte' . . . , die praktisch alle Augenblicke in nackte Bewunderung des Erfolges umschlägt und zum Götzendienst des Tatsächlichen führt." "Vom Nutzen and Nachteil der Historie," *Unzeitgemäße Betrachtungen, Zweites Stück, Werke in sechs Bänden*, Vol. I, ed. Karl Schlechta (München: Hanser, 1980), 263.

[3] Robert Martin Adams, *Surface and Symbol: The Consistency of James Joyce's 'Ulysses'*, (New York: Oxford University Press, 1962), 18-26.

[4] "The glorious, pious, and immortal memory of William III, prince of Orange, who saved us all from popery, brass money, and wooden shoes," J. C. Beckett, *The Making of Modern Ireland 1603 - 1923*, repr. (London:

Faber & Faber, 1971), 139.

[5] *The Complete Writings of William Blake,* ed., Geoffrey Keynes (London: Oxford University Press, 1966), 480.

[6] *Critical Writings,* ed., Ellsworth Mason and Richard Ellmann (London: Faber & Faber, 1959), 81.

[7] "Immer doch
Schreibt der Sieger die Geschichte des Besiegten.
Dem Erschlagenen entstellt
Der Schläger die Züge. Aus der Welt
Geht der Schwächere, und zurückbleibt
Die Lüge."
Bertolt Brecht, *Gesammelte Werke 4* (Frankfurt: Suhrkamp, 1967), 1480.

[8] Christopher Hill, rev. of *The Cheese and the Worms: the Cosmos of a 16th-Century Miller,* by Carlo Ginzburg, *London Review of Books,* 2, No. 21 (6th-19th Nov. 1980), 3.

[9] Bernard J. Bamberger, *The Story of Judaism,* 3rd, augm. ed., (New York: Schocken, 1970), 154.

[10] "In den Lesebüchern
Stehen die Namen der großen Feldherrn.
Ihre Schlachten lernt auswendig
Ihr wunderbares Leben studiert
Wer ihnen nacheifert.
Ihnen nachzueifern
Aus der Menge sich zu erheben
Ist uns aufgetragen."
Bertolt Brecht, *op. cit.,* 1451.

[11] *Critical Writings,* 222.

[12] Cf. Physics, Bk. III, Ch. 1, *The Basic Works of Aristotle,* ed., Richard McKeon (New York: Random House, 1941), 254, and *Metaphysics* Bk. XI, Ch. 9, 864.

[13] *Nichomachean Ethics* Bk. VI, Ch. 2, McKeon, 1024.

[14] *Poetics,* Ch. 9, McKeon, 1463-64.

[15] "Wer ihn besitzt, sagt beispielsweise nicht: Hier ist dies oder das geschehen, wird geschehen, muß geschehen; sondern er erfindet: Hier könnte, sollte oder müßte geschehn; und wenn man ihm von irgendetwas erklärt, daß es so sei, wie es sei, dann denkt er: Nun es könnte wahrscheinlich auch anders sein. So ließe sich der Möglichkeitssinn geradezu als die Fähigkeit definieren, alles, was ebensogut sein könnte, zu denken und das, was ist, nicht wichtiger zu nehmen als das, was nicht ist." Robert Musil, *Der Mann ohne Eigenschaften, Gesammelte Werke Vol I.,* ed. Adolf Frisé (Reinbek: Rowohlt, 1978), 16.

"Words? Music? No: It's what's behind."
Verbal and Physical Transformations in 'Sirens.'

Carl Eichelberger
Philadelphia, Pennsylvania

One of the most challenging and perplexing shifts in Joyce's *Ulysses* occurs in the move from the brief, seemingly objective vignettes of Chapter 10 ('Wandering Rocks') to the fragmented, highly stylized opening of Chapter 11 ('Sirens'). Many critics have all too readily succumbed to the facile generalizations accessible to them through the Gilbert-Linati schema without examining the reasons why Joyce, at this stage of *Ulysses'* narrative development, radically transforms and re-evaluates his notions of fictive language. Critical perspectives generally emanate from the statements that music is the art of the chapter and Joyce's technique is a "fuga per canonem," but my attempt here is to show how musical terminology and forms are hollowed out by Joyce and recast in typographical and linguistic forms which disrupt stock emotional responses by the reader.[1] This ludic transformation of musical superficies into lyrical and poetic linguistic forms exposes the emotional sentimentality of Kernan, Cowley, and other patrons at the Ormond while Leopold Bloom strives to come to terms with Molly's faithlessness on a deeper, less easily defined emotional level.

In the opening of 'Sirens,' which has been referred to as an "overture" or an "orchestra tuning up," sounds function primarily in their power to deceive or mislead, as in the Homeric Siren Song. Through the homonymic correspondence of "blew," and "blue," and "Bloo," sound values remain constant, but typographic and semantic shifts require a movement from visual to aural, to a familiar, yet truncated, version of Bloom's name (see *U* 256).[2] This truncated version of Bloom's name first appears at the opening of 'Lestrygonians,' where his confusion in reading a throwaway leaflet for Dr. John Alexander Dowie's church associates him with Christ's martyrdom:

Bloo . . . me? No.

Blood of the Lamb. (*U* 151.10-11)

These aurally associated, yet typographically differentiated
forms are subsumed by Bloom, whose emotional anxieties
regarding Molly's tryst with Boylan generate the affective norm
of the chapter. This apparently arbitrary sequence of notations
creates an associative ordering which recasts material from
previous chapters and focuses on Bloom's mental processes in
contradistinction   to   the   flirtations   and   sentimentality
surrounding him.

The Sirens of the chapter, Lydia Douce and Mina Kennedy,
are the barmaids at the Ormond, enticing the patrons to alcoholic
self-destruction through sexual flirtation. But their sexuality is
sterile, manifesting itself in voyeuristic (Miss Douce's garter
snapping "Sonnez la cloche" trick for Lenehan) and masturbatory fashion:

> On the smooth jutting beerpull laid Lydia hand lightly,
> plumply, leave it to my hands. All lost in pity for croppy.
> Fro, to: to, fro: over the polished knob (she knows his
> eyes, my eyes, her eyes) her thumb and finger passed in
> pity: passed, repassed and gently touching, then slid so
> smoothly, slowly down, a cool firm white enamel baton
> protruding through their gentle ring. (*U* 286.18-24)

Aside from the masturbatory overtones of the passage,
which foreshadow Bloom's encounter with Gerty McDowell
in 'Nausicaa,' there are several Bloomian associative linkings
of thematic material. A relinquishing of masculine authority
in sexual matters is implicit in the phrase "leave it to my hands."
Bloom's martyrdom through cuckoldry is apparent in his
connection with "All is lost now" and "The Croppy Boy,"
while Boylan and Molly are busy with "La ci darem" and "Love's
Old Sweet Song" (or LOSS acrostically). "Passed" and "re-
passed" are also homonyms for "past," which both Bloom and
Simon Dedalus attempt unsuccessfully to reclaim, and "repast,"
which is Bloom's characteristic compensatory gesture and links
him with Simon:

—To me!

Siopold!

Consumed. (*U* 276.6-8).

The merging of Leopold Bloom and Simon Dedalus is partially based on paternity. Action in the chapter points to a shared past through the phallic "pipes"—Simon plays his and "Bloowho" passes "by by Moulang's"—and the eventually shared child, Stephen (*U* 258.9). Bloom's guilt over his son Rudy's death and Bloom's coincidental reiteration of part of Stephen's discussion concerning paternity in 'Scylla and Charybdis' demonstrates a mystical link between spiritual father and son:

> Do and do. Thing done. In a rosery of Fetter Lane of Gerard, herbalist, he walks, greyeyedauburn. (*U* 202.9-10)

> In Gerard's rosery of Fetter Lane he walks, greyed-auburn. One life is all. One body. Do. But do. (*U* 280. 26-27)

This connection is particularly significant because it is the single link to another living human being which represents the possibility of making Bloo Bloom. Bloom's isolation through cuckoldry and his refusal to participate in the songs of dead or lost feelings creates the possibility for a new, more vital connection to life.

Hugh Kenner has pointed out that the Ormond Hotel, site of the 'Sirens' chapter, is in an area along the Liffey filled with secondhand and miscellaneous shops; these shops contain what is now junk, but were "things that once had the power to summon forth feeling."[3] The verbal and musical debris which constitutes much of 'Sirens' is freighted with significance and feeling, but these responses have long since become sentimental, banal, and trite. The problem becomes how to distinguish moments of genuine feeling from superficial reflex. Lyrics from songs representing loss and martyrdom provide a leaden, reified counterpoint to Bloom's attempts to give articulation to feelings which place him firmly on the side of life and growth, as his very name suggests.

Musical terms descend into the mundane, material world throughout: the scene of 'Sirens' is a *bar*, a teatray is *transposed down,* Miss Douce *tapped a measure* of gold whisky (my italics). Bloom resists the reification process by moving from the piano—confused with a coffin at one point by Bloom—"chords" to the organic, homonymic "cords": "The human voice, two tiny silky cords. Wonderful, more than all the others" (*U* 277.11-12). Bloom's emphasis on the organic dimension of sound production connects him to Stephen whose imaginative cord leads back to the origins of life in a transtemporal telephone call:

> The cords of all link back, strandentwining cable of
> all flesh. That is why mystic monks. Will you be as
> gods? Gaze in your omphalos. Hello. Kinch here. Put
> me on to Edenville. Aleph, alpha: nought, nought, one.
> (*U* 38.1-5)

The hollowness of musical forms in 'Sirens' is characterized by the shell Lydia Douce holds to George Lidwell's ear to hear the ocean; Bloom observes their encounter and connects the shell's "song" back to human perception while realizing the ocean sound is illusory:

> The sea they think they hear. Singing. A roar. The
> blood is it. Souse in the ear sometimes. Well, it's a sea.
> Corpuscle Islands. (*U* 281.29-31)

Stephen has already noted the lifelessness of seashells in his confrontation with Mr. Deasy in 'Nestor' and as they crunch beneath his feet at the opening of 'Proteus.' Just as language dies through fixity in 'Proteus,' attempts to evoke feelings through program music in 'Sirens' fail to entrap Bloom.

Bloom's own "cord" connecting him symbolically to humanity is a "slender catgut thong" which is a labyrinthine conundrum as he plays Cat's Cradle. As Bloom tweaks the thong to join in, it buzzes—echoing Hamlet's "buzz, buzz," meaning "nonsense"—and snaps, Boylan's jingle moves toward Molly, and Lydia withdraws from Lidwell's amorous advances. The empty music, sexual flirtatiousness, and shallow sentimental lyrics in the Ormond give Bloom's emotional disturbances a strong parallel with Circe's warning to Odysseus:

> Square in your path are Seirenes, crying
> beauty to bewitch men coasting by;
> woe to the innocent who hears that sound!

He will not see his lady nor his children
in joy, crowding about him, home from sea;
the Seireness will sing his mind away
on their sweet meadow lolling. There are bones
of dead men rotting in a pile beside them
and flayed skins shrivel around the spot.[4]

Bloom realizes the trap which dead forms and feelings hold for him and decides to leave before the recital finishes; as he departs, he compares his response, in distorted language, to the eccentric Cashel Boyle O'Connor Fitzmaurice Tisdall Farrell who appears as Bloom converses with Josie Breen in 'Lestrygonians':

No. Walk, walk, walk.   Like Cashel Boylo Connoro
Coylo Tisdall Maurice Tisntdall Farrell, Waaaaaaalk.
(*U* 286.31-33)

This temporary madness on Bloom's part strongly evokes the Odyssean warning as he has failed to keep Molly, been unable to consummate his epistolary romance with Martha Clifford, and felt guilt in his inability to keep Rudy alive. Combined with the snapping thong, Bloom's exile is complete, but also provides the source of renewal through spiritual union with Stephen: "Under the sandwichbell lay on a bier of bread one last, one lonely, last sardine of summer. Bloom alone" (*U* 289.12-13).

These verbal and thematic transformations show the degree to which Joyce's fictive methods in 'Sirens' require the reader to reconstruct the linguistic fragments through Bloom's perceptions. As I have said previously, Bloom constitutes the affective norm of the chapter and this assertion is reinforced by the fact that "Joyce appears to have told Gilbert that the tuning-fork could be identified with Bloom."[5] Bloom thereby becomes the center in this chapter which stylistically plays between the parameters of male/female, text/context, speech/writing, and sound/language polarities. These antinomies are brought out by the inclusion of the blind stripling and deaf, bald Pat, the waiter.

The blind stripling is characterized by his cane's "tap." "Pat" is an obvious palindrome of "t-p" permutations in which *Ulysses* embody a number of enigmas. "Tea in both alphabetical and liquid form is one of the objects missing, quested, forgotten,

and made throughout *Ulysses,* and is one of the signs of the
deity."[6]   In 'Sirens,' the blind stripling is defined by sound
and Pat through writing; through their physical presence in
language, they complement and complete each other (much
as Stephen and Bloom will in their "Blephen/Stoom" textual
incarnation). But the "t-p" permutations also form five archaic
verbs meaning "to copulate," linking Bloom's feelings of in-
adequacy with characters whose perceptions are incomplete
by necessity.[7]   Bloom includes all these verbs as he encounters
"Love's Old Sweet Song" (LOSS):

> Bloom. Flood of warm jimjam lickitup secretness flowed
> to flow in music out, in desire, dark to lick flow, invading.
> Tipping her tepping her tapping her topping her. Tup.
> Pores to dilate dilating. Tup. The joy the feel the warm
> the. Tup. To pour o'er sluices pouring gushes. Flood,
> gush, flow, joygush, tupthrop. Now! Language of love.
> (*U* 274.35-40)

This vivid consummation and Bloom's sense of betrayal
move him from a role of passive to one of active paternity. Like
the singers in the Ormond, Bloom is "killed looking back":
Rudy, like Bloom's past, is dead and Joyce has skillfully placed
correspondences which indicate Stephen will become Bloom's
reclaimed son in spirit. The isolation which characterized Bloom
in the first half of Ulysses is intensified in 'Sirens' until his
Cat's Cradle breaks and his movement toward Stephen begins.
Yet Bloom's only happiness in love remains with Molly, despite
her faithlessness.   Bloom has crossed his bridge of "Yessex."
"Yes" is Molly's all-encompassing gesture at the close of
Ulysses and Bloom realizes that Molly is the only "instrument"
he can play "Love's Old Sweet Song" on:

> See. Play on her. Lip blow. Body of white woman, a
> flute alive. Blow gentle. Loud. Three holes all women.
> Goddess I didn't see. (*U* 285.32-34)

The incomplete union through Lydia's shell and Lidwell's ear,
which Joyce typographically casts as "Lidlyd," is counter-
pointed by another incomplete union through sound:

> —Sure, you's burst the tympanum of her ear, man, Mr.

Dedalus said through smoke aroma, with an organ like
yours.

In bearded abundant laughter Dollard shook upon the
keyboard. He would. —Not to mention another mem-
brane, Father Cowley added. Half time, Ben. *Amoroso
ma non troppo.* Let me there. (*U* 270.13-18)

Molly's comments on Ben Dollard's "organ" surface in Bloom's
consciousness here and Ben is eventually included in Bloom's
list of Molly's possible lovers in 'Ithaca.'
      Just as Bloom moves from isolation to reunion and re-
newal, the text of 'Sirens' moves from fragmentation to unity,
from death to life. The reading process in 'Sirens' necessarily
entails an act of rereading. The opening fragments down to
"Done. Begin!" are opaque upon an initial reading due to a
lack of context, but meaning emerges as these threads of
language are woven into the text in a more expansive context
to refamiliarize the reader with them. As their leaden opacity
becomes translucent through Bloom's mental processes, both
Bloom and the reader perceive them as the "bones/of dead
men rotting in a pile," but they serve Joyce well as the skeleton
upon which to hang his stylistic *tour de force* concerning female
flesh. The shifting fields of text and context, combined with
the fragmentation and recombination of linguistic forms, offer
the first indication in Joyce's finished writings of how his talents
for linguistic manipulation would be manifested in *Finnegans
Wake.*
      The most comic (or grotesque, depending on one's sense
of humor) physical transformation in 'Sirens' closes the chapter.
Bloom's response to Robert Emmet's patriotic injunction,
which he recalls as he sees Emmet's picture in Lionel Mark's
window, is a grand burst of flatulence interrupted by the sounds
of a passing tram. This event brings the speech/writing and
sound/language polarities into play in a simultaneous deflation
of political rhetoric, which will be the primary subject of the
next chapter, 'Cyclops,' and Bloom, both literally and
figuratively. Bloom's digestive system has tranformed his mid-
day meal in 'Lestrygonians' into sustenance for life, so it can
now pass into death along with the exhausted forms of
expression which have been transformed into linguistic debris.
The distinction between speech and writing can be seen in

Joyce's ability to capture Bloom's fart in linguistic units through
which this phenomenon is understandable, but cannot be
accorded status as verbal utterance due to the lack of vowels.
The passing tram acquires semantic significance due to its sound
association with preceding material: "Karaaaaaaa" becomes
echoically linked to the phallic "carracarracarra cock," giving
a humorously Bloomian significance to Lenehan's "Got the
horn or what?" This Joycean ability to give significance to
phonemes by echoic linkage shows how the creation of a new
language in an internally referential world provides access to
heterodox realities through the visual and aural properties
of language. The previously discussed homonymic linkages
are applicable here as well.

Another comic element involved in the associational
linkages to previous sections in *Ulysses* is that Emmet is also
referred to by Bloom at the conclusion of 'Hades,' after
speaking to Hynes who misprints Bloom's name as "L. Boom"
in the list of mourners at Paddy Dignam's funeral. The
associational richness created through the recasting of previous
material in what initially appears in abstruse or inappropriate
ways, and its transformation into revelatory delights for the observant reader, demonstrate Joyce's brilliant control throughout
Ulysses. Emmet's inspiring words are eventually overwhelmed by
the life processes of Bloom, and the clatter of technology, all a-
wash together in Dublin's Sargasso Sea:

> Seabloom, greaseaseabloom viewed last words. Softly. *When
> my country takes her place among.*
> Prrprr.
> Must be the bur.
> Fff. Oo. Rrpr.
> *Nations of the earth.* No-one behind. She's passed. *Then and
> not till then.* Tram. Kran, kran, kran. Good oppor. Coming.
> Krandlkrankran. I'm sure it's the burgund. Yes. One, two.
> *Let my epitaph be.* Karaaaaaaaa. *Written. I have.*
> Pprrpffrrppffff.
> *Done.* (*U* 291.3-13)

Notes

[1] See Richard Ellmann, *Ulysses On The Liffey* (Oxford University Press, 1972). The unpaginated appendix between pp. 187 and 189 contains a full working out of the Linati and Gilbert-Gorman schemas with comparisons.

[2] Don Gifford and Robert J. Seidman, *Notes For Joyce: An Annotation of James Joyce's* Ulysses (E. P. Dutton Co., 1974), pp. 56, 239, 240.

[3] Hugh Kenner, *Joyce's Voices* (University of California Press, 1979), p. 104.

[4] Homer, *The Odyssey*, trans. Robert Fitzgerald (Anchor Books, 1963), p. 210.

[5] Colin MacCabe, *James Joyce and the Revolution of the Word* (Barnes and Noble, 1979), p. 84.

[6] Arline R. Thorn, "A Mighty Maze: Word Games in *Ulysses*," *Perspectives on Contemporary Literature* (#6/1980), p. 4.

[7] Gifford & Seidman, p. 247.

Joyce and Metafiction: The Case of 'Eumaeus.'

Carla Marengo
Torino, Italy

In a letter to Stanislaus (28 February 1905) Joyce lists a whole series of books he has read: "I have read the Sorrows of Satan, A Difficult Matter (Mrs. Lovett Cameron) The Sea Wolves (Max Pemberton) Resurrection and Tales (Tolstoy) Good Mrs. Hypocrite (Rita) Tragedy of Korosko (Conan Doyle) Visits of Elizabeth (Elinor Glyn) and Ziska," and adds "I feel that I should be a man of letters but damn it I haven't the occasion yet."[1]

A distinguishing feature of this letter, almost a manifesto, is the casualness by which Joyce establishes a connection between a list of books covering a whole range of fiction and his awareness of having a literary vocation. Joyce's eclecticism and unselectiveness can be noticed both in his avoidance of labels for the literary works cited and in his acceptance of the contiguity of literary genres at theoretical as well as at practical levels. By exploiting the plurilinguism of the genre Joyce is able to experiment with numerous ways in which stories can be told and to show how they can affect one another.

In so doing, Joyce places himself right in the middle of the contradictions of bourgeois literature which, for theoretical reasons, confers value on what is new, original and subversive, while on the other hand it denies value to imitative, repetitive and traditional literature just because it seems to respond only to the demands of the market. By setting out to explore the quality of literariness that belongs both to transgressive work and to the traditional one, Joyce seems more interested in ascertaining what is common to the various traditions and models in terms of their answers to basic needs than in singling out their original and idiosyncratic characteristics.

This attitude entails the awareness that language patterns

and narrative levels are related and interacting. To Joyce, a work of art is dependent on stereotypes and clichés—not to be inserted as quotations or paddings, but to represent the analogues of its own procedure: always reshaping, through the reference to its origins, its own model, apparently reducing the possibilities of language only in order to multiply them again.

Elementary procedures and basic devices together with their unlimited number of combinations carry on the struggle of literature in reaching out to the limits of language, always being tempted by what it does not know how to say, by what cannot be said. Old and new, conventional and unconventional, what confirms and what destroys epic distance, stand side by side in Joyce's fiction, placing the reader in an unstable relationship with the text by which he is at the same time reassured and disturbed, and in which his awareness of fiction as rule-governed is at the same time confirmed and destroyed.

Joyce's involvement with the creative processes of language does not mean that he operates in a totally chaotic or arbitrary reality; he is aware that fictional reality is highly formalized and patterned and submits to it in order to let the casualness of repetition, the combinatory games in which it originates reveal the originality of the work rather than isolated and limited actions on words or structures.

Joyce shows the author to be a function of his own fiction, dominated and controlled by the recurrence of constant features, by the incidence of universals, but at the same time engaged in reconstructing these concretions and patterns, integrating his precarious awareness into the strategies of his work.

The struggle of the author for the appropriation of language and which takes the shape of a struggle for the access to power, is played out through a series of different narrative choices that range from restricting the perspective on the ficitonal *datum,* by providing a maximum of information and explanation, by givings all the keys, to blurring the contours of events and things in order to cast them in a larger perspective by concealing or deleting the signals and indicators that might (otherwise) lead to an easy and univocal interpretation.

No matter how disruptive and ironical a novelist may be, his set task will always be to try and define what reality is through a practical rediscovery of sentiments and emotions, through the re-founding and testing of knowledge in a sort of initiatory rite endlessly resumed as he writes.

The ambiguous balance between a drive towards a total explicitness of intent (as is the case with the popular novel) and its blurred and tentative presentation becomes the background against which the whole structure of one of the most crucial chapters in *Ulysses*, "Eumaeus," must be considered.

The position of "Eumaeus" is crucial, as it is the first episode of the *Nostos* section. After the confusion of Stephen's fight with the two privates and the climax connected with it in "Circe," it is the first one in which we realize that novelistic needs will dictate the end of the literary game and dispel fictional magic. After an episode in which almost all has been enacted, the literary game is here explored and vivisected as though it were for the last time, questioning the intellectual structures and strategies of the work itself. The fictitiousness of narrative is revealed through the adoption of a metafictional mode; that is, the whole process of composing and responding to the text is deeply woven into the verbal texture of this chapter. "Eumaeus" represents the moment in which the work looks at itself and brings to light the tricks, the devices, the obscure labour of the writer by placing the world of words both in relation to and in contrast with other worlds of signs (such as economics, science, photography, history, navigation, music, painting, etc...).

The reason for the opacity, for the murkiness and the garbled style of "Eumaeus" cannot be, as has been suggested, the author's exhaustion: "There is [. . .] a distinct possibility that Joyce's own fatigue played a dominant role, for in the "Eumaeus" notesheets one sees Joyce more dependent than usual on repetitious notes, external structure, and mythological allusion. It is as if his creative imagination were momentarily bankrupt, thus compelling him to work exclusively within the previously erected framework."[2] Nor can it be ascribed to a sustained exercise in the parody of "journalese" in which "Joyce seems to have reached the limit of humiliation of English prose."[3] No particular genre is being parodied; the style rather reflects in—"the widest possible sense" (*U* 644)— the groping progress of the author within his work and his ultimate reduction to a mere junction point in the text, undermining any notion of omnipotence. The striking insistence on Homeric parallels may anticipate one of the chapter's basic issues: everything is a tale already told; its contours and details must be precise—only to be blurred again by the continuous osmotic blending with other tales.

A hazy and garbled discourse which adds irrelevancy to irrelevancy, feeding on blanks and discrepancies, represents the connective link between the various tales. The beginning "Preparatory to anything else" (*U* 613) seems to open up an endless series of fictional (and linguistic) possibilities, as though the end of the book were the beginning. Everything has happened before but everything must still happen or must happen anew—in "Eumaeus" as well as in the whole of literature.

Throughout the narrative signals are scattered to indicate that the main technical problem concerns the modalities by which a literary work can be detached from reality. The concepts of inception and conclusion, which mark the internal frontiers of "Eumaeus" stressing the idea of dimension and the problems connected with it, emerge as landmarks of a narrative and critical attitude. The tendency of the work is to inglobe itself endlessly. The story is always duplicated in terms of directions and of signals and the terminology used bears heavily on the modalities of reading. Terms are borrowed from literary criticism, which apply to the analysis of the structure and pace of discourse such as "in medias res," "finis," "dénouement," "finale form," "entrée," "contribution," "séance" "sequel," "contretemps," "coup d'oeil," or the significantly redundant "termination of [. . .] *finale*." As they often appear in italicized form, they seem to be alienated from the main context and to indicate modalities and principles on which all novels are built.[4] Concepts like "providence" and "coincidence," which intersperse and organize the structure of the stories told, can also be read as metafictional terms.[5]

Words and things often exchange places; the protagonists' reality is consistently replaced by the discourse around it: "We can't change the country, let us change the subject" (*U* 645), Stephen says. So the corpus of fiction is continually expanded by reflexiveness and self-criticism, questioning the concepts of imitation and congruity, of precise and predictable correspondences between the work of art and reality. The principle of discontinuity is brought into the work by the platitudes and generalities introduced by phrases such as "synopsis of things in general" (*U* 644) or "woolgathering," (*U* 630) which break the narrative flow—suspending belief—

and open up fictional possibilities which are never taken up
again, though.

Through the excess of explanation and comment everything is trivialized to the point of being watered down and
actually made nonsensical, empty of meaning and function
as in the phrase "whereas the simple fact of the case was it
was simply the case of the husband not being up to the
scratch. . ." (*U* 651). Thus, the writing of fiction is to be
identified with "fabrications" (*U* 635), with the wording of
illusions, the building up of utopias ("spinning yarns" *U* 635),
the propagation of lies and distortions ("bluffing," "whoppers"
U 635), "sweet nothings" (*U* 650) which take shape in the
conscious manipulation of language. The story of all these
actions and devices of language as medium is progressively
laid bare along with the development of the fragments of
stories proper.

A phrase that was the catchword and the leitmotif of
a minor character, Tom Kernan,—subsequently adopted by
Bloom[6]—becomes a major key to a reconsideration of the
working and the status of fiction in "Eumaeus." Here, the
phrase "retrospective arrangement" is isolated from its original
context and assumes a generality and an absoluteness that is
characteristically blurred by the excess of explanation and a
doubling of concepts: "Looking back now in a retrospective
kind of arrangement, all seemed a kind of dream. And the
coming back was the worst thing you ever did because it
went without saying you would feel out of place as things
always moved with the times." (*U* 651). The neat identification of what could be the mode of fiction inherent in "a
retrospective kind of arrangement" and the desire both in the
author and in the reader to order and appropriate reality is
counteracted by the cliché at the end of the sentence: the
banality (and inherent shocking truth of) "all seemed a kind
of dream" undercuts and negates the conscious process that
seemed at work in the endlessly alert game of recapturing and
reproducing past experience.[7] While common sense and clichéd
knowledge stress that it is illusory and ultimately useless to
recapture and rewind time in everyday life, the suggestion of
the "dream" fosters the idea of infinite repetition.[8] The
problem of defining identity is to be linked with the ordering
of a number of elements to a sequence, as is the case with
Fitzharris: "rumoured *to be* or *have been* Fitzharris" (*U* 641

italics mine). Here, the difference may only be between his identity in the past and in the present, between two separate series that run parallel, as manifestation of the parallactic principle.

The principle is meant to apply primarily to the kind of narrative which feeds on the recollection and rearrangement of things past, the novel, which continually tries to overreach itself by superimposing a climax and letting the last word of the story coincide with the highest crical moment attained in the act of narration.

The finished text will always appear to be immobile, "out of place," irredeemably dated in comparison with the reality that produced it. This idea is emphasized elsewhere in the chapter: "He too recollected in retrospect (which was a source of keen satisfaction in itself)" (*U* 656) closes the circle, exposing the contiguity of reality (the everyday experience of tracing the past) and fictionality (arranging experience in an order that may be satisfactory *in itself*). Reality appears to be totally fictionalized, owing its order to the coincidence principle, which in a stagy way, engenders an infinite sequence of mirrors, without any possibility of reconstructing the original constellation. The literary work, too, continuously mirrors itself, as it does in the second passage about Parnell's hat being knocked off, with Bloom picking it up: this "retrospective arrangement" requires an emphasis on the fact that a similar action has already been described earlier in the book. Therefore the "matter of strict history" (*U* 654)—and of journalistic and ephemeral report—comes alive in the larger context of *Ulysses*: "he turned round to the donor and thanked him with perfect *aplomb*, saying: *Thank you, sir* though in a very different voice from the ornament of the legal profession whose headgear Bloom also set to rights earlier in the course of the day, *history repeating itself with a difference*" (*U* 655, italics mine).

The only reality is the adventure of the book which—as intellectual work seems to take place regardless of the ability of the teller and of his limited awareness: "Nevertheless, without going into the *minutiae* of the business, the eloquent fact remained that the sea was there in all its glory and *in the natural course of things* somebody or other had to sail on it and fly in the face of providence though it merely went to show how people usually contrived to load the sort of onus on to the other fellow like the hell idea and the lottery and insurance, which were run on identically the same lines" (*U* 630, italics mine). To prolong the metaphor, "in the natural course of things," through a kind of natural law, from a strictly deterministic point of view, it appears that adventure-fiction— has to be practiced, although this entails hard labour, a burden to be carried and passed on as a sort of onerous heritage, the concern for which will haunt the inheritor.

Equally binding seem the behaviour and the attitude of the consumer of this adventure, as he requires and imposes the inception of the tale as well as its infinite swelling and growth: "those jarveys waiting news from abroad, would tempt any ancient mariner [. . .] to draw the long bow about the schooner *Hesperus* and etcetera" (*U* 635).

The composition of a novel, is both part of a generalized structure of the human mind and a basic need, a common experience as well as an adventure in language, it is an enterprise in which all agents can feel that they are engaged and capable of contributing something. But the adventure to be experienced and narrated appears to be larger, almost independent and somehow pre-existent to the person who lives through it. So characters will appear to be always overwhelmed by their roles and in their need to adjust themselves to these roles, they make their stories tally as in "the globetrotter went on adhering to his adventures" (*U* 613) or try to be "quite in keeping with [their] character" (*U* 613) or make the ingenious pun of the rover sailing on "the Rover" (*U* 615) come true within fiction; what they do is to try and rationalize chaos.

The seven years' struggle of Murphy, the sailor and story-teller, "tired of [. . .] rocks" (*U* 630)—"My little woman's down there. She's waiting for me [. . .] I haven't seen her for seven years now, sailing about" (*U* 624),—is coextensive with Joyce's labour over *Ulysses*.[9] which can be identified as the tentatively announced "*My Experiences. . . in a Cabman's Shelter*" (*U* 647).[10]   So this book identifies with parts of itself and with other books as well—from *Rip van Winkle* (*U* 624) to *The Arabian Nights' Entertainment* (*U* 659) and *The Last of the Mohicans* (*U* 660),—all books that "can be read in the dark:" not literally or because of special abilities in the reader (though Murphy boasts of them), but precisely because their tale and inner structure coincide with many other tales of the past and of the future.

A passage from another chapter of *Ulysses* seems to be no less suggestive of the self as a fictionally structured universe: "We walk through ourselves, meeting robbers, ghosts, giants, old men, young men, wives, widows, brothers-in-love. But always meeting ourselves." (*U* 213). Joyce himself traces these archetypal qualities in the *Arabian Nights*: "Arabian Nights, serial stories, tales within tales, to be continued, desperate storytelling, one caps another to reproduce a rambling mock heroic tale."[11]

Murphy's tale seems to be carried on, in the letterwriting device, by which it is enclosed and framed: "Bow to the inevitable. Grin and bear it. I remain with much love your broken hearted husband, W. B. Murphy" (*U* 625). The appropriateness of the proverbial phrase "grin and bear it" to the nautical content of the tales also reminds us of the fact that the manuscript enclosed in the bottle will have to travel by sea, risking its own loss and destruction at any moment, at the same time hoping to be stranded on some hospitable and friendly beach where it can be opened and decoded and read.[12]

Fictional traces both of the book and of Bloom can also be found in "Ithaca," where "the optical reflection of several inverted volumes improperly arranged and not in the order of their common letters with scintillating titles on the two bookshelves opposite" (*U* 708) leads to the discovery of "*Laurence Bloomfield in Ireland* by William Allimgham (second edition, green cloth, gilt trefoil design, previous owner's name on recto of flyleaf erased" (*U* 709). The mirror had previously revealed both an animation of objects through the "interchanges of looks [. . .] between [. . .] three objects and Bloom" (*U* 707) and the possibility of an exchange of identities and roles between the embalmed owl whose "clear melancholy wise bright motionless compassionate gaze regarded Bloom" and static Bloom whose "obscure tranquil profound motion less compassionated gaze regarded the matrimonial gift of Luke and Caroline Doyle" (*U* 707). At the same time his "composite asymmetrical image in the mirror" is a guarantee of perpetual movement in a space that continually enlarges itself, a signal that Bloom is not a static reflection of the world or an object among objects, but rather a living illustration of the reality that produced them.

Hugh Kenner suggests that once in *Ulysses*, "Leopold Bloom exists within an episode he actually fancies himself as writing [. . .] and the result is stylistic disaster; the episode is "Eumaeus."[13]   But far from being just the supposed author of "My Experiences in a Cabman's Shelter," Bloom emerges here and features himself as the author of the whole of *Ulysses*, as a character who is both within the book and outside it—just as every author is.

When in this chapter Bloom's passivity is reflected by the rhythm which almost slows down to a standstill, this is not merely a psychological detail, but—together with his "disgusting" soberness and keen attention—the integration of his privileged function as narrator, editor and director.   To assume the responsibilities inherent in this new capacity he must resist and shrug off the author's power to shape his fate; only then can he gain the independence and authority to write his own tale.   His aptitude for exposing disguises, lies and incongruities in other people's behaviour impels him to explore such tricks and approach the very nature of his own fictional reality.   It is meaningful that the revelation of this potential authorship[14] comes immediately after a passage in which Bloom tries to twist his fate in a more favourable way, revolting against a role which compels him to fight, as he can win only through disguised violence,[15] which would bring the action and the book to an ineluctable if untimely end.   Bloom's mind tries to escape from the nightmare of cuckoldry: "Suppose she was gone when he?. . . I looked for the lamp which she told me came into his mind but merely as a passing fancy of his because he then recollected the morning littered bed etcetera and the book about Ruby with met him pike hoses (*sic*) in it which must have fell down sufficiently appropriately beside the domestic chamberpot with apologies to Lindley Murray." (*U* 653).   The apologetic *sic*, which belongs to the editorial work proper, stresses the point that the novel is a written universe; it reveals the creative drive and aspirations in Bloom and is reinforced by the quality of the material to which it applies: the phrase "met him pike hoses" is something we actually only hear in this form as reported by Bloom—possibly Bloom's own invention.   As Hugh Kenner says "The grotesque phrase comes up again and again and again, seven more times in all, till we're quite sure we heard her say it. Her own recall [. . .] runs: that word met something with hoses in it and he came out with some jawbreakers about the incarnation."[16] Assigning roles, giving advice, instructing with an omniscient attitude are aspects of Bloom's Moses-like role particularly in "Eumaeus."

The very chapter which establishes Bloom as possible co-author also denies him the qualities of an entertainer. For Joyce, the flattening down of the author on the level of a character entails the loss of supremacy and privileged insight into the characters. At the same time, the perspective is widened by the identification with his antithetical alter, by the revelatory contiguity of the fate of the common man and the fate of mythical figures like Odysseus.

Bloom's superiority complex and his patronizing attitude in this chapter seem to cast him in a dominant role, but are counteracted by a tendency to efface him, to render him amorphous ("a strange kind of flesh," U 660) and anonymous, blending him with other characters, as the punctilious references to him as the subject of action reveal: "The horse was just then . . . and later on, at a propitious opportunity he purposed (*Bloom* did), without anyway prying into his private affairs. . ." (U 664, italics mine). Or: "And as for the lessee or keeper, who probably wasn't the other person at all, he (*Bloom*) couldn't help feeling, and most properly, it was better to give people like that the goby" (U 642, italics mine).

Just like the language used, characters are changeable, unstable, flimsy, and illusory; their identities are based on the exhibition of papers, and the ones produced by W. B. Murphy (his discharge and the postcard with the name of A. Boudin as addressee) are certainly no more valid or helpful than the newspaper in which Bloom, checking on the events of the day, is confronted with is his name mispelled a L. Boom (U 647). Genealogies are illusory, too elaborate to be credible (as in the case of Lord John Corley, U 616) or entire fabrications (as in the case of the "*soi-disant* sailor," U 630) or, if straight-forward, in direct line, dubious from the very beginning, as in the case of Simon Dedalus whose 'double' appears to have been a performer in a circus. So the characters rather appear unrooted, unburdened of family ties and ties of nationality, of social roles and productive activities which would raise their status beyond that of "nondescript specimens of the genus *homo*," U 621). But this seems to be the state of the human condition in Dublin. Literary, historical and real characters intertwine and overlap indefinitely through the mixing of the sources, as in the characterization of W. B.

Murphy as "ancient mariner" (*U 636*) blending Coleridge and Longfellow (as well as the different terms by which he is denoted: seadog, rover, sailor, seafarer, "old salt" even, which actually denotes a character in one of the stories he tells. The flimsiness of the chapter becomes apparent, when we realize that all the characters involved are in disguise; they belong to various distorting tales, in which they have to fit or to which they must adhere, the differences being only whether it is their own tale or the one other people tell about them: "The lies a fellow told about himself couldn't probably hold a proverbial candle to the wholesale whoppers other fellows coined about him." (*U 636*).

Unruliness, unpredictability, and fraudulence, together with absolute power and gratuitousness, are the distinctive traits of the storytelling figures in this chapter, of which the major ones represent characters: Bloom is called "a born adventurer" (*U 626*), the evoked Simon Dedalus "a born raconteur" (*U 620*).[17]

In order to create fictional reality, a series of tricks is necessary, such as the initiatory confinement in a sort of theatrical magic box[18]—the cabman's shelter,—where every word acquires an illusionistic twist, becoming, as it were, "conspicuous by [. . .] total absence" (*U 648*), and where the various storytellers for once in their lives have the power at the same time to create and dispel reality. The ability to slip in and out of roles—or different tales—is the major feature of the characters in this chapter. And because every role is part of a tale or pantomime or theatrical piece, stereotypes function as well as allround types. In "Eumaeus" the reader witnesses a continuous sequence of imaginative games on a revolving stage, experiencing at the same time the appropriation and sudden deprivation of the fictional world while the devices that establish it are exposed. A continuous fading of character upon character, of situation upon situation is taking place, as in the tale featuring Antonio illustrated through the animation of his own portrait tattooed on Murphy's chest. The communication between the teller ("the communicative tarpaulin," *U 626*) and the audience is tested against the ability to participate in and get out of the action presented in the theatrical terms of a proper *seance* (*U 660*):

"Tattoo, the exhibitor explained.   That was done

when we were lying becalmed off Odessa in the Black
Sea under Captain Dalton. Fellow the name of Antonio
done that. There he is himself, a Greek.
   —Did it hurt much doing that? one asked the sailor.
   That worthy, however, was busily engaged in collecting
round the someway in his. Squeezing or . . .
   —See here, he said, showing Antonio. There he is,
cursing the mate. And there he is now, he added. The
same fellow, pulling the skin with his fingers, some
special knack evidently, and he laughing at a yarn.
   And in point of fact the young man named Antonio's
livid face did acutally look like forced smiling and the
curious effect excited the unreserved admiration of
everybody, including Skin-the-Goat who this time stretch-
ed over.
   —Ay, ay, sighed the sailor, looking down on his manly
chest. He's gone too. Ate by sharks after. Ay, ay."
(631).

Interestingly enough, the tattoo only becomes meaningful and
enjoyable when animated, when the audience is invited to
pay particular attention to the tricks through which the story
is mediated ("squeezing or . . ."; "some special knack"). The
responsiveness of the audience is integrated in the telling of
the tale as well as in its conclusion, when the end of the game
signals the return to the "normal expression of before" (U
615-6); coincides with the information about the character's
death and his subsequent disappearance; "He's gone too" from
the scene. It is the series of curtains and of frames, the various
levels of abstraction—the chest of the sailor just being the stage
of the action,—the isolated chains of action that our attention
is focused on. The technique of representation within representation, the stylistical juxtaposition of contexts and messages
and their hierarchical arrangement, point in the direction of
metafiction. The effort to trace the original stories, the starting
points of each series of artifacts, proves to be meaningless—an
insight which deeply influences the reading process.
   No simple concept of art, such as "mimesis," is allowed
to take root, as reality already is presented as manipulated,
as "unnatural." The reference to an eminently metatheatrical
play, to Shakespeare's *Antony and Cleopatra*, harps on this
point: "His inscrutable face, which was really a work of art,

a perfect study in itself, beggaring description, conveyed the impression that he didn't understand one jot of what was going on. Funny very." (*U* 629). The face already is "a work of art," but—and here the reversal is funny—instead of disclosing knowledge and wisdom, its inscrutability only conceals stupidity and blindness.

Only the story counts and must deliberately be pursued to its very limits; it must be totally exhausted in rehearsal like that story, the protagonist of which is an unknown Simon Dedalus (*U* 623 f.):

>   —I seen him shoot two eggs off two bottles at fifty yards over his shoulder. The left hand deat shot. . . .
>   —Bottle out there, say. Fifty yards measured. Eggs on the bottles. Cocks his gun over his shoulder. Aims.
>   He turned his body half round, shut up his right eye completely then he screwed his features up some way sideways and glared out into the night with an unprepossessing cast of countenance.
>   —Pom, he then shouted once.
>   The entire audience waited, anticipating an additional detonation, there being still a further egg.
>   —Pom, he shouted twice.
>   Egg two evidently demolished, he nodded and winked, adding bloodthirstily:
>
>   —*Buffalo Bill shoots to kill,*
>   *Never missed nor he never will.*

Fiction, as an audience-oriented genre, imposes reality and determines expectations that must be answered ("there being still a further egg"). The action requires to be carried on until it is entirely resolved and becomes self-explanatory and obvious ("egg two evidently demolished"). It is even doubled and enlarged by the reference to the legend of Buffalo Bill. The story originates in a discrepancy over the identity of Simon Dedalus; as in other cases, the layer of documentary information is screened and at the same time multiplied by the additional information gained from the state of the text. So the "not very cleanlooking folded document" (*U* 625) exhibited by the sailor, the "stained by coffee evening journal" (*U* 629) read by a man in the shelter, the "slightly soiled photo" of Molly, on which "the slight soiling was only an added charm" (*U* 653), not only frame an event, linking it up with its original context, but also are the bait for new stories, while the perfection of the "esthetic execution" is sterile.

Thus the most usual things are cast in a light of imprecision and indeterminacy and become sources of surprise, calling for redefinition. This also holds the narratorial impulse in check, paralyzing the characters ("a brazier [. . .] or something like one [. . .] lagging footsteps [. . .] for no special reason" (*U* 615). The gratuitousness of information swells the discourse, interspersing it with irrelevancies; so we hear of "one hearer, who, by the way, seen by the side bore a distant resemblance to Henry Campbell. . ." (*U* 631) or a "lessee or keeper who probably wasn't the other person at all" (*U* 642). The starting point of most stories, the railway station, is shown in all its dead uselessness: "Great Northern railway station, the starting point for Belfast, where of course all traffic was suspended at that late hour. . ." (*U* 614).

The scientific attitude of "looking at both sides of the question" (*U* 643),[19] or of ascertaining priorities ("whether it was the traffic that created the route or viceversa or the two sides in fact," *U* 628), or of verifying and weighing each piece of information under the cover of solitude, proves diametrically opposed to the requirements of fiction. But the detective-like attitude of tentatively reproducing the conditions under which a certain criminal action took place, re-establishes a kind of creativity in the "detective" reader. No "simple" knowledge seems possible at this stage, just as there is no simple expression to it: simple souls who are tempting the old mariner to tell lies (*U* 636), who are "pretending to understand everything . . . not knowing their own minds" (*U* 655)—for whom "ignorance is bliss" (*U* 629)—have a clear idea of the tragic nature of life: "it was simply the case of the husband not being up. . ." In contrast to such simplifications, Bloom's problematic intelligence studiously tries to avoid pseudo-explanations and in his search for the truth accepts approximation and misunderstanding, as in the interpretation of the Latin dictum "*Ubi patria*" (*U* 644), in his misunderstanding of the tenor of the Italian conversation (*U* 622) and of Stephen's comment on names ("sounds are impostures," (*U* 623) as well as in the possibly incorrect quotation of the term "Acztecs" (*U* 636) instead of *ascets*.

Bloom also allows for romance when he asks Murphy about
Gibraltar and the names of the ships, when he introduces
Molly as a Spanish singer; here, he casts himself in the role
of the simple-minded person, while his "utopias" and random
meditations represent the more creative if farraginous aspect
of his mind.

In "Eumaeus," characters merge and overlap,[20] their
values and functions mix, and most of the time they act through
their understudies as Bloom does through Murphy. Their
ways of overlapping and intertwining range from ample
definitions allowing for almost any role ("Mr. Bloom who was
anything but a professional whistler. . ." *U* 613) to the putative
species of all the individuals of the same name ("the Antonio
personage is no relation to the dramatic personage of identical
name who sprang from the pen of our national poet. . .", *U*
636). Identities are assumed and genealogies altered in
theatrical embodiments: Murphy, for example, becomes an
embodiment of Simon Dedalus, Stephen's father, and therefore
threatens Bloom's aspirations to the same role; the character
of "old salt" (*U* 630) represents a self-portrait, which allows
an identification of both Murphy and Bloom ("easily pictur[ing]
his advent on the scene." The sailor is a "bit of a literary
cove in his own small way *U* 659), and just like Bloom, who
in spite of his shortcomings has the "touch of the artist" (*U*
235), he is not affected by the infelicitous performance due
to his stammer, suspicious Bloom is irresistibly attracted to
him, up to the point of excusing him: "the fictitious addresses
of the missive which made him nourish some suspicions of
our friend's *bona fides, nevertheless* it reminded him. . ." (*U*
626, italics mine), and the sailor himself seems to be totally
at ease, too, "Why, the sailor replied, relaxing to a certain
extend under the magic influence of *diamond cut diamond*,
it might be a matter of ten years" (*U* 624, italics mine). The
common denominator is the "average man, i. e. Brown, Robinson
& Co." (*U* 627) who because of his indefinability can be
related to a whole series of historical, mythical, and fictional
characters.

The basis of all fiction is precisely this "distant
resemblance" (*U* 631), which the characters bear in respect to
each other. It is the possibility of error and imprecision, of
misunderstanding that sets fiction in motion. The aspiration
of language towards clarity is continually defeated within a

literary work, just as the choice of the most appropriate diction and of unambiguous stylistic and representational strategies (*appropriate, proper, right* or *pertinent,* for example, being key terms that prove to be inadequate and almost ridiculous if seen in the light of Bloom's "Sherlockholmesing" (*U* 636) attitude in this chapter).

Stephen's question "What's in a name?" and his considerations about the value of sounds—"sounds are impostures"—are transformed in the strategic pattern of the chapter and through the force of exemplification ("Shakespeares are as common as Murphies," (*U* 622) into an exquisitely literary problem. What's in a name giver? Who has the right to give names, what is their function, what is their relationship with reality? "Where did thots come from?" (*FW* 597.25). The vain delight of Murphy in naming things, of Bloom in establishing identities, exposing the imposters and fitting the tale to the teller, of Stephen in being shocking and original, and distinct of the rest of the group, and of Beaufoy in struggling for something unusual -all this tends to show the uselessness of dealing with language as a separate and closed entity. Authors—name givers—are shown to be mere *functions* of the literary game, dependent on the work as such.

The reader caught in this game risks being gulled as he is involved in the tricky game, to which the various elements of the text combine: "So the scene between the pair of them, the licensee of the place, rumoured to be or to have been Fitzharris, the famous invincible, and the other, obviously bogus, reminded him forcibly as being on all fours with the confidence trick, supposing, that is, it was prearranged, as the lookeron, a student of the human soul, if anything, the others seeing least of the game" (*U* 641). The reader must reach the right balance of relaxation and tension, the most appropriate distance and perspective, the most appropriate timing and order of expectations and needs, the exact degree of involvement.

The author and his text, like all characters with public responsibilities, must not "outlive their welcome" (*U* 642), must be aware of how fictional rules impose themselves, shaping their own functions and roles. Every element must be introduced at the right time so that the interest does not begin "to . . . flag" (*U* 637). Exits of historical characters must be carefully planned, because their lives will be registered in terms of

their fictional consistency.   Modern historical characters must
be aware of how modern communication media (journalism,
photography, reportage) may enourmously amplify errors
in timing to the point of imposing their own rhythm and
asserting their independent truths.   Both Parnell and Fitzharris
do not seem to have paid attention to these immutable rules
and have therefore met with untimely and unheroic *exit*.   No
matter what their "historic story," it is their fictional story
that will determine their fortune with posterity, even their
resurrection ("One day you would open the paper, the cabman
affirmed, and read, Return of Parnell" *U* 648).   The power
of the press to manipulate reality is elucidated by what can
be regarded as the most powerful image of the chapter: the
sweeper, the "steamroller," which is capable of putting our
lives in danger and which almost ineluctably evokes the di-
mensions, the power, the function of the rotary presses of
the newspapers, sweeping rubbish into their pages and ennobling
it, shaping it so as to establish ideal patterns of behaviour.
(cf. *U* 662).   Through its oratorical awareness and for all its
limitations, this medium represents another accepted and
widely consumed form of literature, a place where an author
may choose his own liberty, may learn to be "his own master,"
to avail "himself of the right of free speech" (*U* 622).

Journalism becomes a metaphor for metafiction—the
discontinuous discourse from which fiction is generated anew,
dehumanized and desensualized, free from ideological bounds
and disentangled from all codes.[21]

Unlike the traditional novelist who prepares for the last
jump when the end of the book is approaching, Joyce surrenders
to the power of narrative, meeting a definite need, clearly
conscious of what he can effect: he invites to the adventurous
opening of a whole series of chinese boxes where different
skills are required each time, knowing that the pleasure is all
in the opening and not in the content.

Notes

[1] *Letters of James Joyce,* II, pp. 82-3.

[2] Phillip F. Herring, *Joyce's Ulysses Notesheets in the British Museum* (Charlottesville: The University Press of Virginia, 1972), p. 49.

[3] Anthony Burgess, *Joysprick* (London: André Deutsch, 1973), pp. 105-6.

[4] Marilyn French, *The Book as World: James Joyce's "Ulysses"* (Cambridge, Mass.: Harvard University Press, 1976), p. 208, also speaks of "foreign tags" and "italicized words and phrases" to underline the effect of strangeness and isolation of the words in "Eumaeus": "This narrator . . . uses words and phrases that have long since been assimilated into English as if they were strangers to the language."

[5] The same network of allusions and references seems to emerge in a passage of *Finnegans Wake,* 468: "Echo, read ending. Siparioramoci! But from the stress of their sunder enlivening, ay clasp, deciduously, a nikrokosmikon must come to mike.

> —Well, my positively last at an stage! I hate to look at alarms but, however they put on my watchcraft, must now close as I hereby hear by ear from by seeless socks 'tis time to be up and ambling.
>
> In the word "siparioramoci" the reference to the theatrical medium (the Italian "sipario" meaning "curtain") and to the point of the action described (the Italian "separiamoci" meaning "let us part") merge. On the other hand, the whole sentence "my positively last at any stage!" very closely reminds us of this motif in "Eumaeus": "Like actresses, always farewell—positively last performance then come up smiling again." (642)

[6] For an illuminating discussion of this motif see Susan Dick, "Tom Kernan and the Retrospective Arrangement," *J. J. Q.* , 18, 2 (Winter 1981).

[7] The alertness of the style of "Eumaeus" has been pointed out by Fritz Senn, "Bloom among the Orators: the Why and the Wherefore and All the Codology," *Irish Renaissance Annual,* I, 1980: "If he had the resources of a Mr. Philip Beaufoy (or, as he seems to think, of Stephen Dedalus, poet and man of letters), then he might be able to compose such figurative, parabolic, ornate, winged, fumbling, discordant and alert (yes, alert) prose

as the one of "Eumaeus."

[8]The same idea finds a more naive formulation in the clichéd language of "Nausicaa": "Returning not the same. Like kids your second visit to a house." (*U* 77).

[9]The "Eumaeus" episode was finished before April 1921. In a letter to John Quinn, Joyce writes on 24 November 1920: "I began Ulysses in 1914 and I shall finish it, I suppose, in 1921" and he adds "I hope to finish the *Circe* episode before Christmas. Eumaeus, being already drafted, I could send on in January." (*Letters of James Joyce*, III, 1966), pp. 30-1. —The vicious circle in which Joyce himself feels to be caught, is expressed in a letter to Frank Budgen: "All I can do is to slave along at Bloom, curse him" (end of February 1921), (*Letters of James Joyce*, 1957), p. 159.

[10]Cf. the "Nausicaa" episode: "See ourselves as others see us. . . Ask yourself who he is now. *The Mystery Man on the Beach*, prize titbit story by Mr. Leopold Bloom." (*U* 376).

[11]*Scribbledehobble* (Northwestern University Press, 1961), p. 21.

[12]The relevancy of the nautical terminology hardly needs discussion. The sea experience proves to underline the narrative structure of the chapter, starting from the description of Bloom as "all at sea for a moment" (*U* 623), to that of a no better qualified Dublin eccentric, O'Callaghan, "landed into hot water" (*U* 645), ending with Parnell as an outstanding example of shipwreck.

[13]Hugh Kenner, *Ulysses* (London: Allen & Unwin, 1980), p. 68.

[14]Fritz Senn, *Irish Renaissance Annual*, I, 1980, p. 187, "Clearly both "Circe" and "Eumaeus" in their own particular modes hint at a distorted fulfillment of Bloom's rhetorical (and authorial) aspirations."

[15]In a letter to Frank Budgen (end February 1921) Joyce had to admit that violence was well within the scope of the Ulyssean world: "At one time I thought the slaughter of the suitors un-Ulyssean. In my present frame of mind I have modified my opinion," (*Letters of James Joyce*, 1957), p. 160.

[16]Hugh Kenner, *Ulysses*, p. 82.

[17]Cf. Marilyn French, *The Book as World*, p. 215 "We do not trust the narrator and we look to the characters, to their dialogue and to their inner monologue to discover the facts." Fritz Senn is even more radical in his approach "We may not even trust the dashes any longer. . . Sounds and speeches and dashes may be impostures in "Eumaeus," a chapter of guises and subterguges," (*Irish Renaissance Annual*, I, [cf. ann. 7] p. 187.

[18]We are reminded of the incantatory nature of Murphy's dream-like words when Bloom and Stephen have gone out of the magic box: "Ex-Gumley, was still to all intents and purposes wrapped in *the arms of Murphy*, as the adage has it, dreaming of fresh fields and pastures new. (*U* 660,

italics mine). Also, the narrative technique suggests the magic tricks of the camera eye: "A few moments later *saw* our two noctambules safely seated. . ." (*U* 621, italics mine).

[19] Bloom contines, in this chapter the "Mr. Knowall" attitude and unimaginative, matter-of-fact drive introduced elsewhere in the book. (cf. *U* 315).

[20] Shari Benstock and Bernard Benstock link this phenomenon with other representational strategies of this chapter: "The camera's eye never allows us to view the entire scene at once and enumerate the characters present. Nor are most of them clearly defined individuals, and like the metamorphosing dog in Circe they change identities throughout. The two constants are Stephen and Bloom; two defined variables are the grizzled seaman and the shelter keeper, but they are both shrouded in mystery . . . How many casual customers are scattered about is impossible to determine, but the safest assumption is three . . . their occupations if any, are unclear. The narrative voice is uncertain referring to them most often as 'cabbies' (at one time noting, 'the jarvey if such he was'—632), but the trio is also detailed on the same page as 'longshoreman number one,' 'loafer number two,' and 'a third' (the narrative voice simultaneously guessing at a vocation and making a value judgment)." *Who's He When He's at Home, A James Joyce Directory,* (Urbana: University of Illinois Press, 1980), pp. 37-8.

[21] Marilyn French, *The Book as World,* pinpoints this achievement showing that the "loss of the reader's subject matter" is to be linked with "the meandering style" of "Eumaeus" (p. 212) and that the reader, at this point, "is paranoid with distrust" (p. 216), having lost all certainties, having ascertained that language is deception. "Clearly the narrator knows that the reader is involved in the coming together of Stephen and Bloom, and he is mocking him for his interest." (p. 19)

"Ithaca"—An Essay in Non-Narrativity

Monika Fludernik
Vienna, Austria

> Unlike all the other techniques of *Ulysses* question-and-answer (especially question-and-answer of this formality) is not naturally a narrative method; it implies a static situation which is being examined and analyzed rather than the unrolling of a concatenated series of events or developments. There are events and developments in the chapter—some of them important ones—but the method blurs their place in a sequence and deadens their impact; instead it puts all the emphasis on a detached and apparently ill-ordered enquiry into the state of the two men and the nature of their relationship.[1]

The present paper is meant to enlarge upon this perceptive comment by Peake, showing that what he has noticed in his commonsensical way is in fact borne out by narrative theory and a narratological analysis of "Ithaca."

There are several key-words in this passage, but the most important phrase is "not naturally a narrative method." Peake explains that not only is the question-and-answer technique in itself an unfamiliar method of narration, he also tries to establish why, in this particular case, the reader has difficulties in ascertaining the sequence of events (or plot).

It will be advisable to start with a short discussion of the term narrative (versus non-narrative). There is no agreement among scholars as to the precise qualities of the epic versus the lyric and dramatic genres. A few basic propositions, however, are generally accepted. Robert Scholes defines narrative as consisting of a story and a story-teller.[2] Or, as Gérard Genette has maintained,

> Story and narration would not exist for us without the
> mediation of the *récit*. But reciprocally, the *récit*, the
> narrative discourse, can be what it is only by telling
> a story, without which it would not be narrative (like,
> let us say, the *Ethics* of Spinoza), and only in so far as
> it is presented by someone, without which (like a collec-
> tion of archeological documents) it would not be dis-
> course. As narrative, it lives by its relation to the story
> that it tells; as discourse, it lives from its relation to the
> narration that it offers.[3]

Even if most critics would agree with this vague definition,
there is serious disagreement about the qualities of a story
in narrative. It is not absolutely clear what would be the minimal
requirements for a plot,[4] and—as Scholes has admitted himself—
the essentially aesthetic relation between events cannot be
grasped in a purely structural analysis lacking semantic
reference.[5] As has become obvious in recent criticism, the
mere presence of two or more events and their relatedness do
not necessarily establish a plot.

The answer to this dilemma can be supplied by a trans-
formational model[6] in which the plot (or sequence of events)
functions as deep-structure to the actual narrative, the surface-
structure on which the events have been rearranged according
to (admittedly still elusive) aesthetic rules. The teleology of
the narrative will thus admit of considerable disrupture in the
correct chronological sequence of events, a disrupture which,
in itself, is frequently regarded as a criterion of the higher
"literariness" of a text.[7]

Even greater disagreement will be found with regard to
Scholes' postulated story-teller. In the modern epic the story-
teller (first-person or third-person personal narrator) has frequently been eliminated as a distinct personality giving way
to a presentation of events through the consciousness of one
(or more) character(s). As Stanzel has shown conclusively,[8]
however, even in this case events are not presented immediately
but through the mediation of this (these) "reflector(s)."
Stanzel here develops Plato's distinction between *diegesis* and
mimesis.[9]

Whereas drama is seen to be a purely mimetic genre, the
epic is defined as a combination of mimetic and diegetic
elements.[10] Traditionally, dialogue has been regarded as the

main mimetic (or non-narrative) constituent of narrative texts.
Characters' soliloquies, and recently interior monologues, i. e.
characters' inner speech as well as their dialogue, are thus set
aside from the diegetic part of the narrative (narrator's speech).
Instead of defining the narrative text as a combination of diegetic
and mimetic elements, therefore also explain it as the
interlocking of narrator's and characters' speech.[11]   Since
characters' speech is frequently mediated through the diegetical
part of a text (in the form of indirect speech or narrated speech
discours indirect libre, the fundamental difference in status
between narrator's and characters' speech has sometimes been
lost sight of:

> Da sie [K. Hamburger] nun aber nicht zwischen Autor
> und Erzähler scheiden möchte, sondern nur ganz allge-
> mein von einer Erzählfunktion spricht, die eine fluk-
> tuierende sei, weil sie bald Dialogform annehme, bald
> sich in indirekter oder erlebter Rede [indirect speech or
> narrated speech] vollziehe, verwischt sie den *grund-*
> *sätzlichen Unterschied, der zwischen den beiden Sprech-*
> *situationen, derjenigen des Erzählers und derjenigen*
> *der Personen, besteht,* woraus, wie schon in den zwanziger
> Jahren erkannt wurde, gerade die Spezifität des Narrativen
> resultiert, insofern es sich ja *nicht* einfach *um* zwar
> verschiedene, aber *hierarchisch-funktional gleichrangige*
> *Sprechebenen handelt, sondern diejenige des Erzählers*
> *die Instanz ist, die die dargestellte Welt als ganze ver-*
> *mittelt.* (My emphasis)[12]

The co-existence of diegetic and mimetic elements,
particularly in the novel, can also be explained by the historical
development of the novel out of various heterogeneous narrative
forms:

> In this way the novel broke with narrative form and
> became a combination of dialogues, scenes, and detailed
> presentations of decor, gestures, and intonations.[13]

This quotation from Eichenbaum's "Theory of Prose" also
makes clear that—like characters' speech—purely descriptive
passages are not diegetic in themselves but serve as illustrative
adjuncts to pure narration in the same way as dialogue scenes

can be said to illustrate or adorn a narrative.

The above survey of definitions for the term 'narrative' will have demonstrated that no unequivocal paraphrase has as yet been found. In point of fact, the novel has profited to a large degree from the vagueness of its concept and from its affinities to extrá literary genres, and its resistance to catalogization must eventually be seen as one of its greatest merits.

The term narrative is generally used in two radically different senses, either with the connotations of 'diegetic' or of 'epic;' or, if one so wishes, it is used in the narrow sense for those parts of an epic text which 'narrate,' and in a broader sense for the epic genre itself (which, because it is constituted on the basis of story and story-teller, is traditionally felt to be dominated by diegesis or narration).

Since the epic genre and hence the term narrative have developed drastically with regard to form and content from Homeric times merely by virtue of having been distinguished from the lyric or dramatic genres, a discussion of whether a text is narrative or non-narrative can in general be easily resolved with reference to form alone. Critics who maintain that a certain text is narrative or non-narrative, however, usually pass verdict on whether the text in question can still be regarded as a novel in the traditional sense of the word. The novel, as an historical genre of evidently heterogeneous provenance, has always resisted delimitation with regard to form or content. To judge whether something is or is not a novel is therefore usually a value judgment. After Nabokov's *Pale Fire* and similar experiments in the novel one will have to accept a very wide definition of the term 'novel' indeed.

To me, therefore, the only reasonable starting-point for an enquiry into the narrativity of a narrative text seems to lie in the study of diegetic elements, their quantity and their distribution in the text, in this case the "Ithaca" episode of *Ulysses.* This procedure will allow for a more detailed view of the development of the novel into the twentieth century as well. It can prove that in a number of modern novels the diegetic element has been reduced considerably (one need only think of Compton-Burnett's dialogue novels or of Beckett's quasi-pure interior monologues):

> One of these extremes [problem cases with regard to categorization i. e.], familiar in modern literature, consists

of works with a narrative base (such as *Marius the Epi-
curean* or *Ulysses,* to name two different cases), upon
which so many non-narrative elements have been erected
that the work's narrative quality is severely attenuated
for the sake of other qualities.[14]

Returning to Peake's statement as quoted at the beginning
of this paper, it will now have become evident that the question-
and-answer technique is not naturally a narrative method.
Dialogue as the main constituent of drama and as a mimetic
element of fiction is certainly un-mediating and hence, one
should think, non-epic. However, we should beware of taking
the form for the content. Question-and-answer techniques
of this formality are not naturally mimetic either, but in
fact could be regarded as deriving from a model of philosophic
enquiry such as is exemplified in Plato's dialogues. In these
cases dialogue is argumentative and diegetic or didactic (though
on a metalinguistic and metafactual level). It will therefore
be worth pursuing the question whether—irrespective of its
im-mediate form, which is generally employed in mimetic
texts—"Ithaca" contains narrative (i. e. diegetic) elements and
whether (and how) it mediates a story. Pure diegesis, as in
Plato's dialogues, or in any text of referential prose, need not
occur in fiction alone. Discussing the 'narrativity' of "Ithaca"
must therefore involve an analysis of the diegetic elements
in the text as well as eventually an enquiry into the epic
qualities of the episode as a whole.

It will thus be impossible to keep the two connotations
of the term narrative apart as strictly as this could be wished
for in the framework of this study. However, I shall endeavour
to indicate in each instance whether I am using the term in its
restricted or its more general sense.

In an approximate statistic (based on a quarter-line
unit) 14.7% of "Ithaca" as printed consists of questions. Of
the answers, 16.6% describe the actions of the protagonists
Stephen and Bloom and could therefore be termed 'narrative.'
4.4% of the text deal with utterances made by Bloom and
Stephen and 33.5% with the representation of their consciousness. Taking the three together, one can say that 54.5% of
the episode render what we might call the 'plot' of "Ithaca."

However, this leaves us with further 30.8% of the text
to account for. These passages deal with extraneous material

not necessarily related to the actual goings-on in Bloom's house.   I am referring here to passages like the description of the water-way to Bloom's tap, the enumeration of articles in Bloom's drawer, or the philosophical analyses of Bloom's thoughts such as the one quoted below.

> Reduce Bloom by cross multiplication of reverses of fortune, from which these supports protected him, and by elimination of all positive values to a negligible negative irrational unreal quantity.
>
> Successively, in descending helotic order: Poverty: that of the outdoor hawker of imitation jewellery, the dun for the recovery of bad and doubtful debts, the poor rate and deputy cess collector. Mendicancy: that of the fraudulent bankrupt with negligible assets paying ls.4d. in the £, sandwichman, distributor of throwaways, nocturnal vagrant, insinuating sycophant, maimed sailor, blind stripling, superannuated bailiff's man, marfeast, lickplate, spoilsport, pickthank, eccentric public laughing-stock seated on bench of public park under discarded perforated umbrella. Destitution: the inmate of Simpson's Hospital for reduced but respectable men permanently disabled by gout or want of sight. Nadir of misery: the aged impotent disfranchised ratesupported moribund lunatic pauper. (p. 686)[15]

In order to avoid paying too much attention to the form of "Ithaca" instead of analyzing the process of plot transmission, I have found it useful to try to transform the question-and-answer sets into uniform statements as illustrated in the example below.

> Of what did the duumvirate deliberate during their itinerary?
>   Music, literature, Ireland, Dublin, Paris, friendship . . .
>   (627)

transformed into:

> During their itinerary the duumvirate deliberated of music, literature, Ireland, Dublin, Paris, friendship, woman, prostitution, diet, the influence of gaslight or

> the light of arc and glowlamps on the growth of adjoining
> paraheliotropic trees, exposed corporation emergency
> dustbuckets, the Roman catholic church, ecclesiastical
> celibacy, the Irish nation, jesuit education, careers,
> the study of medicine, the past day, the maleficent
> influence of the presabbath, Stephen's collapse.

Examples like the one quoted on the previous page ("Re-
duce Bloom by cross multiplication of reverses. . .") lead
us straight on to another problem connected both with the
subject-matter of such passages and with our tentative transformation of the text into continuous prose. Passages such
as these resist transformation because it is not quite clear
whether Bloom is actually thinking about his possible
penury or whether the generator of these questions is
improvising on the subject of Bloom. Who compiles the
budget? And who has assembled the list of Molly's suitors?
These questions have to be answered if we want to transform
our text into prose. Is it "Bloom compiled a budget as follows"
or "If we were to compile a budget, it would look as follows?"

Critics disagree on whether "Ithaca" has to be seen from
Bloom's point of view. Personally, I adhere to Goldman's
suggestion that "by its fifteenth chapter, *Ulysses* has begun
to provide its author enough in the way of material to become
self-perpetuating."[16]   The form here generates new material,
and this material need not describe what is going on, on a purely
realistic plot level. As Peake phrases it, the text "examines
and analyzes" the reality of "Ithaca," and in doing so adds
much extraneous material and information appropriately clad
in meta-linguistic form and logic.

30.8% of the episode deals with such non-realistic material.
Bernard Benstock has reached similar conclusions in his
article on "Ithaca."[17] His analysis further distinguishes between
passages apparently generated by a camera eye view of things
and passages which he calls "encyclopedia." He also pays
attention to combinations of various forms, for instance "Conversation & Encyclopedia" or "Camera eye and Bloom's mind"
etc.

One encounters similar difficulties at the end of the episode,
which resists transformation because the questions "Womb?
Weary?", "With?", "When?", and "Where?" cannot be interpreted realistically or be made to tally with the preceding des-

cription of Bloom's posture in his bed.

So far we have established that a number of passages resist transformation because their relation to the reality described is problematic. Furthermore, we have found that the reality of which we can get a glimpse in the text is being interpreted and analyzed with the help of much material alien to the minds of either character. But let us treat these passages as scientific (or scholastic) digressions and examine a longer section dealing with the actions of our protagonists in order to ascertain the relationship between the individual 'sentences' of our transformed prose text:

> Having set the half-filled kettle on the now burning coals, he [Bloom] returned to the still-flowing tap to wash his soiled hands with a partially consumed tablet of Barrington's lemonflavoured soap, to which paper still adhered (bought thirteen hours previously for fourpence and still unpaid for), in fresh cold neverchanging everchanging water and to dry them, face and hands, in a long redbordered holland cloth passed over a wooden revolving roller.
>
> In answer to Bloom's offer Stephen answered, declining, that he was a hydrophobe, hating partial contact by immersion or total by submersion in cold water (his last bath having taken place in the month of October of the preceding year), disliking the aqueous substances of glass and crystall, distrusting aquacities of thought and language.
>
> (The recognition of the probable) incompatibility of acquacity with the erratic originality of genius impeded Bloom from giving Stephen counsels of hygiene and prophylactic to which should be added suggestions concerning a preliminary wetting of the head and contraction of the muscles with rapid splashing of the face and neck and thoracic and epigastric region in case of sea or river bathing, the parts of the human anatomy most sensitive to cold being the nape, stomach and thenar or sole of foot.
>
> Similarly he repressed the following additional didactic counsels: Dietary: concerning the respective percentage of protein and caloric energy in bacon, salt ling and butter, the absence of the former in the lastnamed and

the abundance of the latter in the firstnamed.

Confidence in himself and an equal and opposite power of abandonment and recuperation seemed to be the predominant qualities of Bloom's guest.

At the same time the phenomenon of ebullition occurred in the vessel of liquid by the agency of fire. Fanned by a constant updraught of ventilation between the kitchen and the chimneyflue, ignition was communicated from the faggots of precombustible fuel to polyhedral masses of bituminous coal, containing in compressed mineral form the foliated fossilised decidua of primeval forests which had in turn derived their vegetative existence from the sun, primal sources of heat (radiant), transmitted through omnipresent luminiferous diathermanous ether. Heat (converted), a mode of motion developed by such combustion, was constantly and increasingly conveyed from the source of calorification to the liquid contained in the vessel, being radiated through the uneven unpolished dark surface of the metal iron, in part reflected, in part absorbed, in part transmitted, gradually raising the temperature of the water from normal to boiling point, a rise in temperature expressible as the result of an expenditure of 72 thermal units needed to raise 1 pound of water from 50° to 212° Fahrenheit.

A double falciform ejection of water vapour from under the kettle lid announced the accomplishment of this rise in temperature. (633-634).

Some events no doubt occur here, but none of them are presented in their conventional order. Bloom's offer to Stephen to wash himself is left out and only alluded to. The plot is not 'narrated' but taken for granted and analyzed. There is a gap (in logic as well as in presentation) between each segment. Whereas, conventionally, narrative would give us the basic facts ('narrate' them) and then, perhaps, enlarge upon details (commentary, interpretation), this sequence starts with the interpretation of a given sequence of events and so forces the reader to reconstruct what may have happened from the consequent interpretations based on these events. Diegesis, and particularly narrative diegesis, is usually intent on telling its subject matter as lucidly and effectively as possible, as far as this is consistent with aesthetic considerations. This applies to the chronology of events as well as to their consequentiality, both of which are conventionally meant to support the teleology of the narrative. Where a narrative passage tends to be centred on the sequence of events, a didactic passage (referential prose, such as scientific or philosophic argumentation) tends to stress logicality.

Both criteria have been disregarded in our 'discourse.' There is no link between the single statements, which frequently obscure the relevant facts. Bloom's 'offer' is relegated to the verb complement and only Stephen's reaction to it is described. If we were to rewrite this passage intelligently, we would have to insert connective particles and clauses, thus restituting the missing connections.

The logic of the question-and-answer pattern in "Ithaca" resists definition since it does not follow the rules of actual scientific enquiry. If such an enquiry is conducted, it follows inherent logical rules such as spatial or temporal order, cause and effect patterns or the endeavour to complete a given pattern or scheme. Not surprisingly, "Ithaca" as a parody of science grossly violates such implicit rules by the inconsequentiality of its argument, the apparently random questioning.

This illogicality or incompatibility of the sequence of questions is supported by their disparate origin. Some of these questions try to elucidate the plot, some of them are hyper-scientific, some may be termed scholastic, a few could be styled exam-paper questions. As Peake has observed correctly, questions and answers share two characteristics: a recurrent lack of discrimination (the answers are frequently incompatible with the questions, particularly in the amassing of irrelevant detail), and "flat encyclopaedism."[18] Thus the pseudo-scholarly logic of "Ithaca" disrupts not only the sequence of questions but also the proper relationship between questions and answers.

One will have to conclude that "Ithaca," even if transformed into continuous prose, is not a diegetic text. In fact, it seems to have been structured in a way so as to deliberately elude diegetic rules of logic. This lack of connectives is not due to the form of the episode, the question-and-anwer pattern as such, but to the randomness of the questioning. There seems to be a lack of aim at each and every point in the text and hence a wavering between various alternate possibilities. No clear subject-matter of investigation nor a definite method of enquiry have been adopted—with fatal results for the reputation of scholarliness.

"Ithaca" is therefore not a narrative text in the restrictive sense of the term. One could go from here to postulate that it is hence non-epic as well, since a minimum of diegetic text would seem to be an indispensable constituent of the epic genre. However, this stipulation would not be acknowledged without reservations by a great number of narratologists. In the introductory remarks of this paper I came to the conclusion that mediation of a plot can be seen as the main epic feature. Therefore, I will add a brief discussion of the quality of mediation in "Ithaca."

Mediation of a story is traditionally effected by means of a personal narrator (first-person narrator or third-person narrator such as in Salinger's *Catcher in the Rye* or Fielding's *Tom Jones*). In what F. K. Stanzel calls the figural narrative situation,[19] such as *A Portrait of the Artist as a Young Man*, the story is mediated through the consciousness of one or more of the major characters. In such novels events frequently have to be reconstructed from the reactions of the soliloquizing characters; they are not 'narrated.' Mediation thus occurs through a distinct consciousness, that of the protagonist, whereas in more traditional narration the narrator provides the focus of uniform consciousness.

This kind of explanation has been challenged by Dorrit Cohn in her recent review of Stanzel's book.[20] For her, a minimum of diegetic narrative is necessary for mediation. Molly's pure interior monologue, taken out of the novel's context, is thus excluded from her revisionary typological circle.[21] It is difficult to resolve the two interpretations. Faulkner's *As I Lay Dying*, for example, seems to reveal a continuity of experiments with the non-diegetic, but on the other hand texts like these can be seen as "experiments" or border-cases with no general validity. Perhaps one will have to accept the fact that the necessary connivance of the reader in the reconstruction of the plot shifts the centre of mediation from the story-teller to the reader. If this were an essential element of mediation, "Ithaca" would indeed belong to this category, since here as there the reader is required to piece together information concealed in the episode. Mediation would therefore lie in the resistance of the text to its direct perception by the reader as either *recit* (diegesis) or immediate presentation (i. e. illusion of immediacy of presentation), and it would call attention to the text as an intractable medium, a code to be deciphered by the reader.

These suggestions are not meant to provide a definitive third scheme, but in fact present a way of obviating the necessity of designating "Ithaca" as either epic or non-epic. They want to illustrate that—in contrast to mathematical logic—the absence of diegesis for "Ithaca" does not necessarily imply the absolute non-narrativity of this episode. However, it certainly does prove "Ithaca" to be a non-narrative (i. e. non-diegetic) part of *Ulysses.*

For "Ithaca," then, one could postulate something like 'non-diegetic narrativity,' or the constitution of narrativity on the basis of (macrostructural) mediation of plot (through admittedly non-diegetic elements). In "Ithaca" this process manifests itself in a two-fold way. For one, "Ithaca," like "Penelope," is part of *Ulysses* as a whole and hence 'epic' just as dialogue passages in a narrative text are epic. But, more importantly, the plot is mediated through questions and answers about the plot, and so the reader is led to establish the facts for himself.

At this stage a comparison with narrative techniques in earlier episodes of *Ulysses* is due. As far as percentages of narrative statements are concerned, "Ithaca" with approximately 16.6% ranges near the average (about 22% of *Ulysses* consists of narratives in the individual episodes).[22] The problem with the 'narrative' in "Ithaca," however, is its illogicality and inconsequentiality, a problem which seems to be absent from narratives in the earlier chapters of the novel. This impression is shown to be false by a close examination of the narrative in the earlier episodes. In fact, nowhere in *Ulysses* does the narrative approach the diegetic proportions of a conventional narrative text.

Because of their different narrative situations,[23] one has to consider the initial episodes (roughly up to and including "Wandering Rocks") apart from the rest of the novel. In the initial episodes Stanzel's figural narrative situation, in which the story is mediated through the consciousness of Stephen or Bloom, prevails even though an increasing authorial presence makes itself felt. In these episodes the diegetic element is deliberately kept inconspicuous in order to maintain and strengthen the illusion of immediacy in the text. The two main devices for effecting this inconspicuousness of the diegetic are the juxtaposition of short narrative passages with interior monologue and dialogues and, secondly, the stylistic assimilation of the narrative to the main character's idiom (including the appropriation of the characters' idiom by the impersonal narrator).[24]

Juxtaposition is an essentially non-diegetic device since it tries to evade the sequential nature of language and foregrounds the simultaneity of juxtaposed elements. Furthermore, both dialogue and interior monologue are mimetic *per se* and hence the emphasis in the initial episodes is on mimesis even if the framework of the narrative implies a diegetic basis for these chapters.

When an authorial (narratorial) presence makes itself felt in *Ulysses* (first in slightly ironical and over-particular descriptions in "Calypso" and "Lotuseaters"), this does not imply a strengthening of diegetic elements. Up to "Hades" the narrative in itself remains unobtrusive, but its idiom (in part) and some of the juxtapositions with passages of interior monologue or dialogue signal the presence of a non-neutral *arrangeur*. Nevertheless, the narrative is still felt to provide a diegetic framework for these three episodes.

In "Aeolus" the juxtaposition of headlines and narrative as well as the stylistic properties of the narrative in itself (descriptive passages such as the new beginning of "Aeolus"[25] and word-play throughout the whole chapter) increase the importance of the narrator's point of view and suppress (or even obstruct) the diegetic qualities of the narrative. Nevertheless, "Aeolus" can be regarded as a text with a diegetic framework if one considers the headlines as a merely formal super-imposition of non-narrative elements. The *Little Review* version of "Aeolus" did not differ from "Hades" with regard to narrative techniques.

In "Lestrygonians" the diegetic element in the narrative dominates although the peculiar phrasing of various sentences not only indicates the presence of a playful narrator but also disrupts the ideal lucidity of diegesis.

In "Scylla and Charybdis" the extent of word-play in the narrative has reached such proportions that the diegetic quality of the episode has waned to a considerable extent. As in "Proteus," the narrative could even be regarded as a description of Stephen's perceptions in his own vocabulary, which would attenuate the narrative quality of the episode even further.

In "Wandering Rocks" diegesis is reduced by the consistent employment of juxtaposition as a disruptive device both in the individual sections of the chapter and in the episode as a whole. Even in the coda (section xix) discontinuity makes itself felt as the reader is presented with a seemingly random sequence of unconnected portraits and descriptions. In spite of the stylistic conspicuousness of the prose there is no real 'narration of events.'

In the first nine or ten episodes of *Ulysses* mimetic elements can therefore be said to dominate but are superimposed on a conventionally-looking diegetic framework of narrative. Since the reader takes his clues about the plot from the diegetic statements in the text, he is likely to consider juxtaposition and other non-narrative devices as formalistic surface-structure elements not essentially incompatible with the mediation of the plot. The narrative situation has changed from figural to almost-authorial (an elusive omniscient narrator competes with Stephen's and Bloom's points-of-view from "Hades" onward). If we are to believe Cohn, the basic pattern has not changed, since for her the diegetic framework is essential to a figural narrative situation; the change would then ostensibly lie in a change in narrative perspective.

With "Sirens" and "Cyclops" the narrator's (narrators') point(s)-of-view take over completely. However, this does not result in an emphasis on diegesis, as one would expect. The continued and obtrusive playfulness of the narratives, juxtaposition ("Sirens," "Cyclops," "Oxen of the Sun"), and stylistic parody stress the diminishing importance of plot rather than the diegetic quality of conventional narrative parodied in the pastiches. This is very surprising in view of the fact that the episodes from "Sirens" to "Oxen of the Sun" are dominated by (authorial) narrative (45.7% in "Sirens" and over 65% in "Cyclops"—counted, again, on a quarter-line basis). An analysis of the various narratives in "Sirens" and the following episodes shows that most of the narrative is either obtrusively playful (thus emphasizing not the transmission of plot but the medium of language—this is true of the pastiches as well),—or mainly descriptive (description in itself is not diegetic), as in the many mock-epic pastiches in "Cyclops." To some extent this applies to "Eumaeus" as well, an episode presumably foregrounding conventionally narrative (and hence diegetic) elements.[26]

"Circe" and "Ithaca" are episodes mimetic (non-narrative) in form but not necessarily in their content. The stage-directions in "Circe" closely resemble a fantastic narrative, but they are not intrinsically diegetic. In both episodes plot is transmitted through non-narrative forms; in "Ithaca" this is done in a much more radical way, since there are no stage-directions to generate the dialogue and put it into a narrative framework. "Penelope," as a pure interior monologue, however, is purely mimetic. There is no plot to be transmitted in this last episode, except perhaps for Molly's shifting of her position from bed to chamber-pot and back again.[27] The rest is silent—though voluble—thought.

After this survey of narrativity in *Ulysses*, one has to conclude that the novel does not consistently employ conventional patterns of diegesis in its narrative except for the purpose of parody. The absence of diegetic elements does not become evident until "Circe" and "Ithaca," however, because it is in these episodes that non-narrative (i. e. non-diegetic) content and non-narrative form are conjoined. In earlier episodes and in "Eumaeus" diegetic elements exist in varying proportions, but their diegetic effect is disrupted by mimetic interpolations or by the stylistic quality of the narrative itself. Hence, even in these earlier episodes narrativity is constituted in the overall macro-structure of *Ulysses*.

How is this macrostructural narrativity engendered? Does it rest on the diegetic elements in the various episodes, which imply a diegetic framework? The answer to this question is probably in the affirmative. Since the reader of *Ulysses* starts reading a text which he knows to be fiction, he will expect a story to be told. He will therefore take the diegetic elements in the text as clues to an implicit diegetic framework not explicitly laid out in the text and he will regard narrative as diegetic even if it has been distorted almost beyond recognition by the playful stylistics of the narrator (as in "Sirens"). This instinctive need of the reader to work out a plot, even if narrative (i. e. diegetic) elements are missing or scarce in a given text, makes the reader the one mediating instance (or consciousness of mediation) in those kinds of fiction not easily ascribable to either the mediation of personal narrators or the consciousness of one (or more) of its characters. In this way "Ithaca," although non-narrative in form as well as content, could be regarded as a narrative (i. e. epic) text. This interpretation also helps to explain some of the features of earlier episodes which seemed to contradict the thesis that Stephen's or Bloom's point-of-view was dominant from "Telemachus" to "Hades." Although— on a microstructural level—narratorial omniscience can be shown to compete with Stephen's and Bloom's point-of-view (particularly so in "Telemachus" and "Hades"), on a macro-structural level it is the reader who, in his need to find a simple, dominant perspective, transfers Bloom's (or Stephen's) point-of-view even to neutral passages presumably originating with an omniscient (impersonal) narrator. It is, thus, the reader who constitutes the narrative (epic) quality of *Ulysses* by inter-preting disparate diegetic and non-diegetic elements in the text as clues to a story which is not told conventionally but has to be re-written or re-performed by the reader in the act of reading.

In this way *Ulysses,* like *Tristram Shandy,* reveals itself as a self-analysis of the novel rather than a purely narrative text. Of course, few narratives are consistently or purely diegetic (perhaps with the exception of folk-tales); however, the amount of non-narrative elements in *Ulysses*, even at the very start of the novel, is worth specific consideration. "Ithaca" is the last episode to constitute narrativity (mediation of the plot) on a macro-structural level. ("Penelope," I think, should be consider-ed as a coda without narrative content.) "Ithaca," Joyce's favourite episode, then, marks the climax of a development beyond the borders of the narrative genre, or, as W. A. Litz has put it, "In its radical form 'Ithaca' bypasses the familiar conventions of nineteenth-century fiction and shows us another way in which the novelist's passion for omniscience can be achieved without violating our sense of individual and local reality."[28]

Notes

[1]Peake, C. H., *James Joyce. The Citizen and the Artist*, (London, 1977), 283.

[2]Scholes, Robert, and R. Kellogg, *The Nature of Narrative*, (Oxford 1966, repr. 1971), 4.

[3]Quoted from the translation by Robert Scholes (*Structuralism in Literature. An Introduction*, [London, 1974]), 165; cf. also Genette, Gerard *Narrative Discourse. An Essay in Method* (Ithaca, NY, 1980), 29.

[4]Cf. Scholes, *Structuralism in Literature*, 95-96.

[5]Ibid., 102.

[6]Cf. Stanzel, F. K., *Theorie des Erzablens*, (Gottingen, 1979), 31; English translation by Charlotte Goedsche: *A Theory of Narrative*, (Cambridge, 1984), 16-18.

[7]Cp. the formalist/structuralist concept of "deviation."

[8]Cf. Stanzel, A Theory of Narrative, 9-21.

[9]Cf. Ibid., 65-66.

[10]Cf. Ibid., and 245, footnote 12.

[11]Cf. Lämmert, Eberhard, *Bauformen des Erzählens*, (Stuttgart, 1955), 201.

[12]Hempfer, Klaus W., *Gattungstheorie*, (Munchen, 1973), 173-174 (italics M. F.).

[13]Eichenbaum's statement is quoted in Todorov, Tzvetan, ed. *Théorie de la littérature*, (Paris, 1965); it was taken here from Scholes, *Structuralism in Literature*, 87.

[14]Scholes, *Structuralism in Literature*, 95.

[15]All quotations in this article are from the Bodley Head edition of 1937, repr. 1955.

[16]Goldman, Arnold, *The Joyce Paradox: Form and Freedom in His Fiction*, (Evanston, Ill., 1966), 99.

[17]The paper referred to was read at the Dubrovnik Joyce Seminar and has meanwhile been published; cf. Benstock, Bernard, "Dateline *Ithaca*: The News from Eccles Street," *Modern British Literature*, 5 (1980), 29-42.

[18]Peake, *The Citizen and the Artist*, 285.

[19]Cf. Stanzel's *A Theory of Narrative* and "Second Thoughts on *Narrative Situations in the Novel:* Towards a 'Grammar of Fiction!'" *Novel. A Forum on Fiction*, 11 (1978), 247-264.

[20]Cf. "The Encirclement of Narrative. On Franz Stanzel's *Theorie des Erzablens*," *Poetics Today*, 2 (1981), No. 2, 157-182.

[21]Ibid., 169-170 and 179.

[22]The statistical unit is, again, the quarter-line. 'Narrative' here includes everything which is neither dialogue nor interior monologue.

[23]Cf. Stanzel, F. K., *Die typischen Erzablsituationen im Roman: Dargestellt an "Tom Jones," "Moby Dick," "The Ambassadors," "Ulysses" u. a.*, Wiener Beiträge zur Englischen Philologie, vol. 63, Vienna & Stuttgart, 1955. English translation by James P. Pusack: *Narrative Situations in the Novel*, (Bloomington, Indiana, 1971).

[24]In German narratology the term "Ansteckung der Erzahler- durch die Figurensprache" ('contamination of narratorial idiom by characters' speech') has become the standard. (Cf. Spitzer, Leo, "Sprachmischung als Stilmittel und als Ausdruck der Klangphantasie" *Germanisch-Romanische Monatsschrift (GRM)*, 11 (1923), 193-216. In English studies there is no standard term. Page has called the appropriation of characters' idiom by the narrator "submerged speech," Cf. Norman Page, *Speech in the English Novel*, (London, 1973), 32, and Hugh Kenner has recently dubbed it the "Uncle Charles principle" (*Joyce's Voices*, London, 1978, 18).

[25]Cf. Bodley Head, 108, lines 1-21. This was added in the revisions of 1921 (cf. in the *placards*, *The James Joyce Archive*, ed. Michael Groden et al., [New York & London, 1977-1978]; vol. 18, *ULYSSES: 'Aeolus,' 'Lestrygonians,' 'Scylla and Charybdis,' & 'Wandering Rocks.' A Facsimile of Placards for Episodes 7-10, 3 and 13)*.

[26]Cp., e. g. the term "Narrative old" in the Gilbert/Gorman *Schema*.

[27]Bodley Head, 728-729; cf. also Cohn, Dorrit, *Transparent Minds. Narrative Modes for Presenting Consciousness in Fiction*, (Princeton, NJ, 1978), 223-224, 226-227.

[28]Litz, A. Walton, "Ithaca," in: Hart, Clive, & David Hayman, *James Joyce's "Ulysses." Critical Essays*, (London, 1974), 385-405; 405.

Transparent or Opaque? The Reader of *Ulysses* between Involvement and Distanciation

Sonja Bašić
Zagreb, Yugoslavia

> ". . . those themes-forms, those two-faced structures in which are articulated the choices from language and the choices from existence that linked together compose what tradition has luckily so equivocally called a *style*. . ."
>
> Gérard Genette

Critics nowadays often distinguish between transparent language that pretends to be a window through which the reader can look at the world and opaque language, which, drawing attention to itself, complicates the reader's affair with referents and meanings.

As a critical term opacity may seem a vague, ambiguous, and therefore dangerous word. Owing to its metaphorical extensions it can, however, indicate and even embrace numerous other terms of the modern critical vocabulary such as artifice, mannerism, *espace littéraire*, poetic, lyrical or self-conscious novel, irony, parody and, coming closer to linguistics, signifier-signified, foregrounding and de-familiarization.

In critical theory we find the terminological pair transparent-opaque in the structuralist writings of the sixties. Especially interesting in this respect are several essays by Tzvetan Todorov collected in his *The Poetics of Prose*.[1] Todorov argues very forcefully that our civilization may just be at the end of an anti-verbal period which has lasted for no less than twenty-five centuries. Throughout that period men had been led to believe that discourse was a "docile reflection of events" and that words were "simply the transparent names of things."

In opposition to that belief Todorov affirms that words organized into discourse acquire an independent value and "form an autonomous entity" (80), they become opaque. And opaque texts "do not refer to a meaning independent of them, the form chosen is the only form possible" (29). We must therefore disengage language from its illusory transparence (80) and learn that discourse is not governed by a correspondence with its referent but by its own laws. Opacity, then, is a constitutive element of discourse, a quality that liberates it from the tyranny of the referent and from the traditional realistic demands of verisimilitude.

From the structuralist point of view, referentiality and the transparence it entails sometimes seem just some kind of necessary evil. In an attempt to achieve some kind of balance Todorov, following Benveniste's linguistic model, sees the literary text as a speech-act with two levels. Referentiality points to exterior reality and belongs to the level of narrative in the sense of story or *fabula*. Literary tropes or auctorial intrusions are properties pertaining to the level of discourse or *sujet*. The degree of opacity of the literary language is determined by the proportion of the two speech-act levels. However, "discourse has the superior autonomy for it assumes its entire signification starting from itself, without the intermediary of an imaginary reference" (25-26). The more obvious the discourse, the greater the opacity of a text. Todorov seems to suggest that opacity is everything adding to, detracting from or altering the substratum of the story.

Although this schema is meant to apply to all kinds of literary discourse, its anti-referential bias has often turned it into a means of condemning the alleged transparency of realism as "mere" imitation and favouring the fabulators of earlier (and more recent) times and, above all, the artificers of modernity. Yet even in rejecting this anti-realist bias, the literary scholar must be aware of the possibilities offered by such critical views in his approach to the literature of modernism in general[2] and James Joyce's *Ulysses* in particular. Although no zero point of realist transparence can be located in literary practice, *Ulysses* might profitably be studied as a series of variations on and departures from a set of norms characterizing (even if only hypothetically) the fiction of realism. Especially useful in this respect is an additional, more strictly linguistic or formalist definition of realism offered by David Lodge in

his *Modes of Modern Writing.* According to Lodge, realism
is "the representation of experience in a manner which approxi-
mates closely the descriptions of similar experience in nonliter-
ary texts of the same culture."[3]   Often the notion of realism
is made to depend on a general and unqualified demand for
verisimilitude and an equally restricted repertoire of referents:
recognizable, ordinary, everyday events, especially unpoetic,
trivial or unpleasant ones.   In this regard no novel is more
realistic, or even naturalistic, than *Ulysses.*   Its literary discourse, however, very often diverges from its story.   And it
is in this dialogue between its discourse and its story—in what
Todorov would term the "proportion between them"—that
Ulysses is perhaps most "modernist," as it points at what is
perhaps the greatest paradox of the art of literature: the fact
that no art is so close to life and at the same time so distant
from it, with words both linking it to and screening it from
the world in such an absolutely unique way.

The divergence of modernism from the norms of realism
has also been stressed by Roland Barthes.   Modern literature,
says Barthes, is distinguished by the effort "to substitute the
instance of discourse for the instance of reality (or of the
referent) which has been and still is a mythical 'alibi' dominating
the idea of literature."   Barthes maintains that the field of
the writer is "nothing but the writing itself . . . as the only
area for the one who writes"—his famous *espace littéraire!*
"These facts of language," however, "were not readily
perceptible so long as literature pretended to be a transparent
expression of either objective calendar time or of psychological
subjectivity, that is to say, as long as literature maintained a
totalitarian ideology of the referent, or more commonly speaking, as long as literature was realistic."[4]   There is no doubt, at
this stage at least, Barthes' attitude towards the transparence of
realism was also derogatory.

This line of reasoning has clearly influenced some
approaches to James Joyce published more than a decade later.
Colin MacCabe's controversial book *James Joyce and the
Revolution of the Word,* for instance, is an attempt to see
Joyce from a position combining marxism and psychoanalysis,
and obviously biased against the transparence of representational
realistic writing which is dismissed as a meta-language.[5]   Joyce's
language, on the contrary, in his opinion refuses the very
category of meta-language and becomes an "object-language"

containing obscurely figured truths which defy the division between World and Word. A "classic realist" text, a novel by George Eliot, for instance, reflects the "conviction that the real can be displayed and examined through a perfectly transparent language." Fielding, on the other hand, "placed his fictions as fictions," bringing into the foreground, as Joyce later did himself, "the play of the language." Hugh Kenner presents a similar argument in his book *Joyce's Voices,* applying it directly to Joyce's work. It runs as follows: in *Dubliners* Joyce had kept his language transparent on the whole—a medium through which we can perceive the goings-on, and which therefore enables us to comprehend them as the characters do not. Joyce, Kenner continues, begins *Ulysses* with this in mind, plus interior monologue, his "chief new device"

> But with the eleventh episode, called "Sirens," something changed, and so radically that the author's staunchest advocate, Ezra Pound, was dismayed. (Would these events really lose, Pound wrote to ask, by being told in "simple Maupassant?") For no longer do we see the foreground postures directly, in order to see past them perhaps to Homer. Our immediate awareness now is of screens of language, through or past which it is not easy to see. The language is what we now confront. . . .[6]

Language through which we see—screens of language—along with Barthes and Todorov, Kenner is also in fact speaking about transparent and opaque language, about ways in which Joyce's discourse differs from the discourse of realism, supporting or defying the illusion of reality. Instead of "classic realism" which MacCabe pinned, derogatorily, on George Eliot, Kenner talks about "objective realism" which he pins, with only qualified praise, on Swift—as the first in a line of writers who based their narrative on scientific observation and experiment tending to equate experience with the discrete reports of the senses.

Coming closer to the central concern of this paper, I also wish to relate opacity to what John Fletcher and Malcolm Bradbury have called the introversion of the modernist novel, its two introversions in fact: One of them moving towards subjectivity, the flow of consciousness—in many cases that of the author as writer himself, the other tending to stress that the novel is an artificial game, a kind of substitute reality. The result of both is "a progressive fading of that realism which has long been associated with the novel; language ceases to be what we see through, and becomes what we see. The novel hangs on the border between the mimetic and the autotelic species of literature, between an art made by imitating things outside itself, and an art that is an internally coherent making."[7] Or, as Hillis Miller has formulated it: "There may be a new interest in the way a narrative is a product of a desire on the part of its author to create a supplementary reality . . .Present. . . . is one form or another of the opposition, fundamental in literature, between mimetic realism and some conception of a narrative as a fabric of language generating meaning from the reference of words to other, anterior words."[8]

In order to effect both of these introversions in *Ulysses* —that into the mind and that into the book—Joyce has created a repertoire of extraordinarily rich, varied, complex and quite undisguised shifts in literary technique. In discussing the opacities created by them we should also remind ourselves of two terms used by older formalist/structuralist criticism: actualization or foregrounding and de-familiarization or making strange. Actualization is a term introduced by the Czech structuralists in the thirties and defined by Mukařovsky as the "aesthetically intentional distortion of linguistic components." In a revealing and critical interpretation of this term Jiři Veltruský warns us of the danger of using it as a general aesthetic criterion, mainly because it lays too much stress on the concept of deformation as a constitutive element of art.[9] Veltruský also draws our attention to the similarities between Mukařovsky's concept, especially in its first sense (de-automatization), and the concept of making strange or de-familiarization which was used by the Russian formalists and most systematically expounded by Viktor Shklovskij, who wrote as far back as 1917 that the technique of art was to make objects unfamiliar. In the essay discussed by Veltruský ("Iskusstvo kak priem"), Shklovskij characterized de-familiarization as a device which enables art to "recapture the feel of life." This is analogous to Stephen Dedalus' wish to "recreate life out of life." It asks for "enhanced effects," for expressiveness and involvement. Yet Shklovskij also stresses that a poetic idiom is a constructed idiom, that literary artifice is something that "arrests or retards perception." Shklovskij, in fact, already seems to be speaking of artistic opacity. Even if no longer considered as quite adequate by contemporary theorists, these two terms seem to be particularly expressive of many of Joyce's tendencies and views and can help in analyzing some of his devices. Actualization in the sense of foregrounding might, for instance, be of practical use to us even if only in a limited and modified way. A foreground always implies a background—linguistic or otherwise against which it is highlighted. Even while ignoring it as an aesthetic criterion, we can use the term to denote any significant shift in technique, tone or attitude to be found in a literary text. But it is the quality, nature, effect and especially the frequency of these shifts (which in their constant flux create an extremely puzzling, yet unique blend of human contingency and literary artifice) that constitute one of the central concerns of this paper. *Ulysses* can thus be viewed as a novel that destroys one type of foregrounding as soon as it has been created, and then replaces it with another. In the course of this process the foreground becomes the background which in turn reappears again as foreground. In this way the cycle is repeated, though always with new variations. Because it veers between the psychological and non-psychological function, it flouts nearly every traditional rule of verisimilitude and literary decorum and pushes the strain between unity and diversity to the extreme limits of the humanly acceptable, *Ulysses* can be considered the most heavily foregrounded novel in the history of literature.

II

Rather early in *Ulysses*, on the fifth or sixth page of the first chapter, there is a passage beginning with a quotation from Yeats' poem "Who Goes with Fergus?" and followed by Joyce's text:

> *And no more turn aside and brood*
> *Upon love's bitter mystery*
> *For Fergus rules the brazen cars.*

> Woodshadows floated silently by through the morning peace from the stairhead seaward where he gazed. Inshore and farther out the mirror of water whitened, spurned by

> lightshod hurrying feet. White breast of the dim sea.
> The twining stresses, two by two. A hand plucking
> the harpstrings merging their twining chords. Wave-
> white wedded words shimmering on the dim tide . . .
> Fergus' song: I sang it alone in the house, holding down
> the long dark chords. Her door was open . . . (U 9)

Hugh Kenner has suggested that *Ulysses* begins as a homage
to objective realism but then proceeds to kick it to shreds.[11]
One of his reviewers, Shari Benstock, has pointed out that it
would be wrong to interpret the styles of *Ulysses* as merely a
series of aberrations from some abstract and in fact nonexistent
"realistic" norm. Her point is well taken. It seems to me,
however, that the mainstream of the 19th century realistic
novel did establish reading expectations and certain conventions
against which *Ulysses* may be profitably measured. It is also
a fact that in the early pages of *Ulysses* (admittedly very few
pages) Joyce has more or less followed some of these conventions. (He has, for instance, firmly established numerous
unambiguous referents such as characters, times or places).
Most of the passage following Yeats' lines can easily be
assimilated into that convention. In it we recognize the
"poetic," richly metaphoric style we have already met in *The
Portrait of the Artist,* including some of its "purple passages"
("wavewhite wedded words shimmering. . ."—isn't this somewhat overdone?)—which we are not perhaps to take too
seriously, knowing what we do about Joyce's views on the
Celtic Twilight. The first sentence beginning with "Woodshadows . . ." by comparison seems a kind of circumstantial
introduction into the poetic reverie and remembrance that
follows. It is certainly a simple sentence, quite transparent
at first look, and the reader begins to sort it out like any
basically referential sentence: the morning peace, the stairhead, the sea and the woodshadows seem to belong or refer
to the "real" world outside. The hurrying feet and twining
stresses are easily recognized as metaphors. On second thought,
however, the reader may remember that there are no woods
near Joyce's Martello Tower at Dun Laoghaire. And he *should*
remember the remaining lines of Fergus' song:

> *And rules the shadows of the woods*
> *And the white breast of the dim sea*
> *And all dishevelled wandering stars.*

The reader then understands that these woodshadows are a kind of hoax, a cuckoo's egg in a nest of swallows. They float so vividly in Stephen's memory of the poem that for him they have apparently become a part of reality. Yet Joyce has not prepared us for this, he has given us no signal. These woodshadows are sprung at us as if out of ambush—the ambush of another convention.[13] I cannot be too emphatic in stressing Joyce's slyness at this point. This seems to me to be the first clear sign in the novel that Joyce does not play by the old rules and that the text of *Ulysses* is in fact a stylistic mine-field: we never know when we are going to fly into the air or be rammed into the ground. The sentence which seemed so simple at first sight is in fact more opaque than those following or—opaque in a different sense. It seems to be a spoof on the subject of realistic illusion, part of a game on the part of the novelist who is "flaunting his artifice."[14] At second look, the sentence also seems a little strange and awkward, not quite grammatical: "from the stairhead seaward where he gazed . . ." The structure of the sentence seems to imitate the floating of shadows or memories. Both these elements are signs of opacity different from the more obviously and traditionally literary and "poetical" elaboration that follows.

These woodshadows, then, are not woodshadows of the world, but woodshadows of the mind. At the same time they are woodshadows of literature: their primary source is neither outer nor inner reality, but a book. They are, moreover, put into the text as a clearly literary sign in order to obstruct and "screen" our view of reality. Both as rendered experience and as written text the woodshadows are intruders. They disrupt a code and shatter the convention of stylistic unity—in this case the convention of what, lacking a better term, Kenner has called objective realism. Metaphorically speaking, they are twice removed from the objective world—extracted from a book and refracted through the mind.

Apart from being an instance of opacity they are also emblematic of the two types of introversion both of which are typical of modernism—as we have said—but coexist in a unique relationship within *Ulysses*. One is the psychological shift, the voyage inward, into the Mind. The other is the formalist's enclosure into language, the voyage from the World into the book. In *Ulysses* each of these two introversions tends to use its own techniques, its own forms of artifice. As we know, the stylistic devices used by the first include interior monologue and/or stream of consciousness, the breaking up of chronologically ordered narrative and syntax, Leitmotifs, "spatial form" and "poetic" devices such as figures, tropes, sound effects etc.,—mostly in a psychological function, i. e. as functions in regard of some character or his/her consciousness. The second introversion is not psychological as a rule but, rather, "literary" and formalist: in *Ulysses* it is marked by the use of irony, clichés, puns, allusions (very complex) and quotations, references to various spiritual disciplines (religion, criticism, philosophy, science, esoteric lore etc.), imitation of English literary styles and genres, mostly in the form of parodies and pastiches, or of catechism, dramatic dialogue, journalese etc. Each of these have been frequently discussed by critics. Not enough has been said, however, about their interrelationship within the text and the extent to which they both reveal and hide the world through the literary forms they create. Further, not enough has been said about how these on the whole, divergent claims of "formal wholeness and human contingency"[14] function in practice in the text of the novel. And finally, not enough has been said about their effect on the reader.

Simplifying very much, we might state that the first introversion tends to involve the reader and further his identification with the characters, their problems and emotions, while the second tends to distanciate him. This is a very important distinction which in fact lies at the root of one of the greatest feuds among Joyceans. The first tendency is used as the starting point by those readers and critics (and they are legion) who in spite of everything, see *Ulysses* primarily as a novel of human contingency: a book about human fate, an epic of man's body and spirit, a novel about the City, about the Artist, about Common Man and Woman. The other tendency would answer for what John Gross has called "the element of icecold detachment in the book as a whole."[15] In my belief it is essential for our understanding of the novel to see *Ulysses* as the supreme example of the co-existence rather than the fusion of these opposite tendencies. Through one of them Joyce is religiously using the Word to strengthen the illusion of reality, "to recreate life out of life." Through the other he is continually debunking it—with tongue in cheek, potato in pocket and, as Kenner wittily remarks, forty stylistic variations "in utero" in one chapter alone, "Oxen of the Sun."

The former tendency can be connected to what has been called the illusionism of realism, to what Todorov speaking of Flaubert has called his "sensationalism."[16] *Both* tendencies, however, can be traced back to the heritage of impressionism and symbolism. It has been pointed out by Clive Scott, most significantly for our present argument, that "literary impressionism is, not surprisingly, a matter of linguistic techniques, the attempt to make language the act of perception rather than analysis of the act, to make language *experiential activity rather than description of activity.*"[17]   This is what Henry James meant when he said: "Don't state, render." This is what Ezra Pound had in mind when, talking about Shakespeare's "dawn in russet mantle clad," he said in "A Retrospect": "There is in this line of his nothing that one can call description: he presents."   On the other hand, impressionism has its solipsistic, self-reflexive side which stresses the process of artistic composition, and the religious aestheticism of its symbolism is also tinged by irony. Along with other influences, it is this latter aspect of impressionism and symbolism that went into the making of Joyce the parodist, the self-conscious ironist and cold artificer, Joyce the distanciator. On one hand language as experiential activity, on the other, language as artifact: Fire and Ice. At one end of the continuum the author involves us, draws us into his artifice, and through it into the characters' psychology and the recreation of experience; at the other he keeps us at bay, plays, ironizes, hides behind his devices.

And yet, all is not as simple as it seems. We all know that interior monologue, which is supposed to recreate the inner life of the characters, prevails only in the first third of the novel, and that in the remaining, much larger part of the novel, direct access to the human contingency of the characters is impeded by distanciating techniques. In spite of that—doesn't Bloom grow in stature as the novel proceeds, just as Joyce had intended him to?   In the remaining two thirds of the novel referentiality is certainly obscured by "screens of language," by opacity. Yet opacity is a feature of the early part of the novel as well. The second part of the novel is dominated by the distanciating techniques of irony and parody. Yet—as I shall try to show later on—interior monologue, as well as description and dialogue, are also often shown in an ironical perspective and even turned into parodies. When the writer wishes us to "experience" something related to Bloom or Stephen, he often uses "poetic" devices which involve us as a rule. Yet—aren't these devices another way in which language is drawing attention to itself with renewed modernist awareness of aesthetic distance? Aren't they also artifacts? Does their opacity, however, have a different effect on the reader than, say, the opacity of parody and if so, what does the difference consist in?

Before proceeding, one should pay tribute to the advocates of the unity and coherence of *Ulysses*. Unity is certainly there in its story, idea, theme, mythic reference, structuring of its motifs and symbols, its dominant ironic tone etc. In many ways *Ulysses* is certainly much more tightly structured than most novels that preceded it. Its two introversions and the extraordinarily numerous, often conflicting discourses they entail, however, act as disrupting forces. From this point of view the basic division of *Ulysses* into two parts is justified. The first third of the novel is dominated by one type of opacity characterized by interior monologue, mainly psychologically motivated; here, language assumes the status of experiential activity and tends to involve the reader. The remaining two-thirds of the novel are not psychological; they are visibly "made," their dominant techniques are artificial and cold, they distanciate the reader. In spite of Joyce's irony, the reader can easily identify himself in the first part with Bloom feeding his cat, frying the kidney, worrying about his wife, meditating on the destiny of the Jewish race. In the second part, Bloom becomes a musical motif ("Sirens"), a grotesque puppet ("Circe") and a secondary theme of literary parody ("Oxen of the Sun"); he moves from the space of the world into the space of literature.

This division is useful, however, only as long as we use it in the most flexible manner, allowing for the most unexpected reversals, fusions and confusions. At the moment of our strongest identification with Bloom in "Lestrygonians," for instance, the hidden author-narrator distanciates us by means of irony. In spite of the coldness of the catechistic manner of "Ithaca," Joyce suddenly draws us into an intense human and mythic identification with Bloom and Molly. One and the same "foregrounding" device sometimes serves different ends, while different techniques may be used to achieve one and the same effect. The agglomeration of images characteristic of stream of consciousness, for instance, can at one moment enhance our involvement with Bloom's state of mind. In a different context, the same device does not represent anybody's consciousness; psychologically, it may be completely unrepresentative, becoming the structural intersection of certain motifs and themes as summed up by Joyce outside and apart from the characters' minds. On the other hand, maximal identification with Bloom is achieved both in a rather transparent, direct and only occasionally poetically charged discourse (e. g. in "Lestrygonians") and in the pseudo-scientific and mythic opacity of "Ithaca." It is on representative examples from these two chapters that I now propose to support the following argument: Each of the two introversions of *Ulysses* is dominated by certain types of foregrounding leading to different types of discourse. The two shifts—from the World into the Book and from the World into the Mind—are accompanied by shifts from transparent to opaque language. The first relies on the games of artifice, the second on realistic illusionism and poetic recreation. Each of these is, however, rarely found in a pure state. BOTH types of introversion in *Ulysses* can be coloured by the "poetic" or by the parodic and ironic, thus creating some very unexpected combinations. *Ulysses* is thus in continual flux and reflux between the two poles, with each thrust very often containing the germ leading to a potential counterthrust.

III

The "Lestrygonians" episode is both thematically and stylistically a chapter of involvement. From the narrative point of view it is dominated by interior monologue (direct free style), alternating freely with descriptions in the third person, that pass into indirect free style, including a few grammatically indeterminate sentences which are difficult to pinpoint in this respect. (Thus, for instance, "Glowing wine on his palate lingered swallowed" *U* 175, or "Dribbling a quiet message from his bladder to go to do," *U* 176, are technically not interior monologue because Bloom is referred to in the third person, although we may suppose that it is coloured by

Bloom's voice.) To the constantly alternating narrative points of view are added other stylistic devices which stress the role of language as "experiential activity" or an instrument of expression. Prevalent in the chapter is also the psychological motivation in accordance with the traditional demands of characterization, creation of atmosphere and plot-structuring. Central to it are Leopold Bloom, whose feelings and thoughts, rendered and recreated so as to enter "under the skin" of experience, become its verbal equivalent. An interesting example is the passage in which Bloom is looking at women's clothing in shop windows with both sensuous and sensual effects and associations, veering from ecstasy to disgust aroused by the eating scene at Burton's restaurant (U 168-9). A few pages later, seated at Barney Kiernan's, drinking wine with his sandwich, Bloom remembers the day when he first made love to Molly. Then he exits into the yard on his way to the toilet (U 174-7).

This part of the chapter has several climactic moments. The first culminates in the sentence "Perfume of embraces all him assailed" (U 168)—in which the second part is even grammatically incorrect and is therefore not just an example of poetic inversion as suggested by some critics, but of a more significant stylistic deformation characteristic of modernism. It is interesting to note here that in the immediate context of this sentence Joyce has in fact reversed the conventional notion of direct free style as an expressive device demanding "poetic" treatment. Here these "minimally narrated" forms are either stylistically neutral or just thematically suggestive, while those sentences that are most highly charged poetically and most heavily foregrounded linguistically and syntactically are in fact the "narrated" ones: "A warm human plumpness settled down on his brain. His brain yielded. Perfume of embraces all him assailed. With hungered flesh, obscurely, he mutely craved to adore" (U 168). Here language is trying to merge with experience, and experience trying to flow into the images, rhythms, assonances and the syntax which is as mixed up as Bloom is at the moment. The covert narrator "recreates life out of life" (renders, presents, gives us the feel of something that lies beneath and beyond consciousness, approaching in this way even the threshold of unformed, inchoate states of being). The sentences become opaque, artifical. However, they direct our attention to their elaboration primarily in order to draw us into the experience rendered, to involve us, to force us to commit and identify ourselves. (The same happens in Burton's restaurant although the scene is unpleasant and disgusting).

Reading this cluster of sentences in just a slightly larger context, however, we become aware of a countercurrent running through it as well. Subversion follows immediately after the climactic passage. It begins to be set into ironic perspective by the short, clipped laconic stage directions in direct free style immediately following. The ensuing interior monologue also operates on a diminishing scale: kissing is lovely in deep summer fields, but seems less attractive in trickling hallways of tenements and on creaking bedsprings. The reader's involvement gets progressively deflated like a bicycle tire: pfff! Another deflating device are the five names invoked (remembered or imagined and—presumably—revived in Bloom's stream of consciousness). *Who* are Jack and Reggy? And what vulgar names! How separated on the page, not "streaming" into each other at all! Not knowing who Jack and Reggy are or, indeed, if they "exist" at all on the same level of reality as Bloom, we miss an important psychological motivational link which obstructs our involvement as readers. Jack and Reggy are not related to the "human contingency" of the situation. Their exclamations have something of the gratuitous "dialogues" in "Circe;" they undermine our involvement, clip the wings of our illusion; they are artificial and distant, leaving us cold.

On the whole, however, recreation of experience prevails in "Lestrygonians." One of the great examples is the sentence: "Wine soaked and softened rolled pith of bread mustard a moment mawkish cheese" (*U* 174). Who is the narrator of this sentence? Is it a recreation of Bloom's sense impressions from the inside, or a presentation from the outside? The sentence is syntactically unformed, distorted, incomplete. Characteristically, there are no pronouns, and what are the verb forms? Could they perhaps all be past participles? In that case we might consider this sentence as evading the clutches of point-of-view compartmentalization and trying to transcribe an experience, an experience lying much deeper than words, certainly not interior monologue, perhaps stream of the senses, where the words, devoid of rational and syntactic links, are rolled in their unstructured liquid sentence like bits of food in liquid saliva. And then, after a page of rather transparent

and matter-of-fact interior monologue without many poetic
devices, the ungrammatical sentences "Glowing wine on his
palate lingered swallowed" (*U* 175)—who swallowed?—the
subject is missing!) and: "Crushing in the winepress grapes
of burgundy. Sun's heat it is. Seems to a secret touch telling
me memory. Touched his sense moistened remembered . . ."
(*U* 175-6). Undeniably there are changes in pronouns here
which do matter for the narration, although I am not suggesting
that they are of primary importance. Yet they contribute to
our impression that Joyce is working his theme both from the
inside and the outside, trying to achieve some sort of impossible
unity of language and experience, turning each of them inside
out. In these sentences, Joyce seems to have reached the climax
of expressiveness of the illusionistic type by involving the reader
in the personal fate of the protagonists through the use of
interior monologue as the central technique. This might also
be considered as a definition of the discourse dominating the
first third of *Ulysses*. And it reappears in a decidedly unpoetic,
metonymic form in the last chapter, which from that point
of view is also subversive). As in the previous example, however,
here again we find devices running in the opposite direction
and distanciating the reader. After about one page of text
Bloom, the lover, must go to the toilet. Here irony does not
seem to suffice, and Joyce resorts to parody, perhaps of Hamlet
("to go to do not to do") or perhaps of Pythia's "ibis redibis."
Furthermore, he employs an entirely misplaced mock-heroic
cliché (does one have to be "a man and ready" to go where
Bloom has to go?), followed by another similar, equally arbitrary
cliché ("drained his glass to the lees, *U* 176), before Bloom
quite unclimactically exists into the yard. From the point of
view of narration this last passage is stupendously muddled.
The first sentence is in the third person, while the end of the
second one is probably an insert of Bloom's stream of consciousness. The text in between is narrated by the covert
narrator-author, but there is no point in calling him omniscient.
He is the artificer playing with language, using irony, parody
and cliché which, since they do not further the progress of
Bloom's story, add nothing to the motivation of his character.
Here Joyce is throwing the ball directly at us, by-passing Bloom,
and telling us: "See, I am *making* all this." And this attitude
marks the other introversion, the shift into the book.

    Joyce has further subverted the notion of stream of consciousness in *Ulysses* by producing something we might call a mock version of it. We have already stated that this technique is by definition related to psychological presentation which mostly draws us into a character's experience. However, this is not quite true in the passage towards the close of "Nausicaa" which reproduces what is supposedly passing through Bloom's mind while "snoozing off" (cf. *U* 382). In the crowded density of its motifs, this passage strikes us as more visibly constructed. By analogy with earlier examples one would expect that Joyce, imitating Bloom's "drowsy numbness," would have created more fully the illusion of reality. In contrast to them ("Seems to a secret touch telling me memory . . ."), one wonders whether the imitative reconstruction of the flow of the mind has not been forgone here in favour of extremely free linguistic structuring only partly motivated by psychology. I should say that construction has here imposed itself on psychological motivation instead of the other way around. Because of this, the passage strikes us as a psychologically arbitrary sum of motifs, more important as part of the thematic structure of the book than as the expression of an individual state of mind. Along these lines it is extremely interesting to study the "bang fresh barang" (*U* 579) passage from "Circe." In *Ulysses*, as in other modernist novels, such agglomerations of motifs are usually a signal that we are dealing with stream of consciousness. *Ulysses* in fact only uses such sentence structures when rendering allegedly pre-verbal, pre-rational states of mind.[18] The example from "Circe," however, is not stream of consciousness: Stephen has not heard the bell in front of the auction room, and we know that the image of the cod-doubled bicycler is Bloom's image, not Stephen's. Critics have suggested that this passage might represent some kind of collective stream of consciousness. Even if we accepted this possibility, the passage would still strike us as extremely artificial, primarily owing to the quantity of animal allusions it contains. These allusions cannot be fully justified by the psychological context of the novel. They must also be seen as part of the deliberate and undisguised literary design of the chapter (homeric parallel, metamorphosis theme) and as being related symbolically and obliquely rather than directly and psychologically to the characters.

   To sum up: The stream of consciousness technique in *Ulysses* is preeminently psychologically motivated. It ranges

from fairly transparent forms to poetically strongly foregrounded, opaque ones, and functions as one of the preeminent
vehicles of language as experiential activity capable of involving
the reader. As a result of the novel's affair with artifice, however, the mind sometimes disappears as the background of
this device. What remains is a tangle of images and motifs,
a grid, often coloured by irony and parody and estranged from
psychology, which disengages us from the fate of the characters, relevant for the overall thematic structure of the novel,
as it brings the Mind to the side of the Book.

IV

Although the shift into the Book as artifact, signalled
by Yeats' woodshadows, can be noticed at the very beginning
of *Ulysses*, we have pointed out that it begins to prevail more
massively somewhere after the first third of the novel. Among
the distanciating techniques we must certainly single out
parody, not just in groups of phrases, short dialogues or passages,
as in the earlier chapters, but in numerous long paragraphs in
"Nausicaa" and "Cyclops," or even in entire chapters such as
"Ithaca" and "Oxen of the Sun." As a literary device, parody
is perhaps least suited to the demands of a story of human
contingency. It is, however, the ideal medium for word games
and stylistic virtuosity. In *Ulysses* parody occasionally separates
itself from the story, but it is usually woven into the thematic
or structural framework of the novel. It can be used, for
instance, to make fun of the characters (as aspects of life) or
of styles (as aspects of literature). In the first section of
"Wandering Rocks" parody is, thus, used both to make fun
of snobbishness (Father Conmee meets "the wife of Mr. David
Sheehy M.P.," *U* 219), and of realistic descriptions in literature
("a blue ticket tucked with care in the eye of one plump kid
glove, while four shillings, a sixpence and five pennies chuted
from his other plump glovepalm . . ." *U* 222).
    One of the early passages in "Cyclops" describing "the
land of holy Michan" (*U* 293), is thus a parody in no direct
relation to Bloom. Indirectly, however, it is related to the
Citizen who is Bloom's antagonist. It is an irresistibly funny
text derisive of primitive nationalist notions and styles, while
at the same time skirting the limits of pure nonsense. The

concluding passage of the same chapter, in which Bloom is shown escaping from the pub, deals directly with him, but prevents the illusion being created by parodying the biblical style and vocabulary, which is ironically foregrounded by the scientific measurement of the angle of his supposed ascent into heaven, which is in turn set into ironical perspective by a colloquial phrase ("like a shot off a shovel," *U* 345). As parody is usually considered to be a stylistic device of the second order, we cannot but admire the varied and important uses it has been put to in this novel.

Parody is rather easy to diagnose as a stylistic device. It is much more difficult, however, to define the discourse of "Circe," to my mind one of the coldest, most artificial and distant chapters in the novel. Although couched in dramatic form, it is as removed from Aristotle's concept of mimesis as are the parodies in "Oxen of the Sun." This "drama" consists almost entirely of stage directions which are repulsive, grotesque, often burdened with the most arbitrary, yet pedantic detail (e. g. Molly attended by an obsequious camel and likened to Flaubert's description of Saint Anthony's vision of the Queen of Sheba, cf. *U* 439). The descriptions contained in these stage directions do not satisfy the minimal requirements of verisimilitude, not only in the "hallucinated" scenes (e. g. Bloom with Bello), but even in the scenes which are supposedly closer to reality (the descriptions at the very opening of the chapter). Joyce who, when he tries, can catch the colloquial cadence of speech better than any writer in the language, writes dialogue here that no one has ever spoken or will ever speak. The "speakers" are kisses, wreaths, shorthand and long-hand, which can never even remotely come to life, indeed, they are not even meant to. What is more, the living characters also appear unreal, dead. Bloom and Stephen are present on nearly all the pages of this overlong chapter. Yet they behave like alienated wooden dolls. We are introduced to disgusting scenes at the very beginning of the novel. But when the stench of Burton's restaurant is described in "Lestrygonians" we know that it is experienced by Bloom and this motivates the disgust. In "Circe" experience is rendered in the coldest, most round-about manner. When the navvy "ejects from the farthest nostril a long liquid jet of snot," (*U* 433), the stylistic devices are identical to those used in "Lestrygonians," but the effect is quite different. There is no identification (even if with something unpleasant), this is happening nowhere and to no one, the action is isolated from the experience of the protagonists, it forms part of an impersonal structure. I must state at this point my full awareness that Joyce is doing this on purpose and that my analysis is not a criticism but, rather, an attempt to unravel the distanciating techniques used in this chapter. The descriptions in "Circe" are extremely exaggerated to the exclusion of all verisimilitude. The dog is of a different breed each time it is seen, the children from "Nausicaa" appear in improbable roles. Such scenes are often called hallucinations. It should be stressed, however, that the dog metamorphosis, even if it were hallucinated by Bloom, has no psychological foundation, but is a part of the Homeric pattern. Even when the supposedly psychological link exists (Bloom metamorphosed into a female, Stephen seeing his dead mother as an ugly monster), the characters seem divorced from their emotions in a somewhat Brechtian sense.

In the "Circe" chapter the borderline between reality and illusion is particularly elusive. The reader is supposed to pick out a few things that have "really" happened: Bloom has followed Stephen to the brothel, spent some time there with him, later saved him from the soldiers who attacked him. The shades of fantasy are, however, thrown over all of the action. Arriving in Nighttown, is Bloom stuffing bread and chocolate into his pockets, on the same level of probability with his feeding the cat in "Calypso?" Does he "really" buy that pig's crubeen and sheep's trotter (sprinkled with pepper? at midnight, on his way to a brothel?) The very absurdity of the questions tells us that, whatever our final judgment of formalism and structuralism in literary criticism, they have exposed some fallacies of literal referential reading! As Kenner remarks on another scene in this chapter: "This is bottomless!" Here we had better remember what Todorov has told us: verisimilitude is out!

In "Cyclops" and "Oxen of the Sun" Joyce has removed the characters from us through parody; in "Sirens" they have become functions of the "musical" form. In "Circe" they walk and talk before us as if on stage, but they are estranged from each other and from us; there is absolutely no communication. Characteristic in this respect are the games played with Bloom's name: Bloom stops being a person and becomes a series of sound variations (Jollypoldy the rixdix doldy," *U* 434). Transparence has been replaced by the opacity of parodic foreground-ing. Even if "Circe" often appears to be a hallucination re-vealing the shameful corners of Bloom's and Stephen's nature and of human nature in general, in it we must not look for direct psychological motivation and referentiality. It is, rather, a stylistic exercise, a distant approximation of experience, both expressionistically hysterical and coloured by *Verfremdung*, willfully, even perversely constructed by the author.

Yet we know that *Ulysses* is a minefield. We know that in it nothing is quite what it seems. There is hardly any aspect, device or motif in the book which can be separated for pro-longed inspection without bringing us to its negation, turning us round and round. Even in these examples, deliberately selected for the coldness of their artifice, we encounter elements that "humanize" Joyce's approach. In spite of the irony and parody which screen Bloom from us in these late chapters, we can detect in them the usual countercurrent. Embedded in the middle of "Cyclops," for instance, we find the moving scene in which Bloom talks about "love, . . . the opposite of hatred" (*U* 333). We see him painfully confused when meeting Boylan or thinking of him. Even the parodies of "Oxen of the Sun" give us glimpses of "meek sir Leopold . . [by] love led on" and "woman's woe . . . pondering," (*U* 388). In spite of the wandering rocks of artifact the human story remains afloat.

V

In what directions did listener and narrator lie?

Listener, S.E. by E.; Narrator, N.W. by W.; on the 53rd parallel of latitude, N. and 6th meridian of longi-tude, W.: at an angle of 45° to the terrestrial equator.

In what state of rest or motion?

At rest relatively to themselves and to each other. In motion being each and both carried westward, forward and rereward respectively, by the proper perpetual motion of the earth through everchanging tracks of neverchanging space.

In what posture?

Listener: reclined semilaterally, left, left hand under head, right leg extended in a straight line and resting on left leg, flexed, in the attitude of Gea-Tellus, fulfilled,

recumbent, big with seed. Narrator: reclined laterally,
left, with right and left legs flexed, the indexfinger and
thumb of the right hand resting on the bridge of the
nose, in the attitude depicted on a snapshot photograph
made by Percy Apjohn, the childman weary, the man-
child in the womb.

Womb? Weary?
He rests. He has travelled.

With?
Sinbad the Sailor and Tinbad the Tailor and Jinbad
the Jailer and Whinbad the Whaler and Ninbad the Nailer
and Finbad the Failer and Binbad the Bailer and Pinbad
the Pailer and Minbad the Mailer and Hinbad the Hailer
and Rinbad the Railer and Dinbad the Kailer and Vinbad
the Quailer and Linbad the Yailer and Xinbad the Pht-
hailer.

When?
Going to a dark bed there was a square round Sinbad
the Sailor roc's auk's egg in the night of the bed of all
the auks of the rocs of Darkinbad the Brightdayler.

Where? (*U* 736-737)

In *Ulysses* there is much that is disjointed, fragmented,
artificially kept apart. Each theme, tone, attitude, impression
and device is destroyed or put into ironic perspective by what
follows, then rebuilt and reconstructed only to be destroyed
again. The book is pervaded by a great centrifugal force. Yet,
I should like to conclude by commenting upon a passage that
seems to be absolutely centripetal. It is the close of "Ithaca,"
the penultimate chapter of the novel. It also seems to unite
most elements discussed in this paper and some of those that
have not been mentioned. This passage is a companion piece
to the climactic passages in "Lestrygonians" that I have interpreted above: in it Joyce seems to have reached the climax
of expressiveness involving the reader with the protagonists
on a level which seems to transcend their personal fate and
acquire a mythic dimension.
    Critics have pointed out that this chapter is written in

the so-called catechistic manner, a style characterized by a normative rather than speculative nature. From this formal and propedeutic side "Ithaca" is a parody. On the level of content it seems to be primarily preoccupied with "objective" data—from the contents of the sideboard in the Blooms' kitchen to a treatise on the origin of the water flowing from the faucet. The parodic character of the chapter is underlined by the discrepancy between the apparent aim of the chapter—to give us as much information about the characters as possible—and the catechistic method which admittedly is not the best vehicle for a meaningful and profound insight into human nature. This is further underlined by the pseudo-scientific content which is imposed on the discourse. In this chapter Joyce certainly does flaunt his artifice, with a difference, however, because he miraculously succeeds in turning it into a most touching expression of human contingency. At the very close of the chapter the coldness of parody seems to be humanized through a fusion of numerous, apparently disparate elements. Joyce describes Molly and Bloom lying in bed as if he were a Martian seeing the scene for the first time.[19] This puts us at a distance from a situation which would otherwise seem very normal, even banal. It is, however, this very distance that unexpectedly and touchingly reveals their frailty, reminding us that the security of the bed, the marriage bed in particular, is illusory in more than one way. They are individually located and identified in greatest detail as Leopold and Molly Bloom, of 7 Eccles Street, Dublin, in the early hours of June 17, 1904. At the same time, they are just two tiny, nameless atoms, hurtling with their planet through a dark universe.

In this passage the fusion of contrasting tendencies can be traced down to the smallest detail. The universal perspective tends to dwarf Molly and Bloom. By measuring the angle of their position with respect to the equator, and recording the geographic latitude and longitude of their bed, the author sets them in a comic, even grotesque light. On the other hand, the two of them are travelling "through everchanging tracks of neverchanging space," thus becoming, metaphorically at least, part of allspace and alltime. The movement of the text from scientific precision to unintelligibility imitates the movement of Bloom's consciousness while falling asleep (the last sentence could in fact be stream of consciousness). Yet this text also connects his personal destiny with the universal, mythic cycle of birth, copulation and death: Bloom lies curled like a foetus in the womb and is weary, Molly is filled with seed; the Joyce-coined composite words seem to combine the helplessness of a child before birth with the weariness of a man on his way to death ("he has travelled"). At the same time, the pathetic, funny link with everyday reality is maintained through the reference to an existing snapshot of Bloom made by someone called Percy Apjohn! Molly and Bloom also find their place in language, in the language and style of *Ulysses*, but also in the oral and written tradition: in the story of Sinbad, the sailor from the Arabian Nights and the bird Roc (whose egg he apparently finds in the tale) which takes us into the world of fable and legend, of Keats' "perilous seas in faery land forlorn;" in the language of nursery rhymes, counting-songs and puns, veering between wit and nonsense, between the poetic and the ironic. Falling asleep, Bloom loses his identity and consciousness and this is reflected in the sentences, as rational meaning and syntax are dissolved in wordplay. At the same time images allude and suggest, grow into symbols, perhaps even archetypes. "Darkinbad the Brightdayler"—these names actually combine nonsense with the first terms of Genesis: night and day! The night of the bed is perhaps darkly symbolic, the "roc's auk's egg" with its small "r" and its double genitive is both tricky and mysterious at the same time, but the language seems to fuse them all into some kind of final metaphoric identification in which Bloom is Odysseus is Sinbad is Roc-and-the-egg is man is child is sleep is the universe is language is the silence following the final unanswered question: "where?"

Let us remember the text from "Lestrygonians," which exemplified the poetic actualization of the single, individual consciousness prevailing in the early chapters of *Ulysses,* stressing the use of language as a psychological, expressive medium recreating experience and involving the reader. The passages from "Cyclops" and "Circe," which followed, exemplified the "cold" techniques of the book as construction, as artifice. Yet in "Ithaca," the chapter which, owing to many of its thematic and stylistic qualities, should distanciate us as well—Joyce deceives—or enlightens us again. For a moment at least prose has become poetry, the personal has been fused with the general, the everyday with the mythic. Parallel to the key passages from "Lestrygonians," this example from

"Ithaca" is also one of the highlights of the novel, this time creating involvement of a larger, more universal scope.

Ulysses, however, does not end with "Ithaca." Its end is not marked by silence, but rather by a landslide of words. After the "Where?," which remained unanswered, we are not confronted with the final void; the "Where?" is just one more question in a line of questions and answers which could be prolonged indefinitely. The silence of the end of "Ithaca" is not a sign that time has stopped; it is only a pause, a short respite, after which the novel is resumed in "Penelope." At the end of "Ithaca" Northrop Frye's monad, the notion of the final and ultimate unity of all existing things, imposes itself even against our will, and threatens to take us too far in the direction of Frye's idealistic vision. Molly's chapter sets us on our feet again. In spite of its apparent lack of rational or syntactic order, its narrative is soothingly, reassuringly down-to-earth. Technically so extreme at first sight, it is in many ways the easiest and simplest to read of all the chapters in *Ulysses*. Joyce has deceived us again, but we do not mind it any more. This is just one more reversal reminding us of Joyce the supreme acrobat forever precariously balanced between Art and Life, Substance and Sense. Perhaps we should remember at this point that Gérard Genette has defined the job of the critic as looking for "those themes-forms, those two-faced structures in which are articulated the choices from language and the choices from existence that linked together compose what tradition has luckily so equivocally called a *style*."[20]

Through Joyce's two introversions we get involved with the world and distanciated from the world, but we never reject the world. Speaking of form, we speak—or wish to speak—about sense. Joyce's choice from language is for us equally a choice from life.

Notes

[1] Tzvetan Todorov, *The Poetics of Prose,* (Cornell University Press, 1980). Page references marked in the text.

[2] The applicability of formalist and structuralist methods in the study of modernism has been demonstrated and discussed in David Lodge, *Modes of Modern Writing,* (Edward Arnold, 1977).

[3] Lodge, *op. cit.,* p. 25.

[4] Roland Barthes: "To Write: An Intransitive Verb?", *The Structuralist Controversy,* ed. R. Macksey and E. Donato, (Baltimore, 1972). Quoted in Lodge, *op. cit.,* p. 60.

[5] Colin MacCabe, *James Joyce and the Revolution of the Word,* (Macmillan, 1978), Ch. II, "The End of a Meta-Language: From George Eliot to Dubliners."

[6] Hugh Kenner, *Joyce's Voices,* (Faber & Faber, 1978), p. 41. Significantly one of the chapters is entitled "Beyond Objectivity."

[7] John Fletcher and Malcolm Bradbury, "The Introverted Novel," *Modernism* [editors the same], (Penguin, 1976), p. 401.

[8] J. Hillis Miller, ed. *Aspects of Narrative,* (Columbia University Press, 1971).

[9] For a disscussion of foregrounding cf. Lodge *op. cit.,* pp. 2-6 and passim. Shklovsky's terms retranslated from Croatian Viktor Sklovskij, *Uskrsnuće riječi,* Stvarnost, Zagreb, pp. 48-9 & 50. Jiři Veltruský, "Jan Mukařovský's Structural Poetics and Esthetics," *Poetics Today,* (Winter 1980-81), p. 134-5.

[10] Kenner, *op. cit.,* p. 94.

[11] *Modern Fiction Studies,* (Summer 1979), pp. 81-3.

[12] It is interesting to note that Kenner also refers to these woodshadows. He does not, however, refer them to Yeats, but discusses them with regard to free indirect style. About the same passage he says rather ambiguously: "These thoughts of woodshadows floating are not Stephen's, not quite, but the sentences that brush them in absorb Stephen-words and Stephen-rhythms, moving us imperceptibly into Stephen's thoughts." (*op. cit.,* p. 71).

[13] Cf. Robert Alter's definition of the self-conscious novel as one that "systematically flaunts its own condition of artifice and by so doing probes into the problematic relationship between real-seeming artifice and 'reality'

quoted in Seymour Chatman, *Story and Discourse,* (Cornell University Press, 1978), p. 250.

[14] Fletcher/Bradbury, *op. cit.,* p. 398.

[15] Quoted by Maurice Beebe in *Ulysses: Fifty Years,* (Indiana University Press, 1974), p. 181.

[16] Todorov, *op. cit.,* p. 151.

[17] Clive Scott, "Symbolism, Decadence and Impressionism," *Modernism,* p. 222.

[18] As this is not the primary theme of my paper and the terminological disputes have not been settled so far, I have used the terms "stream of consciousness" and "interior monologue" rather indiscriminately, although I have occasionally distinguished between "narrated" and "minimally narrated" forms or "free direct" and "free indirect" speech, using terms from Chatman's *Story and Discourse.* I am also familiar with Gérard Genette's attitude expressed in his *Narrative Discourse. An Essay in Method.* (Cornell University Press, 1981). It is interesting to note at this point that Genette rejects Dujardin's definitions formulated in his work *Le Monologue intérieur* (Paris 1931), dismissing the connection of this technique with pre-rational inchoate states of mind as a prejudice of that time. He proposes the term "immediate speech."

[19] The same approach used by Tolstoy to describe an opera performance is singled out by Sklovskij as a key example of *ostranenie!*

[20] Genette, *Figures II,* (Editions du Seuil, 1969), p. 20.

Ulysses as Human Comedy

Jasna Peručić-Nadarević
Zagreb, Yugoslavia

Comedy is an art form representing not certain inherently funny subjects, but a certain attitude to life, it is a *mode* whose essential *method* of operation is laughter. But the discussion of how "comedy" works is clearly quite different from the discussion of how laughter itself works. The psychology of laughter, in a word, is distinct from the criticism of comedy. That the former has so often been unwittingly substituted for the latter is perhaps due to the ambiguity of the word "comic." Since it can mean "laughable" as well as having "to do with a comedy," it may well underlie the common confusion between investigating the nature of laughter in a person (i. e., doing psychology) and investigating its use in a literary form (i. e., doing criticism). This essay is concerned with the criticism of literary comedy.

Comedy as a literary mode should be distinguished, in particular, from *farce*[1] ("Comedy with the meaning left out"), a mode that uses laughter purposively rather than simply inducing it for its own sake, and from non-comic *satire,* a mode whose mockery is milder. We should note, however, that a single work considered as comedy might well contain passages of farce and bitter satire as component parts of the comic whole. Furthermore, some satire may be sufficiently genial in its attack to be considered as satiric comedy. Farcical comedy, on the other hand, i. e., comedy containing a high proportion of farce, lies at the other end of the comic spectrum, with celebratory comedy quite close to it. Comedy, as defined, then, requires a certain distance, for it is to be appreciated as well as experienced.

In *Ulysses,* the aesthetic distance resulting from the so-called "mechanical" structure and texture is also an essential part of the comic distance. Note here how Joyce associates beauty and the "joy" of comedy with "rest":

> . . . a comedy (a work of comic art which does not urge
> us to seek anything beyond itself excites in us the feeling
> of joy . . . . comedy the perfect manner in art. All art,
> again, is static . . . This rest is necessary for the appre-
> hension of the beautiful—the end of all art, tragic or
> comic—for this rest is the only condition under which
> the images, which are to excite in us terror or pity or
> joy, can be properly presented to us and properly seen
> by us. (*CW* 144-45)

This essay, however, is not concerned with *Ulysses* as an aesthetic artefact, save in so far as the distancing structural and textual forms that make it one are also those that enable its totality to convey both the vitalist theme and the "luminous stasis" of joy that makes it a "proper work of comic art."

The comedy that is most *obviously* comic and not farcical is satiric comedy—the most clearly intentional sort—but what is most *centrally* comic is, perhaps, celebratory comedy, despite its kinship to farce. It is genial, compromising and, taking life as a whole, life-accepting—and this is what most principally distinguishes comedy from tragedy. Tragedy represents the virtues of the warrior, comedy those of the cultivator. Tragedy moves us to defy the inescapable, comedy encourages us to accommodate ourselves to it. Joyce's philosophico-historical beliefs, based on the assumption that nothing fundamentally changes, are essentially anti-utopian; therefore he could not be didactic or reformist, with only the modes of tragedy or comedy being available for his vision of humanity, he chose comedy.

In *Ulysses* Joyce himself became silent to allow the epic comedy of humanity to be heard. This withdrawal behind his handiwork makes the book less *personal* only that it may thus become all the more epically *human*. Joyce's work is clearly an example of imposed rather than organic form, for Joyce like Shakespeare, believes in *art* as specifically human and natural to human beings ("the art itself is nature.")[2] The imposed form is in fact the aesthetic representative of the mode of *Ulysses*, comedy—which needs a degree of detachment—and indeed of a particular kind of comedy: in the last analysis, celebratory. The celebratory quality is embodied not only in the vitalist theme that leads to the final "yes." This theme is seen in the constant opposition of forces of life to those of death. The "life-force" theme can be found in the vitality expressed through the variety of styles, as well as in the vitality shown in each; formally in the many protean word-games; in Bloom's resilience and Molly's earth-mother characteristics, and even in Stephen's self-critical wit and ultimate injunction to hold on to "the now, the here" (*U* 186); and finally in the suggestion of the mythical systems running parallel with modern Dublin: thus continuity *and* change are shown to be fundamental to life. The essential human resilience that enables man to dodge or fight back is the condition for continual resurrections after the apparent triumph of death-forces. In other words, this vitality is found in structure, texture and character—indeed in the whole of that aspect of art which works in the service of life and is itself an expression of its creative energies.

Ulysses is "human" in three separate, though interrelated senses: as opposed to *divine,* to *inhuman,* and to *guiltless.* Thus, its comedy is universal, celebratory, and tolerant. *Ulysses* is firmly rooted in the secular world. There is a "coming down to earth," a bringing down of all that is highfalutin over-spiritual, ideal, abstract. For Joyce, the human spirit is always embodied in the particular, "the now, the here." However confused and imperfect the ordinary world may be, it is the world in which our values exist. Its confusions and imperfections, indeed, are the soil in which grow those humane values that *Ulysses* both portrays and embodies. *Ulysses* confirms that *Errare humanum est,* in other words, that nothing human should be alien to man. However ludicrous, the characters are seen as human, not monstrous in their faults, sufferings, and hopes.

Some confirmation that the comedy of *Ulysses* does combine these three aspects of the "human" is given by the fact that they correspond, as much as might reasonably be expected, to three main elements of its composition. The *symbolic structure* comically universalizes local and temporal content, extends the depth, richness, and universality of Joyce's reading of life. The *stylistic* gusto and panache give its Dublin drabness a celebratory vitality, while revealing through its variety the arbitrariness of any one viewpoint, whether cultural, historical or personal. And finally, the treatment of the *characters*— especially Leopold and Molly Bloom—reminds us that "to understand all is to forgive all."

Ulysses, then, shows humanity as pretentious, absurd, and full of frailties, but does this with a cosmic humour that accepts the world and humanity, and, in full awareness of time, death, and the "incertitude of the void" (*U* 697) with its final YES to life.

Ulysses is not only a unified aesthetic whole in the comic mode but also a concrete comic presentation of the whole of essential human experience: a work at once unified and various, universalized and particularized. A thread of sameness, in the form of protean theme and energy, runs through the differently woven episodes as a unifying and vivifying element.

Every discussion on comedy in *Ulysses* should start with Joyce's own argument on this topic. In his Paris Notebook Joyce, attempting to create his own aesthetic, argues for the superiority of comedy over tragedy.

> An improper art aims at exciting in the way of comedy the feeling of desire but the feeling which is proper to comic art is the feeling of joy. Desire, as I have said, is the feeling which urges us to go to something but joy is the feeling which the possession of some good excites in us. Desire, the feeling which an improper art seeks to excite in the way of comedy, differs, it will be seen from joy. For desire urges us from rest that we may possess something but joy holds us in rest so long as we possess something. Desire, therefore, can only be excited in us by a comedy (a work of comic art) which is not sufficient in itself inasmuch as it urges us to seek something beyond itself—but a comedy (a work of comic art) which does not urge us to seek anything beyond itself excites in us the feeling of joy. All art which excites in us the feeling of joy is so far comic and according as this feeling of joy is excited by whatever is substantial or accidental in human fortunes the art is to be judged more or less excellent: and even tragic art may be said to participate in the nature of comic art so far as the possession of a work of tragic art (a tragedy) excites in us the feeling of joy. From this it may be seen that tragedy is the imperfect manner and comedy the perfect manner in art. All art, again, is static for the feelings of terror and pity on the one hand and of joy on the other hand are feelings which arrest us. (*CW* 144-45)

In the light of such a theory it is easy to see why Joyce chose the *stasis* of comedy. It suited his aesthetics. The detachment of comic vision of life clearly invites artistic detachment, a balanced view invites a controlled form. And a euphoric condition of freedom from desires is consonant with an art that is "nature methodiz'd," an art aesthetically matching various forms with varied content, protean structure with protean theme, with a tension of symbolism and realism.

If the origin of comedy resides in attitude rather than in subject (Walpole's epigram "Life is a comedy to the man who thinks and a tragedy to the man who feels" comes to mind), it is not the events in themselves which are comic or tragic—it is the way they are looked at. Thus death is no less matter for comedy than for tragedy. The *Hades* episode in *Ulysses,* for instance, reveals the power and status of comedy in what could have been a tragic, or at least sombre setting and context. It proves that the radiance and the ironic wit of comedy can transfigure a potentially tragic situation. In fact, the comic qualities of the cemetery scene result precisely from the ludicrous treatment of basic preoccupations with death and sexuality that are usually treated in deadly earnest. Joyce chooses not to dwell on the pain and suffering in any overemotional way because he realizes there is another way out. If we cannot change the world much he can help us, through comic vision, to accept it as it is. So *Circe,* that potentially horrible nightmare, is paradoxically, like *Hades,* one of the most comic episodes in *Ulysses.*

In *Ulysses* one is often aware of the tragic lying beneath the comic surface and, indeed, sometimes breaking through briefly. The ocmic incongruities of human failings and absurdities have often been combined with tragedy before (witness the gravediggers in *Hamlet* or the Porter in *Macbeth*). In *Ulysses,* comedy often requires a contrasting, and thereby intensifying, seriousness.

The "Telemachia," for instance, seems to offer cogent evidence against the case for seeing Joyce's *Ulysses* as a comic epic. Yet without it, so stylish a comedy could have come to appear superficial; and indeed, upon consideration, even the opening section reveals itself not as contrary to comedy but as one of the main factors giving it depth. Just as shadow is an essential part of a painter's sunlit scene, so a certain sombreness is required in great comedy, especially celebratory comedy, for such comedy easily moves towards farce.

The "Telemachia," however, is not merely a large structural component functioning as ironic contrast to the main body of the work. Joyce, like a good painter, leavens his shadow with subtle infusions of lighter colouring, so that it remains recognizably summer shadow. That is why we feel no lack of aesthetic coherence upon moving into the complementary world of Bloom, where a generally warm and mellow atmosphere is discreetly shaded with touches of melancholy.

Even in the opening section, the most sombre in the book, textural infusions of comedy are to be found—in fact, they are surprisingly frequent. Sometimes they are blatantly obvious, like Buck Mulligan's bawdy balladry or his imitation of old mother Grogan: "When I makes tea I makes tea. . . And when I makes water I makes water" (*U* 12). Structurally, however, they contrast with Stephen's sombre brooding in a way that models the larger contrast of the "Telemachia" and the "Wanderings." And they are comparable with similar contrasts elsewhere, for example those between the well-pleasured Molly and poor Josie Breen, whose husband goes to bed "with his muddy boots on when the maggot takes him just imagine having to get into bed with a thing like that, that might murder you any moment. . ." (*U* 744) or between young, brash, and monied Blazes Boylan on his way to that pleasuring and sad Leopold Bloom, "A darkbacked figure under Merchants' arch" (*U* 227).

At other times, a less blatant comedy of character infuses the opening section. There is a comic mood contained in the bright, mocking laughter of Buck Mulligan, who seems to laugh with the world and at it.

Commonly, however, these infusions are of a subtler kind, hardly to be separated from the surrounding gloom engendered by Stephen's broodings on death, religion and guilt. Of course, these broodings, in the larger context of the work, are shown to have an unserious side. They differ sharply, for instance, from those of Bloom at the same hour. He, too, has his sorrows: the suicide of a father, the death of a son, the unfaithfulness of a wife and the alienation of a Jew in Catholic Ireland. But wily old campaigner that he is in the mock-battle of life, he has got his priorities right. At this hour, his broodings are only on breakfast. He may be less brilliant than Stephen, but is more mature; a better example of survival-value despite his lack of heroics—or because of them.

On a smaller scale, similar comic differences occur within the episode itself—similar, not, monotonously, the same: Joyce always writes variations on his themes. Take, for instance, the opening pages: Stephen sees but does not feel the sunshine "merrying" on the sea; indeed, for him it recalls with bitter irony the bowl of green bile at his mother's death-bed. Buck Mulligan, with typical self-preserving insensitivity, merries with the sunshine on the sea—at the same time making a pagan mockery of orthodox religion.

> Solemnly he came forward and mounted the round gunrest. He faced about and blessed gravely thrice the tower, the surrounding country and the awaking mountains. Then, catching sight of Stephen Dedalus, he bent towards him and made rapid crosses in the air, gurgling in his throat and shaking his head. (*U* 3)

This contrasts not only with Bloom's tolerant, but equally life-centred, scepticism, but also with Stephen's more negative, jesuitical atheism.

Ripeness, as represented by Bloom, is much, but in *Ulysses* relativity, it seems, is all. For each character is shown, relative to the others, to be all too "human" in his limitations, which are hinted at throughout.

Keenly aware of the follies of mankind, Joyce, an almost inhumanly detached spectator of absurdity, is nevertheless capable of producing comedy which provokes compassionate laughter, a humane certainty of redemption, thus discovering a common humanity in the ridiculous.

If humour and language are the essential qualities that distinguish us from animals, the Joyce, one of the greatest masters of both, might well be expected to write the most human of comedies—one that interprets, sustains, and comforts our life. Henri Bergson is particularly relevant here:

> The first point to which attention should be called is that the comic does not exist outside the pole of what is strictly *human*,[3]

because man is the only animal which laughs. He goes on to say:

Language only attains laughable results because it is a human product, modeled as exactly as possible on the forms of the human mind. We feel it contains some living element of our own life; and if this life of language were complete and perfect, if there were nothing stereotype in it, if, in short, language were an absolutely unified organism incapable of being split up into independent organisms, it would evade the comic as would a soul whose life was one harmonious whole, unruffled as the calm surface of a peaceful lake. There is no pool, however, which has not some dead leaves floating on its surface, no human soul upon which there do not settle habits that make it rigid against itself by making it rigid against others, no language, in short, so subtle and instinct with life, so fully alert in each of its parts as to eliminate the ready-made and oppose the mechanical operations of inversion, transposition, etc., which one would fain perform upon it as on some lifeless thing. The rigid, the ready-made, the mechanical, in contrast with the supple, the ever-changing and the living, absent-mindedness in contrast with attention, in a word automatism in contrast with free activity, such are the defects that laughter singles out and would fain correct.[4]

This explains why Joyce's protean "life" theme is so appropriate for an epic comedy, and why his encyclopaedic erudition succeeds best when his linguistic inventiveness and exuberance are used for comic effects—very often effects that spring from a mockery of "mechanical," "ready-made" uses of language.

There is clearly a danger in considering *Ulysses* from three separate "aspects," even if we emphasize the two ever-present constants of the symbolic scheme and the protean life-force theme. Any over-schematic approach to literature runs the risk of sacrificing intuitions and subtleties too fine for the conceptual mesh. And *Ulysses* is a work of synthetic complexity *par excellence*, a substantial unity in which various elements are finely blended. In no way does its structure resemble that of a Neapolitan ice. The division made in treating different aspects of *Ulysses* is, then, admittedly somewhat arbitrary, valid only in so far as it helps to bring forth the full richness of Joyce's "human" comedy. To demonstrate this richness clearly, it is necessary to be analyzed—but without forgetting that we are ultimately concerned, as always in Joyce's work, with variety-in-unity.

Ulysses, though structured on Homer, does not give the impression of an action-packed odyssey. Story looms small. This is partly owing to the strong element of time-shifting, which tends to substitute a spatial interest ("next to what?") for the usual temporal suspense ("what next?"), but this is mainly due to the fact that Joyce is a master in the use of language, *Ulysses* is fundamentally a comedy of style. Elaborated language—spoken and written communication across space and time—is *the* essentially human characteristic: more than anything else it can render humanity from within *and* without, *and* in relation to ideas, and to both past *and* future.

Take, for instance, the "Cyclops" episode: not only are Joyce's irreverent catalogues, particularly abundant here, justified as part of the intentional amplification, but action and story-suspense *have* to be sacrificed as they are incompatible with Joyce's aim here. The book would actually be a less complete comedy with them than without them, as Joyce would then have had to jettison various kinds of comic effect like parody, inflation etc., thus sacrificing something of the distance required for the *comic* appreciation of the theme for the dubious benefit of story involvement—more appropriate for a farce. It is precisely the marriage of burlesque and parody, with the cyclopean exaggeration and grotesqueness, that turns the episode into a masterpiece. It fully demonstrates the fact that superlatives, hyperbolical expressions, and high-faluting rhetoric more often mask than model truth and reality in this unideal world.

As the linguistically most varied and stylistically most masterly of novels (with a larger vocabulary than any other), *Ulysses* exemplifies its own theme through style rather than incident: that humanity and its predicaments ultimately are things to be rejoiced in, because they *are* comic in an especially human way. This, rather than by *saying*, is his main method of conveying the idea that the human condition is essentially, and sometimes sadly, comic. Many episodes are almost wholly rendered in this form of presentation. In the "Aeolus," "Oxen of the Sun," "Cyclops," "Nausicaa," "Eumaeus," "Ithaca" and—to a lesser degree—"Penelope" episodes this is the case; the human comedy is focused on the ways humanity uses or misuses language.

Throughout *Ulysses* there is constant interest in language, be it straight, twisted, serious, playful, elevated, debased, blarneyed, or halted. It strikingly draws attention to itself in *Aeolus,* for instance, with much of the comedy arising out of one of the chief modern ways in which language is misused. Joyce is here aiming towards a direct correspondence between subject-matter and style. Form mimics reality, as it were, being at the same time the vital part of Joyce's scrupulous aesthetic ordering. There is a new awareness of the extent to which the world we inhabit is a linguistic product, language being more than simply a means of expression. Consequently, false language falsifies our lives. However, the linguistic exuberance of the "Aeolus" episode, though incorporating the false rhetoric of journalism, is paradoxically a part of its comic vitality. Used not mechanically, but with conscious art, that false rhetoric becomes part of true comedy.

In the other episodes parody and pastiche crop up frequently as well. Furthermore, the contrast of eighteen different major styles in dealing with one day's reality is surely the most striking feature of the book. As a matter of comic surface it conveys man's protean attempts to disguise his basic reality; attempts doomed to failure, because reality constantly shows through. But there is a deeper comic implication, for such protean art also conveys—by its own *being*, no matter what its content—the adaptability, vitality, and creativity that are conditions for the survival of man as a *civilized* animal. On this level are justified Joyce's final "Yes"—*and* our final acceptance of *Ulysses* as a celebratory comedy.

The naturalistic parts of *Ulysses* render one aspect of human beings their uniqueness and mortality, as separate creatures, in a particular place and time, subject to local and specific absurdities. The symbolic parts render another aspect their typicality and immortality, as representatives of a protean humanity, absurd in general and comparative ways. The protean quality itself, whether individual or representative, is specially human, as beasts as individuals or species cannot try to be other than they are, and therefore cannot become absurd. It is, of course, admirable to try and change for the better. This is perhaps why one can celebrate this capacity, although it can lead to absurdity or falsity (as shown in the excesses, evasions and lapses in some works of rhetoric). This protean quality—

always changing yet in the end remaining inescapably the same—resembles the way the English language itself has evolved while always remaining "English." What knits together the naturalistic and the symbolic, the absurd and the celebratory, the particularity and the representativeness of characters and incidents is, of course, language. And it is language used in a host of ways to render these aspects comic (in principle, they could be otherwise, as nothing is *intrinsically* comic). Appropriately, therefore, an essentially "human" comedy is conveyed mainly through the comic use of the two essentially human characteristics: protean language and a sense of humour.

Ulysses, then, though partly a comedy of observation, incident and ideas (some things invite a more comic response than others, though nothing *necessarily* does so), is basically a comedy of *style*, or as Joyce says in the *Wake*: "A comedy of Letters."

Structure:

The great literary artefacts of Homer and Shakespeare, and the Bible figure most coherently as the universalizing frameworks in *Ulysses*, suggesting timeless "humanity." They make *Ulysses* a symbolic expression of certain constant patterns of human experience underlying historical change and the apparently random events of daily life; an expression, as it were, of universal, historical and psychological laws, lying beneath the contingencies of a humdrum world. It is in this sense that the symbolic structure corresponds formally to the understanding that the book is a "human" comedy by virtue of its content: the sense in which it is *not* Dantean.

Joyce has attempted to find the universally human in ordinary experience. Through the symbolic deployment of Homeric myth he has developed a critical irony that mediates between the legendary and the contemporary. The discrepancy between the two results in a form of universal comedy—of this world, not of any hypothetical one. Joyce's irony, of course, is double-edged; it is directed at the past as well as the present. If it reduces the characters to mock-heroic absurdity, it also magnifies them, treating their most trivial habits as profound rituals, attaching a universal significance to the most minute particulars. If it reduces *Ulysses* to Bloom, it also exalts

Bloom to *Ulysses*: they are the same kind of person. In this way, the Homeric world is kept in mind as a reminder that man's basic attitudes may change but are never eliminated— again a matter for celebration, not regret.

By insisting on these parallels, Joyce has made *Ulysses* articulate some of the cardinal patterns of our common culture, has made us aware of the continuing validity, the living truth, of Homer, Shakespeare, and the Bible. His essentially comic approach has brought them closer to us, making them more human than ever before.

Several other humanly basic themes operate, somewhat less obviously, within the general framework. These themes are often ingeniously and elaborately woven into the verbal texture—indeed, the protean theme is not only woven into the texture, it *is* the texture itself, seen as a purposefully variegated whole. Apart from the fact that he describes one day of eighteen hours, in which he symbolizes all the main facets of human life, Joyce's treatment of the major themes throughout the book makes it necessary to apprehend *Ulysses* as a multi-faceted world, a three-dimensional human comedy celebrating those imponderable aspects that history cannot *fundamentally* change.

Symbolic structure, however, is not the only one in *Ulysses*. It may not even be the most important structural contribution to the comedy, though it is the main structural contribution to its quality as a worldly epic. Certainly, there are other formal characteristics that link structure with comedy of style and of character more indissolubly, and are almost as important as the symbolism in bringing about the sense of relativity that is so central to the comic nature of *Ulysses*.

The traditional novel by means of continuous narrative and coherent style, normally aims at leaving the reader with certain aspectual abstractions: precipitates of memory, concepts arising from narrative and style but no longer intimately con-nected with them. Indeed, the prime purpose of continuity and coherence is, self-effacingly, to lead to such aspectual abstrac-tions as character, plot, and theme.

Ulysses is unusual in its use of *dis*continuous narrative and disparate styles, making narrative jump-cuts—temporal or spatial or both—from episode to episode, emphasizing them by striking changes of style. This protean activity is the opposite of self-effacement. As the artist disappears, "like the God of creation," behind his handiwork, the artistry becomes more prominent. And so the precipitates of memory come to include those arising from a consciousness of startling changes of structural and textual style, of apparent incoherence.

Such a method clearly diminishes the role of plot and story, and seems to diminish that of fixed character as well. But it augments the basic comic postulate: that mankind is pointlessly intolerant about essential differences between human types within each period and self-deceiving about the essential continuity within each type from period to period.

The first aspectual abstraction we apprehend is that of *relativity*: characters inhabit different worlds, perceive or can be perceived in different styles—scientifically, rhetorically, metaphysically and so on. This results in dramatic irony: we often know what the characters do not, for they usually think and act as if their inner and outer worlds were unitary, whereas we see both changed by time or circumstance. The paradoxical point is that we are made *continually* aware of this through discontinuity; the characters, immersed in their daily routine, are only rarely aware of it if ever.

The second aspectual abstraction is that of *overlapping perspectives*. Here style meshes with symbolism: Through stylistic archaisms we see that other ages have behaved in fundamentally the same way, though made to seem fundamentally different by radical differences of style, again rarely perceived by the characters. This, of course, is most apparent in the parodies of the "Oxen of the Sun" episode.

The third aspectual abstraction from this method is that of *thematic transcendence*. We finally perceive a unity in discontinuity, a theme of persistence. The different aspects surround a solid reality; in our own lives we may not be able to grasp reality as a whole, because it is not possible to see all aspects at once one cannot be young and old, detached and involved at the same time. This work of art allows us to do so by deducing reality from its aspects. Similarly, we see that the differences of style are differences of *style*, not of substance that the characters, in different worlds—even in that nightmare—do have a persisting core (in *Ulysses* psychology is more basic than sociology). And this work of art, which insists on itself as a *work* of *art*, shows that man can transcend the ludicrous combination of real differences and delusory deceptions, could turn the savage farce of his existence into a human comedy.

Ulysses does not suggest that the facts can be fundamentally changed. However, it does imply that man's—or at any rate some men's comprehension of them may be broad enough, being the prime example itself. Its own activity is an example of basic life-energies comprehended, controlled, and transformed into art. So it is able to say *Yes* to life as a whole, ludicrous though it is.

Style:

Undoubtedly, Joyce's symbolism has to be considered as only part of the total meaning of the whole book. To read it in purely naturalistic terms would be equally fallacious.

The withdrawal of the author "like the God of creation," who remains "within or behind or beyond or above his handiwork, invisible, refined out of existence, indifferent, paring his fingernails" (*Portrait* 215), the absence of any one "Joycean" style, actually results in an enhanced awareness of the shaping artist, and therefore makes the book noticeably a triumph of human creative energy.

A wholly naturalistic book might seem to have written itself, to be a photographic record of reality, in which the reader could become so immersed that he would note only the fictional work of art and not the artistry. This could never happen with *Ulysses*—so that *if* it *is* impersonal it is not non-human. On the contrary, this style deploying the specifically human gifts of creativity, elaborate language and humour—is precisely what renders *Ulysses* "human" in our second sense. It is very much a man-made artefact, but not a "subjective" one in the Romantic fashion. The author is clearly a creative human being, not a camera, and through different styles shows various sides of life (including the inside), but on the whole does not *take* sides. A full-length study would be necessary for a true philosophy of Joyce's style and of the prodigious creation of language which has never seemed better adapted to its subject. But for the moment, it is sufficient to note that form in *Ulysses* usually enacts content in some way.

Joyce found inherent comedy in language, especially its misuses; everything, even the grim, the morbid, and the pathetic, is presented in terms of total, cosmic humour. Joyce shared the

Shavian notion that it is proper to treat the most serious subjects with levity. The *vis comica* operates consistently throughout his work. Given enough distance in time or space, no subject is too grim for laughter, and death itself has a special corner. In "Hades," for example, or the ghostly apparitions in the "Circe" episode, the potentially solemn or morbid is turned to the grotesque through the deployment of comic techniques.

If in *A Portrait* the language changes with the growth of the protagonist, Joyce takes his mimetic form a step further in *Ulysses*: style and technique change as the subject changes. Each character, each place, each hour of the day speaks its own language, possesses its own syntax, its own vocabulary. Each episode, with its original style, colour, and rhythm, appears expressible only in this particular style, colour, and rhythm. Every style, furthermore, is adaptable to some local and specific effect, suggesting at one moment the movement of water, at another the stale air of a brothel. It is passionate, sentimental, violent, obscene, frivolous, sophisticated, scientific, and exquisite in turn. And throughout, Joyce's comic inventiveness, ludicrous wit and sane humour, as part of the human survival-kit, keep breaking in.

There is a kind of comic lyricism in "Proteus," and there is as much mockery in the opening of "Calypso" as in the opening of the book. The windy metaphors in "Aeolus," the culinary and cannibalistic allusions in "Lestrygonians," the Shakespearean phraseology in "Scylla and Charybdis," the sonic and musical organization of "Sirens," or the bombastic parodies of "Cyclops," for all their would-be serious intentions, keep exploding in comic absurdities. There is still the same comic inventiveness in the "Oxen of the Sun" parodies, in the hilariously clumsy and flabby style of "Eumaeus," in the pedantic precisions of "Ithaca," in the hectic swirling movement of "Circe," or in the "unfeminine," bawdy language of "Penelope."

In the "Circe" episode, for instance, life is viewed surrealistically, as in the "Ithaca" episode it is viewed scientifically—and in each case the reader sees that it is viewed one-sidedly and therefore absurdly. Each view reveals something of value; what it mocked is its partiality.

Joyce's comedy generally lacks the commitment of satire, it is usually not "getting at anyone," but rather tends to celebrate the absurdities of human life seeing them as only minimally amendable. Joyce saw them expressed all around him, in literature as well as in life, and expressed not only in the greatest works of literature—by Shakespeare, or Dante, or any of the authors whose styles are parodied in the "Oxen of the Sun" episode—but also in lesser works, that were very much part of the current popular culture. If he was going to write about life, "real life," he had to represent "culture" in the most inclusive sense of the word.

In the "Oxen of the Sun" episode, for instance, Joyce goes beyond the virtuoso pattern of words to a stage where literary tradition and aesthetic delight combine to make parody a part of the structure of the book, rather than a device for its own sake. As well as being a virtuoso display, the "Oxen of the Sun" episode is most impressive in its comprehensive and uncensorious vision of humanity. It shows ethical and emotional attitudes apparently transformed by style alone—though in fact the comic tension is usually set up by mingling some uncharacteristic content with the period style. These attitudes range from the heroic to the anarchic. In part, the styles are humorously inappropriate: the comic nature of the episode derives mostly from the inability of the language of the past to reflect the present without *obvious* distortion. This implies, though, that style always unobstrusively distorts human nature. So it is, then, that the comedy often springs form the instant recognition of incongruity between language and content: low events described in lofty language, for instance, imply a mockery of narrattive convention.

Clearly, this episode confirms that Joyce can do anything with language, not only as a mere display of ingenuity but also as proof that *Ulysses* both continues the line of English literary tradition and contains it. The unity of this technique is brought about by the coherence of Joyce's comic vision. The distinction between what language expresses and the meanings it creates by its patterning is one of the main features of Joyce's comic style in this episode. Comedy is induced in a potentially serious context through the detachment of parody, which demands to be read with tolerance, a sense of humour, and delight in the playful use of language. Parody, of course, is a form of falsification—but that, in a way, is the great literature parodied here, too. The parodic falsification, however, is also clearly an achievement; and therefore these parodies of great literature result in the near-paradoxical mode of *celebratory* mockery, rather than in a bitter satire of humanity's habit of trying to soften—or escape—reality by adopting a period style. They are celebratory because they acknowledge the imaginative achievement of great literature—and incidentally the protean adaptability of humanity—and mocking because they see the tendency of men to be *poseurs.*

Primarily, the parodies are a particularly human manifestation of the life-force, a striking exemplification of the protean energies of language. While they acknowledge the literature out of which *Ulysses* has emerged, they also seem to confirm the necessity of a new literature, of a literature more aware of the human tendency to stylize experience, of *Ulysses*, in fact. Through these parodies, one recognizes the pretentiousness, pomposity, and absurdity of the ways people prefer to see themselves. Strip the style off them and there are no heroes, no perfections but only a vast comic humanity trying different ways of coping with the same old problems. The parodies also function in a structural way, as linguistic transformations. In the end all the parodies taken together seem to express the conception of art as the distillation of history, the growth of the process of life, an expression of the protean life-force: "In woman's womb world is made flesh but in the spirit of the maker all flesh that passes becomes the word that shall not pass away." (*U* 391)

Evidently, the purpose of the parodies is not merely to show off Joyce's skill as a parodism and pasticher, or even to tell a story, but to enrich our experience of the characters and to keep it comic. We see them under a vast number of social and mythical aspects, like in a historical pageant. The parody ensures that we do not take them too seriously, which other writers might have done—and thereby would have made them the less human.

Joyce, then, presents life in its many-sidedness, viewing it from different points of view, comprising a full range of human activity (such as education, science, medicine, and so on), adopting different styles, filling everyday life with surprising vitality and significance. Thus, he confirms his early belief that

> The great human comedy in which each has share gives limitless scope to the true artist. Today as yesterday and as in years gone. (*CW* 45)

Character:

It is in the tolerence and uninhibited inclusiveness of its characterization that *Ulysses* is most clearly "human" in the third sense: man's inevitable and therefore forgiveable imperfection. But just as the three senses shade into one another, so character—even more evidently than structure and style—shades into other aspects of the work.

In *Ulysses* all the formidable narrative techniques serve a thematic purpose, as well as they give depth to the individual characters *and* show universal humanity through unique individuals.

Joyce's uses of myth and symbolistic vision cannot be understood as absolute; they gain significance only when seen in the light of the naturalistic temporal perspectives of the characters. Although Joyce's treatment of his characters is basically ironic, by reason of the different perspectives they are seen in, he does not fail to acknowledge Bloom's integrity and the importance of Stephen's struggles towards maturity, thus celebrating the vitality of ordinary humanity. To say that *Ulysses* is not as rich in "psychological insight as in technical brilliance" is to deny the fact that both symbolism and technical brilliance are more often than not means of creating characters. Thus the triumph of Joyce's art is not technical virtuosity as an end in itself, but as a means to create, among other things, the ridiculous, quixotic, middle-aged Leopold Bloom, the intelligent, brooding Stephen Dedalus, the voluptuous, all-embracing Molly Bloom, and a whole series of minor characters. The result is a sense of the variegated richness of life as well as its ironical paradoxes, its paralysis and its vitality. It is almost a rule that the themes and images radiate from the minds of the characters, which makes the story come alive most complexly.

The constant background irony resulting form the symbolic structure and ready-made rhetoric is never so strong as to reject the characters entirely. Joyce's naturalism portrays them as imperfect contemporaries, absurd but "only human" in their limitations and their pretentious tendency to view themselves as Ulysseses, Hamlets or Christs, and still living individual beings. A master of mimicry and caricature, Joyce is not mainly satirical in his characterization; his method is one of comedy evoked by the implicit affirmation of the permanent life-supporting values inherent in his comic stance.

It has already been stated above that it is in Bloom that the comic vitality of *Ulysses* most clearly resides, not necessarily in his somewhat absurd, pathetic and quixotic figure, but in what is revealed through him. Admittedly, his backslidings and his disorganized notions are a major source of amusement in the book, but the comedy is induced through Bloom rather than at his expense. Retrospectively, Stephen's torments and philosophizing become comic by contrast with Bloom's materialism; not in the sense of being funny, or even absurd in the normal sense, but absurd in a larger sense which is part of the sad human comedy: man being the only animal to suffer for abstractions without any real purpose for life. In this sense the comic can co-exist with the admirable—another fact that is an ironic part of the human comedy.

It is interesting to see how Joyce developed his technique in the direction of a comic vision. A passage from "Hades," which is a rewritten, polished up version of a passage in *Stephen Hero,* can admirably serve to indicate the quality of the later work.

In *Stephen Hero* Joyce describes the funeral of Stephen's sister Isabel:

> The mourners scattered in the seats and knelt timidly on their handkerchiefs. A priest with a great toad-like belly balanced to one side came out of the sacristy, followed by an altar boy. He read the service rapidly in a croaking voice and shook the aspergill drowsily over the coffin, the boy piping responses at intervals. (*SH* 172)

Joyce's final draft, as it were, in *Hades* reads as follows:

> The mourners knelt here and there in praying desks. Mr. Bloom stood behind the font and, when all had knelt dropped carefully his unfolded newspaper from his pocket and knelt his right knee upon it. He fitted his black hat gently on his left knee and, holding its brim, bent over piously.
>
> A server, bearing a brass bucket with something in it, came out through a door. The whitesmocked priest came after him tidying his stole with one hand, balancing

with the other a little book against his toad's belly.
Who'll read the book? I, said the rook.

They halted by the bier and the priest began to read
out of his book with a fluent croak.

What we first notice is the fact that the "Hades" passage is longer, thus allowing the development of character absent in the *Stephen Hero* passage.   By mingling direct interior monologue with plain narrative it contributes to the more varied and lively surface characteristic of the *Hades* episode.   Its textual detail is more accurate, appropriate, and economical. Compare, for instance, "scattered" with "knelt here and there"; the odd "toad-like belly balanced to one side" with "balancing . . . a little book against his toad's belly"; "sacristy" and "aspergill" with Bloom's uncatholic vagueness: "a door" and "a brass bucket with something in it"; or "rapidly in a croaking voice" with "fluent croak."   Note also the introduction of minor psychological points in the "Hades" passage, such as "Who'll read the book? I, said the rock."   And finally, while the *Stephen Hero* passage is descriptive, the "Hades" passage is more dramatic as well as more comic.   Indeed, it is more comic *because* more dramatic.   Joyce is reported to have said: "I find the subject of Ulysses the most human in world literature."[5]   Judging by his own *Ulysses*, as I have attempted to demonstrate, Joyce seems to have found it also the most comic—indeed, he seems to have found both to be in the broadest possible sense—practically synonymous.

Notes

[1] For amplificaiton of these points see Allan Rodway, *English Comedy: Its Role and Nature from Chaucer to the Present Day,* (London, 1975), Chaps. 1-3, passim, and L. J. Potts, *Comedy,* (London, 1946), Chaps. I and II, passim.

[2] The Winter's Tale, IV.4.

[3] Bergson, *Laughter: An Essay on the Meaning of the Comic,* transl. by Brereton and Rothwell, (London, 1911), p. 3.

[4]Ibid., pp. 129-130.
[5]Richard Ellmann, *James Joyce*, (New York/London/Toronto, 1965),
p. 430.

Islam and Creation Myths: A Reading of Page Five of *Finnegans Wake*

Leonard H. Somers
FUNDP, Namur, Belgium

That Islam is a theme of some importance in *Finnegans Wake* was demonstrated by James S. Atherton when he examined the position it occupies in the *Wake*.[1] I should like to follow up his analysis, trying to link the Islamic elements to other themes and beliefs in the book in order to illustrate Joyce's attempt at blending all religions into one.

A first hint in the direction of Islam is given in the first part of the H. C. E. formula on page 4: 'Haroun Childeric Eggeberth' (4.32). Here Master Builder, Finnegan, mentioned at the beginning of the paragraph, is associated with the Caliph of Bagdad, a Frankish king, and the king of the West-Saxons, plus a Roman emperor hidden in the verb 'caligulate' (4.32). The first ruler, Haroun, used to go about the town in many disguises, assuming like Joyce's main hero a variety of identities and reminding us of the wanderers in *Ulysses* (see Bloom in the "Circe" episode). The other two names have been chosen because they contain three times the idea of generation in the syllables *child, egg* and *berth,* quite appropriate in a section dealing with the creation myth. Haroun then prepares us for the next page where the tales of the *Arabian Nights* remind us of his reign.

A very extensive reference to Islam is to be found on page 5, where a connection is established between the fall of the Master Builder from his ladder, while constructing a very Parisian 'eyeful hoyth entowerly' (4.36), and the fall of Adam and Eve, 'the municipal sin business' (5.14).

The first Islamic reference is to the Ka'aba, the sanctuary supposedly built by Ibrahim and his son Ismail, literally translated as 'our cubehouse' (5.14). It contains the 'whitestone' (5.17), white as milk when it came down from Paradise, but now all blackened by the sins of mankind. It is 'blackguardised' (5.17) or spoken of in foul or abusive language all 'through successive ages' (5.15). We can still hear the 'shebby choruysh of unkalified muzzlenimiissilehims' (5.16). The (Christian or Greek) *chorus* makes a (German) *Geräusch* or sound like the thin or *shabby* bleating of *sheep*. *Shabby* also suggests the Egyptian *shabti* (like in 25.2), statuettes found in Egyptian tombs whose function was to perform tasks for the deceased person in the underworld. This reference also links up two additional allusions to Egyptian mythology: Horus, the hawk-headed god of day, light and the good, turns up in 'choruysh', while 'mastabatoom, mastabadtomm' (6.10), the tragicomical end of the passage, contains the ancient Egyptian word for tomb, *mastaba*.

'Unkalified' (5.16) is easiest understood as 'unqualified' but it suggests 'illegitimate' as well since the caliphs were the sometimes contested successors to the Prophet. A brief allusion to the Hindu religion should also not be overlooked here: *Kali* is the name of the goddess of destruction.

Christianity, too, may claim two references: first the 'rock' (5.14) on which the Church was built. According to Anthony Burgess[2] we cannot quite forgive Christ for (as Joyce himself put it) founding His Church on a pun. 'Rock' functions here as a noun and a verb and alludes to Peter, the Church, the Ka'aba and the stones with which Abraham drove the devil away and which the Muslim pilgrims throw during the pilgrimage ceremony of 'pelting the devil.' The latter are the Muslim missiles in the long word of (5.16) 'Muzzlenimiissilehims,' which sounds like the call of the muezzin (of the first syllable!) and reminds one of the chanted *dhikr* (= remembrance) *Lā ilāha illa llah,* "There is no God except God." But 'Rock' also has another important connotation: it is the title of a Sura, or Chapter, of the Koran, Nr. 15. *Al-Hijr* relates the story of the creation and Satan's vow to seduce mankind and cause its downfall.

The second Christian allusion lies in the second element of 'hurtleturtled out of heaven' (5.17) where 'turtle' stands for the Holy Spirit, represented by a dove. 'Turtle', however, leads us to a whole series of other myths of creation. The Maidu Indians of California e. g. see in him (the reptile) a mediator, who in the time when there was only water, would dive from a raft to the bottom of the river and bring up earth to the surface under his fingernails. This earth Earth-Initiate, the creative principle, would roll in his palm into a ball and make it grow to form the Earth.[3] The Pygmees also use a turtle to explain the creation of man: in the beginning a turtle swam in the primal waters, laid its eggs in them and hatched all the animals and the first human couple.[4]

A different kind of African creation myth, however, also seems to be quite relevant here. Let's begin with the cosmogony of the Boshongo, a Central Bantu Tribe of the Lunda Cluster.[5] "In the beginning, in the dark, there was nothing but water. And Bumba was alone. One day Bumba was in terrible pain. He retched and strained and vomited up the sun. . . (he) vomited up the moon and then the stars. . . Still Bumba was in pain. He strained again and nine living creatures came forth. . . ." Similar beliefs were noticed by Haroun Terzieff, the vulcanologist, according to which all living things found their origin in the excrements of the gods projected through the craters of the volcanos. The Kawillewille of the Songe tribe vomited the first two women and then gave birth to the other human beings through his anus (Frobenius, *Atlantis 18*, p. 93).[6] The creation of man according to the Edo tribe contains similar elements. Ogiwu, the god of thunder, keeps all the blood and the sap of the trees in his possession. Without these Osa, the Supreme Divinity, is powerless and cannot create the first human beings. In a quarrel, however, Ogiwu wounds his wife Obieni with his sword so that she can never bear children again. Now the Omonusa spirits come to the rescue and form the first human couple out of the excrements of the gods. Ogiwu gives them their blood and Osa their breath.[7]

All these myths can be linked up not only with the second excremental element of 'hurtleturtled' but also with some anal references in other places: 'nathandjoe' (3.12), the two combined names standing for Jonathan Swift: the one hundred letter thunderclap (3.15); the onomatopaeic 'pftjschute of Finnegan' (3.19); the 'cubehouse' (5.14) seen as a toilet; the two last syllables of 'the thunder of his arafatas'; the question whether the Ka'aba might 'half been a missfired brick, (think of 'Bygmester Finnegan' 4.18). . . or it might have been due to a collupsus of his back promises, as others looked at it' (5.24-26). At the same time the tone of Book I is one of reservation over the accuracy of its contents.[8] Joyce seems

to make fun of those historians who always want to know
what 'agentlike' (5.13) happened—or *wie es eigentlich gewesen*—
and seem engrossed by a narrowing speculation over the irre-
trievable past events they study. He begins the next paragraph
with the exclamation 'Shize?" (6.13), questioning the validity
of what preceded with a rude German expression, our last
anal reference of the lot.

Let us at this point turn back to the world of Islam. We
know how its beliefs and practices can be read from the five
fingers of the upturned hand, reminding the faithful of the
five pillars of their religion: 1) the belief in one God only and
in Mohammed, His Prophet: 2) the obligation to pray five times
a day; 3) the obligation to give to the poor; 4) the obligation
to visit Mecca and the holy places once in a lifetime; 5) the
obligation to fast during the month of Ramadan. Apart from
the last one, all these points are in one way or another interwoven in the section beginning with 5.13.

1) The chant of the muezzin proclaiming the greatness
of Allah Akbar (the Greatest) has already been mentioned
(5.16). God is further invoked in line 5.18 as the 'Sustainer'
one of the many names he is given in the Koran. The name
of Allah, himself, however, is not used in *Finnegans Wake*.
Adaline Glasheen[9] lists over a dozen Arabian names but could
not find the (forbidden? unspeakable?) name of God. But
we do know His power: Sura 13, *Ra'd* or "Thunder," evoked
in 'thunder' (5.15) and 'hurtleturtled' (5.17), reads: "It's He
who makes the lightning flash upon you, inspiring you with
fear and hope, as He gathers up the heavy clouds. The thunder
sounds His praises, and the angels too, for awe of Him. He
hurls His thunderbolts at whom He pleases. Yet the unbelievers
wrangle about Allah. Stern is His punishment."[10]

Mohammed himself appears several times: he is called
'nabir' (5.21) (*nebi* is Arabian for prophet, heavenly messenger);
we see him as a 'provost' (5.22) ready to dominate the whole
Mediterranean world from east to west (5.22), or from the
rock (= jebel, 5.23) of Gibraltar to the Egyptian sea (jpysian
sea, 5.23). He is also hidden in the expression 'Cropherb the
crunchbracken' (5.23), where a hint is given at Mohammed's
slight hunchback (in reality not more than a wart!) or phrophet's
deformity. The more sadistic elements 'crop,' 'crunch' and
'broken' call at the same time the Master Builder's fall to mind.
Finally, the name of Mohammed's own clan, Quraysh, (e. g. in

Sura 106) can be heard in the word 'choruysh' (5.16).

2) The *Sabat* or list of obligatory prayers contains five instances which at first sight don't quite coincide with the ordinary set times. However, Atherton pointed out that 'what time we rise' (5.19) means noon to Joyce[11] and 'when we take up to toothmick' (5.19) means the evening meal. 'Toothmick' suggests Mohammed's habit of picking his teeth up to the day he died! 'Before we lump down upon our leatherbed' (5.20) is the evening prayer; 'in the night' (5.20) must be the prayer before retiring to bed and 'at the fading of the stars' (5.21) indicates the first prayer of the day before dawn. The Christian missal is not being referred to here, as only the five times of Muslim tradition are mentioned. Catholic practice knows eight, and we can agree with Atherton, who sees in it a proof of Joyce's assumption that all religions should be treated on the same footing and there was no reason to start *Finnegans Wake* with a Christian prayer.[12]

3) A reference to the *Zakat,* or obligation to give to the poor, can be found when we read out aloud sentence 5.21: 'For a nod to the nabir [neighbour] is better than a wink to the wabsanti [absent], represents a Christian as well as a Muslim appeal for brotherly love. The long Sura 9, *'Al-Tawba,* Repentance, refers to it in several places. We chose this one because it also sheds light on 'she allcasually ansars helpers' (5.25). Repentance, v. 100, includes the word *ansar,* which is the name for the group of Mohammed's supporters in Medina who gave him asylum (charity) and "nobly followed him."[13] Sentence 5.21 mentions charity ('helpers') and cleverly knits in the Moorish word for palace, *alca-sar.*

4) The *Hadj*, or obligation to go on a pilgrimage to Mecca and visit the holy places at least once in one's lifetime, is clearly being attended to in the first part of the paragraph. Not only the Ka'aba is described in detail (see above), but also Mount Arafat (5.15), the hill outside of Mecca which must be climbed by the pilgrims as part of the ritual. Furthermore, the ceremonial stoning of the devil is contained in the long compound 'muzzlenimiissilehims' (5.16) (see also above).

5) The absence of any allusion to the month of Ramadan, during which the believers refrain throughout the day from eating and drinking and also from sexual intercourse, is striking. Perhaps we can assume that Joyce disapproved of such austerity and didn't want to include it in his religious compendium? I

couldn't take a possible disapproving shot at *absynthe*
('wabsanti,' 5.22) as sufficient evidence for Joyce's accepting
fasting or mortification. There is another allusion to Muslim
celebrations, though: 'Then we'll know if the feast is a flyday.'
(5.24). It must have been inspired by Sura 62, in the Koran,
Al-Juma, Friday or the Day of Congregation, which exhorts
the faithful to refrain from trading on Friday and to hasten to
remember Allah because "that which Allah has in store is far
better than any merchandise or merriment."[14]
    We haven't exhausted our stock of oriental elements yet.
In the same line as the above mentioned *alcazar,* we find a
sheik ('seek onsite' 5.25), or religious leader. Life in the dessert
is evoked by the *bedouin* ('bedoueen,' 5.23, with the ending
of 'between' and the Irish diminutive at the same time) and
their *dromedaries* ('dreamadeary,' 5.26).
    But the last two items are important for another reason:
'bed' and 'dream,' tied in with the popular expressions 'nodding
off' and 'forty winks' (5.21), fix the basic notions of dream
and sleep, the book's ultimate justification.
    One loose end of our oriental rug, however, needs tidying
up: Haroun-al-Rasjid, the enlightened monarch who mingled
with his subjects in order to listen to their moods, and who
serves as a disguise for Joyce, himself, is also the prince in whose
caliphate many of the tales from *Arabian Nights* are set, the
'one thousand and one stories' alluded to in line 5.28-29. For
one thousand and one nights king Shahryar (357.19) listens
to Sheharazade (32.8), our 'gifted' (5.25) 'dreamydreary' who
knows all answers (5.25). They are 'all told, of the same' (5.29),
making up the many layers of *Finnegans Wake.*
    —As sure as God made little apples, we would sigh at
the end of all this! But the same sentence through Joyce's magic
pen tells us the story of Adam and Eve and the Fall ('abe ite
ivvy's holired abbles,' 5.29-30, sure and 'sore' 5.29, a real
'tragoady' 5.13). We knew this had to be included: wasn't
the Koranic chapter in which this episode is related already
mentioned in the word 'arafatas' (5.15)? Indeed Sura 7 is
called *Al-Araf,* the Heights, and relates the same story we already
know from the Bible. Finally, one finds on the same page,
preceding Mount Arafat, references to two additional mountains
both of which have connexions to the Fall via two other
religions, the Hindu and the Old-Germanic. 'Himals and all'
(5.1), referring to *Himmel,* the German word for 'heaven,'

also suggests the Himalayas, whereas the *Riesengebirge* in Germany is presented as 'Riesengeborg' (5.6), the 'Fortress of the Giants.' The former is connected with the Builder's fall and the latter reminds us of Wagner's Ring and the Fall through gold. The 'horrors' of 'Wallhall' (5.30) make a long list taking up more than ten lines and which associates man's Fall with the corrupting influence of civilization and the evils of the cities built by the Bygmester. Back where we started— with a 'wink' at the Master!

Notes

[1] James S. Atherton, *The Books at the Wake. A Study of Literary Allusions in James Joyce's Finnegans Wake*, (London: Faber & Faber Limited, 1954), pp. 210-211.

[2] Anthony Burgess, *Here Comes Everybody. An Introduction to James Joyce for the Ordinary Reader*, (London: Faber & Faber, 1965), p. 267.

[3] Roland B. Dixon, "Maidu Myths," *Bulletin of the American Museum of Natural History*, XVII, No. 2 (1902-7), pp. 33-118.

[4] Hermann Baumann, *Schopfung and Urzeit im Mythus der Afrikanischer Volker*, (Berlin: Verlag von Dietrich Reimer, 1936), p. 198.

[5] Maria Leach, *The Beginning*, (New York, 1956), pp. 145-5, translated and adapted from Z. Torday and J. A. Joyce, *Les Doshongo*.

[6] Quotes in: Hermann Baumann, *op. cit.*, p. 114.
[7] Hermann Baumann, *op. cit.*, p. 238.

[8] Roland Mc Hugh, *The Sigla of Finnegans Wake*, (Austin: University of Texas Press, 1976), p. 5.

[9] Adaline Glasheen, *Third Census of Finnegans Wake. An Index of the Characters and Their Roles*, (Berkeley, Los Angeles, London: University of California Press).

[10] *The Koran*, translated with notes by N. J. Dawood, (Harmondsworth: Penguin Books, 1974), p. 144.

[11] Atrerton, *op. cit.*, p. 246.

[12] *ibid.*, p. 211.
[13] *The Koran, op. cit.*, p. 331.
[14] *The Koran, op. cit.*, p. 105.

"All the errears and erroriboose"
Joyce's Misconducting Universe

Fritz Senn
Zurich James Joyce Foundation

Mistakes are everywhere and errors abound. Things have a way of going wrong. This is shown by Joyce and it happens *to* him. In almost any thumb-nail biography, or encyclopedia entry, chances are that some facts are misrepresented: Joyce is turned into a student of medicine, or married off in 1904, or made blind. Or remember the title of his last work as it generally finds its way into print, *Finnegan*-apostrophe-*s Wake.* The centenary is a great opportunity for new journalistic fumbles as the calendar seems to provoke erudite utterances. For many reasons then, errors seem to cluster around Joyce, more than other writers. It is annoying, and it is wholly appropriate.

The eighth International Symposium provides an instructive example. A transformation of a whole chapter of *Ulysses* into an unusual but relevant medium was staged—into a city walk within Dublin's labyrinthine surface. The chapter was naturally the one called, at Joyce's instigation and by critical near-consensus, "Wandering Rocks." It deals with 19 smallish sections at different places, its main feature, locomotion and juxtaposition and the interlocking of various actions, offers itself for acting out and for visualization. The fictional characters, impersonated by actors (including some Joyce scholars with a newly found vocation) were walking the streets at the respective spots, according to the itineraries mapped out in the book and a time schedule worked out by Clive Hart—who fittingly initiated the performance as Father Conmee, S. J., from the presbytery steps in upper Gardiner Street, at five to three p.m.

Such a collective ambulatory-staging of one whole chapter (disconcertingly accompanied by a reading of the text as heard through transistor radios, the spoken text of course never matching the scene) made evident to its spectators some platitudes that we had become accustomed to. One is that reading a story can give us the impression of being where in actual fact we could never be, in different places simultaneously. The city reenactment demonstrated that no single observer was able to witness more than a small part of the entire procedures, whereas a reader moves effortlessly from one location to the next, almost imperceptibly and, oddly enough, without surprise. By putting oneself into one section, one automatically excluded all the others, except those taking part in the vicinity. The mere necessity to choose one place of observation made it clear that linear language in what is called "story," or "tale," or even "narrative," can streamline spatial variety into one comfortable sequence that we take for granted. Which taught us the irony that a chapter that is also an extreme of surface realism poignantly falsifies its realities and tricks us into a multipresence impossible to experience in real life.

There were other displacements. The *Ulysses* characters were dressed up in colourful period costumes to make them distinct from the crowds of onlookers and the ordinary Dubliners who were, somewhat irreverently, using their city as though it were not the scene of a chapter in a fiction. This naturally amounted to a reversal of the novel's reality, for its characters, with a few well-marked exceptions, are rather drab and inconspicuous, in fact precisely not to be distinguished from the fellow-citizens, except of course through the author's singular attention to them. The medium, in other words, aiming for visibility, imposed its own rules which in turn warped the realism that the whole event was intended to document. And since the centre of Dublin 1982 is a more congested place than it was in 1904, the various character could not proceed at their prescribed pace (the viceregal cavalcade even had to reroute itself completely to comply to traffic regulations) or were actually impeded by clusters of spectators. Leopold Bloom, remarkable in the book for being chiefly neglected and overlooked, drew the largest crowd, which occulted him most of the time—another paradox of congenial reenactment. And, inevitably, some pivotal meeting points were missed, which simply shows that urban navigation, logistics, surface interlinkings—major concerns of the chapter—are irreproducible.

My own chosen sight was Crampton Court (in ruinous condition), from where Lenehan and M'Coy take their departure, turning first south, then east, then north, then west and finally north again (section 9); this would bring me to Wellington quay and, ultimately, close to the Ormond Hotel in time for the final confluence. But the timing went wrong, and the two characters arrived too late at Merchant's arch to find Bloom inspecting the books. He had already left, and so there would have been no reason for Lenehan to boast of a minor adventure with Molly, or to comment on a "touch of the artist about old Bloom" (U 235). So the book's tight cross-referential network was being minutely disrupted.

Moreover, the actor playing Lenehan did not, as the script demanded, pop into a bookmaker's shop (one good reason being that it no longer exists) to enquire about the betting odds of the Ascot Gold Cup race which is being run at, more or less, this moment in distant England and which seemed to involve practically every Dubliner of 1904. Not much of an oversight this, perhaps, but just the sort of thing a pedantic Joycean comma-hunter (in 1982) would pick out to cavil at.

Well, perhaps it is not just pedantry, for in his pursuit of betting information Lenehan in *Ulysses* is told that Bloom (who ought to be hovering nearby) has given out a tip on the rank outsider that will actually win the race. This is based, as we know, on a misunderstanding, but Lenehan will pass on the rumour and help create an envious notion that the sly stingy jew has won a sizeable amount of money and will not even stand a drink. The rumour is believed and will result in much verbal, and some physical, assault and co-determine much of the action of the "Cyclops" chapter. In other words, because of a wholly minor omission the whole subsequent mechanistic chain of events is disrupted. A later clashing scene would become pointless. The plot has been derailed. Causal links have been severed, the clockwork has become defective. If Lenehan was not misinformed, the rest of *Ulysses* would have become a become a different book.

Because of trivia like that, large later portions would be affected. Intertexture is in disarray, this in a chapter that highlights mechanistic causality and is designed like clockwork ("Very large and wonderful and keeps famous time," U 242), or like a military campaign, with map and compasses. Did then the whole experiment—to turn a whole episode into concrete, mobile, interlocking actions—fail? It didn't, because derailment, deviation, dislocution, omissions, chance delays and collisions, accidents—failure itself—are part and parcel of the chapter's intrinsic malfunction. The points being missed add up to the point the chapter is trying to make, among others: places and times are out of joint. The centenary reincarnation of a Dublin miniature was out of gear, and this perversely proved it true. Joyce presents an erroneous universe on a local scale. It works, but never quite as expected or wanted. There are spanners in the works, the machinery is warped, and in bad repair.

Joyce found alternative ways of reminding us that the Universe itself resembles its Dublin microcosmos. As Genesis tells us, it got off on a bad start soon after its seventh day. Our ancestors did what they ought not to have done, they fell, and some remedial plans had to be substituted. Joyce, whose prose began with the mischance in a priest's life, put original sin which necessitated the divine undoing of that initial damage, into one of the energetic non-centres of *Finnegans Wake*. A *felix culpa* varies from a parochial transgression in a park, "O foenix culprit," to "felicitous culpability." It may become a psychologically "freudful mistake" or a "fatal slip," even a "foetal sleep," with other translations like an apparently Chinese "Fu Li's gulpa" thrown it. The felicitous original misconduct suffuses Christian faith and keeps the *Wake* shapes fumbling. So Lenehan's double's failure to hit upon a non-truth is also exemplarily apt in a flawed cosmos.

Joyce's early terms for an imperfect world tended to be medical (or biological), *"paralysis,"* or theological, *"simony"*; and they, together with an illustrative cue from geometry, *"gnomon,"* have been perpetually used by us as significant levers for multiform human blunders. If things in our lives didn't go wrong, there would be no stories, neither of Father Flynn, nor Odysseus, nor Adam, nor Oedipus, nor HCE. Joyce exemplifies this with a broader than the customary spectrum. At the naturalistic end we have defective objects, a humpy tray, a chipped eggcup, a creaky and soiled funeral carriage, a "onehandled" statue, or a cup "held by nothandle." Bloom's latchkey is disturbingly absent. All of which may also reflect a domestic, and a national, and a cultural situation. The process of thinking itself is naturalistically rendered as chancy, haphazard, beyond the reaches of our notions of correctness. In *Ulysses* Joyce had perfected his devices for evoking the imperfections of our mental gropings; they seem to go on very much in analogy to the actions narrated in "Wandering Rocks": a path is pursued, deviated from, interfered with. There are distractions, confusions, misdirections, illusions; hopes, fears, and escape techniques, repressions, odd coincidences. This must also affect language itself, neither words nor syntax remain untampered.

Strange to observe then how some scholarly, superior readers of *Ulysses* condescendingly tend to pass misguided judgments of "correctness." Leopold Bloom, in his private ramblings or instant speeches, does not get things immediately right—as though we ever did! He feels the warmth on his black clothes: "Black conducts, reflects (refracts is it?) the heat" (U 57). Memories of physics linger, too many. From our leisurely distance we may correct him by recalling that it is light, radiated by the sun, that can be reflected, or refracted, but that heat is conducted, and what Bloom tries to remember is the optical term "absorb"; but the fumble is appropriate since colour, light, and heat all come into play. The scientifically correct term is occluded by similar Latin compounds. Bloom could only be wrong if he offered a conclusive choice in public, or signalled some complacency. Phases of consciousness are not posing as scholarly statements. Bloom has been blamed for erroneously claiming that there are no rhymes in Shakespeare. But not even in the intimacy of his own mind does he ever claim this. He merely modifies his own hasty generalisation that poets write in "similar sounds," typically checking himself: "But then Shakespeare has no rhymes: blank verse" (U 152). As a cautious qualification this is correct and could be "wrong" only if isolated as a critical statement (and even then it would be acceptable in the sense that "no rhymes" is in fact what Shakespeare "has" in the vast majority of his passages). Joyce devised a defective shorthand for the often random, tentative processes of thinking. Once some of them have to be released into public speech, as it happens to Bloom in his more unguarded moments, they may become factually wrong: "Mercadante. . .was a jew" (U 342). And it seems to occur in all forms of communication. In the newspaper account of Dignam's funeral which puts Stephen, C. P. M'Coy and M'Intosh, to say nothing of L. Boom, among the mourners present at Glasnevin cemetery, we may learn what happens in reports. *Finnegans Wake* goes on to treat all events and reports, facts or fictions, history or myth, eyewitness accounts, rumours or legend, as hardly distinguishable. No utterance or document deserves trust any more. Language itself has given up all pretense to conform. What in Bloom's day still looks like a frequent exception has become a natural state of confusion in *Finnegans Wake*.

This might be in tune with the transition from the daylight that still illuminates an important first half of *Ulysses* into a nocturnal or even dreamlike opaqueness. Noon day clarity or meaning have given way to a "nooningless knockturn" (FW 64.15); and it is the knocks and turns that meanings take which interest us here. A glutted adverb like "nichthemerically" (FW 185.29) tantalizingly flashes suggestions of how either *Ulysses* or the *Wake* itself appear to have been produced. Less by day (as through Greek *hēmera*), than by not-(German *nicht*)-day (and a slight transposition from a Scottish looking "nicht" to "night" reinforces the nocturnal reading defectively). Or we may choose to approximate the whole conglomerate to a genuine Greek word for a night and a day, *nychthēmeron*. This is a trifle more than the temporal scope of *Ulysses*, but also a term that St. Paul, a latter-day, converted Odysseus, used to describe his being shipwrecked "a night and a day in the deep" (2 Cor. 11:25). *Ulysses*, depending on one's perspective, is either Homeric(al) or "nicht-Homerical"—if not downright nihilistic (German *Nichts* would fit this view). The heterographic chiaroscuro taunts such significations into spectral being: and by any normative standards it is simple to prove that none of them are present. We tend to shape graphic errors into plausible near-truths. *Ulysses*, in fact all the earlier works, have prepared us for teasing patterns out of textual disorder.

When things go amiss, language cannot remain unaffected according to standards of schoolmasters or proofreaders. Bloom, early on, takes his hat from the peg in the hall and reads its legend: "Plasto's high grade ha" (U 56). This is primarily an instant of being faithful in recording what is there, the hatband, belying its "high grade" quality, no longer contains the terminal letter "-t," and it is not for the author to interfere and to mend matters. Sherlock Holmes, we may remember, was an ingenious student of objects like hats suffering wear and tear; like him, the reader of *Ulysses* can draw conclusions

about its wearer. Bloom's defectively lettered hat keeps sur-
facing, and the missing *t* may have strange power over our
reconstructive minds. Is a "Ba" similarly deficient (occurring
three times in short succession, p. 377-8), a similarly truncated "Bat?" One will soon be flying around Bloom. Or is
it some kind of stifled exclamation? Do we determine that
by consulting the two "authorized" translations? The French
team offers "Ahââ" (*Ulysse*, Paris, Gallimard, 1948); Georg
Goyert settled for "Na." (*Ulysses*, Zürich: Rhein Verlag,
1956). The later Italian translation, benefiting from decades
of scholarship, decided in favour of "Pip" as a particle of
"Pipistrello probabilmente" (*Ulisse*, Milano: Mondadori,
1968, 510; "Bat probably"), and Bloom's high grade "ha"
may well have been instrumental to this reading. But not
even every "ha" in *Ulysses* need be an imperfect hat.   A
fourfold "Ha ha ha ha" in the Circe episode does not denote
headgear but the derisive amusement of Zoe and Florry as
they are watching Bloom watching (in one of the phantasies)
Blazes Boylan vis-à-vis Molly (U 565). Even so it is intriguing
that, just a few lines afterwards, Boylan hangs *his* "hat smartly
on a peg of Bloom's antlered head." In the morning, when
Bloom returned from the pork butcher's, it had been Boylan's
letter (U 61) that had made him forget what he did with his
own de-lettered hat, as he later remembers (U 68); it is equally
odd that it was right after passing "Plasto's" shop, on the way
to Glasnevin, that he first caught sight of Boylan (U 92). Somehow the missing terminal letter seems to make us more aware
of potential connections.

   As readers in search of pertinence we may align Bloom's
incomplete "ha" with his whole situation.   Once we become
alerted to a letter that is not there, especially when a terminal
omission seems to be emphasized by an *"initialed . . . over-
coat"* (U 56), we notice it all the better when it is. "See blank
tee what domestic animal?" is a puzzle whose answer rhymes
with "hat." In such ways we learn, as readers, to pay attention
to blanks, and to "See blank tee" (U 283), or to supplement
"Tee dash ar." Simon Dedalus takes off—not a hat, but—Larry
O'Rourke "to a tee" (U 58), and one implication seems to be
that a small difference may really matter.   In another context
the same letter may function as a merely opportune strategem
of transatlantic information: "T is viceregal lodge" (U 136),
a somewhat arbitrary assignment.

A letter missing in one place may be matched by one intruding somewhere else: "Do ptake some ptarmigan" (U 175). This reminds us of the relation between sounds and letters, and the vagaries of English spelling. In Joyce's dystypographical universe we must not be misled by appearances. "See you in tea" (U 497) appears to announce a vision and a beverage, but naughtily reveals itself as a suggestive sequence of letters. And what then is to detain us from an analogous semantic faking and playing off Mulligan's making tea with Bloom's missing "t?" Mulligan's impersonation is conspicuous: "When I makes tea I makes tea, as old mother Grogan said. And when I makes water I makes water" (U12). Such conflation of liquids, along with its blasphemous escalation in "water . . . That I make when the wine becomes water again" (U 19), seems to receive involitional clerical sanction by the mere name of "the Rev. T. Waters" present in a list of ecclesiastical dignitaries (U 317). But Mulligan's quip has nothing whatever to do with Bloom's ha, nor does Mrs. Cahill's retort: "God send you don't make them in the one pot" (U 12), except that Bloom, "nursing his hat" in a bench of the church of All Hallows, muses: "These pots we have to wear" (U 80). Later on "teapot" will become a suggestive word in turn—a blank to be filled—in a parlour game: "I confess I'm teapot with curiosity to find out whether some person's something is a little teapot at present. . . I'm simply teapot all over me" (U 445). Immediately afterwards Bloom is wearing "a purple Napoleon hat."

All of which merely goes to say that an omission, an absence, may reverberate considerably, and a letter that is not there may become very officious and unsettling. Joyce makes t's tease us into dubious semantification long before *Finnegans Wake* spells O. U. T. as "oh you tease" (461), or warns us to "tot the ites like you corss the tees" (542), when the decencies of typographical norms are no longer observed. A little *t*—conspicuous, absent or superfluous—can go a long way, from next to nothing to totality: "T" may be an abbreviated Latin *totum,* which led to "teetotum": "As we there   are where are we are we there from tomtittot to teetootomtotalitarian. Tea tea too oo" sets off the scholarly tenth chapter of the *Wake* (260), but Molly Bloom had already thought of Patrick Dignam as a "comical little teetotum" (U 774).

Instances of erratic t's have been paraded here as equivalent substitutes for the much better advertised odyssey of the letter L, which potently turns a strong "word" into a cosmic "world" in Martha Clifford's letter or, inversely, demotes Leopold ("—L, Mr. Bloom said. Leopold," U 111) Bloom to "L. Boom" in irreverent print (U 647). In Hebrew (Stephen's inattentive remark on the onomastic insult contains "that first epistle to the hebrews," U 648) "*el*" can mean God ("El, yes," U 71). Disorderly shapes like "ha" or "Boom," at any rate, invigorate or discompose precarious textures. In the semantic ecology of Joyce's erroneous universe they can be read as minor losses easily rectified, and multiple gains due to our corrective urges and our tendency towards systematic completion. Mistakes, errors, misprints, defacements and the like also behave tangential new creations. They generate new meanings or microcosmic sidespins.

By such inadvertence a budding artist named Stephen Dedalus contaminated something heard,

> O, the wild rose blossoms
> On the little green place

into

> O, the geen wothe botheth. (p. 7)

("geen" is what Joyce wrote and meant, precisely noting infantile articulation; it was the copyists who standardized the adjective to "green" in all editions, dictionary norms prevailing over the empirical observation that children in their first phonetic ventures usually have a hard time with the liquids). Stephen's condensation of the two lines is, pardonably, inept and faulty. It is also a variant creation. Two separate elements, a wild rose and a green place, have been faultily amalgamated into something doubly non-existent, lexically and botanically. But a new shape has been offered as well, something that language—or the imagination—can produce much more effortlessly than even nature. A "geen wothe" is a fabrication (a Greek term would have been *poiēsis*) beyond the jurisdiction of biology (that the infantile and Joycean word "geen" chances to be a botanical term as well, also spelled "gean," a wild cherry, looks like the kind of gratuitous philology that we tend to utilize in *Finnegans Wake* when it suits our hermeneutical aims). Treated as a suggestive non-word in need of semantic supplementation, "geen" would be appropriate for *Finnegans Wake,* where in fact it does turn up: "As soon as we sale him geen we gates a sprise" (606), yet awaiting plausible clarification.

Similarly "wothe botheth," a mere defect of articulation, consists of non-words, of which at least the second one seems oddly appropriate. For Stephen in his single botched line has indeed "bothed" the two lines of the original, he has similarly conflated two distinct items, the flower itself and its location. We are faced with *both* an erroneous imitation and, perhaps, the signalling of an artefact. We have, in other words, both *less* than reality (a linguistic and conceptual defect), and *more* than it, a reaching out into what we may call symbolic ramification or a provocation of interpretative projection. We can construe the mistakes into a foreshadowing of the artist. The ultimate development of such conflations is *Finnegans Wake,* a work characterized by significant *bothings* throughout, an animated jumble of either linguistic shortcomings or teeming plurabilities.

Our lives, the world we live in or that of the *Wake,* made up of "errears and erroriboose of combarative embottled history" (FW 140.32), Dublin of 1904, the Bloom ménage, are all like Home Without Plumtree's Potted Meat—Incomplete. This leaves us with the intriguing, fascinating, and ever frustrated task of completing, straightening, modifying, clarifying, improving, systematizing it, which we inevitably perform in our own idiosyncratic likeness, propelled by our own brand of curiosity and ignorance.

COMPARATIVE AND GENERAL APPROACHES TO JOYCE

James Joyce as Emblem for the Modernist Age

Morton P. Levitt
Philadelphia, Pennsylvania

> What does our cowardice matter if on this earth
> there is one brave man,
> what does sadness matter if in time past
> somebody thought himself happy,
> what does my lost generation matter,
> that dim mirror,
> if your books justify us?
> I am the others. I am all those
> who have been rescued by your pains and care.
> I am those unknown to you and saved by you.
> —Jorge Luis Borges, "Invocation to Joyce"

Probably the most influential writer of the current, allegedly post-Modernist literary age is the Argentine poet, essayist and short story writer Jorge Luis Borges. The writer James Joyce—similarly blind, similarly an exile—appears in several of the stories of Borges, and, in a generalized sense, we can find in these stories something of the narrative presence of Joyce: in Borges' use of a subjective time, in his unreliable narrators and in his self-reflexive technique. But Borgesian time has philosophical implications much deeper than anything in Joyce; his bookish, unworldly persona has more in common with Chaucer's persona than with Stephen Dedalus or Leopold Bloom or H. C. E. or James Joyce himself; and his obsession with the potentialities of reflexivism goes far beyond the simple reflexive ending of ULYSSES or of "Shem the Penman" in FINNEGANS WAKE. There is, in fact, nothing significantly Joycean about any of Borges' fiction—neither in technique, nor in theme, nor in a view of the world.

Yet there remains the wonderful "Invocation to Joyce." What is it, precisely, that Borges is paying homage to in the life

and work of the Irish novelist?   Superficially, he is acknowledging Joyce's blindness, erudition and exile ("that exile,"
the poem says, "which was your chosen and detested
instrument")—all Borgesian conditions.   More significantly, the
poem celebrates the Joycean example of the life dedicated to
art, to discovering, as the "Invocation" puts it, the rose at
"the center of your maze": the rose of knowledge, of beauty,
of art itself, of the dedication to art, of the life revealed by
art.   It is not Joyce as influence whom Borges celebrates but
Joyce as emblem, as metaphor of the Modernist endeavor.

It is not any specific Joycean technique which Borges
would praise but rather the new concern for technique as a
means of understanding and communicating a new reality (the
same concern expressed by Virginia Woolf in the famed essay
"Mr. Bennett and Mrs. Brown"), the new world confronting
artists at the end of the First World War, that world which
the politicians at Versailles, with their Victorian omniscience,
had refused to perceive.   Further, Borges seems to me to be
celebrating the new Joycean worldview itself, or, more specifically, what is not new in that view, the ties that Joyce retains
to the humanist tradition.   We see these ties, very briefly, in
the humanity of Bloom; in Molly's loyalty to her husband—her
continuing sadness over Rudy, her memories of Howth, her
respect for Poldy; and in Stephen's willingness to be touched
and informed by their lives, as an artist at least, if not as a man.

What I am suggesting, then, is that the "Invocation to
Joyce" perceives what the early critics of Joyce—and some of
the later ones, as well—could not see: that his novels are far
more traditional than they once seemed; that the very radicalism
of their technique is at the service of traditional, humanistic
themes (so that the point of view, for example, is not aloof
and distant, as the immature Stephen claims in A PORTRAIT,
but designed to involve us).   Thus, it is not irony that I see at
the heart of Joyce's use of myth, but the traditional, communal,
life-giving properties of myth, even if they are ironic, even if
they are diminished in a world of diminished potential.   This
is the Joyce, as I see it, who serves for certain so-called post-
Modernist writers as a literary and moral exemplar of Modernism.   His work is their "talisman," Borges says: "I am those
unknown to you and saved by you."

II.

In such a context as this, the customary forms of what may be termed "influence studies" seem inherently limited. There remains a place, obviously, for biographical studies such as Ellmann's or for collections of new secondary materials—the letters to Nora, for instance and, of course, the notebooks—or even for supposedly new schemata. Such works may help us to understand that process of transmutation by which Joyce overcame his sources. But they are likely to prove of limited value in comprehending this emblem of Borges', for this Joyce is more metaphor than literal figure. Nor is he to be found in books such as Robert Martin Adams' *AfterJoyce*: for how can we prove influence per se? who can doubt the profound influence of Joyce on Faulkner, and who can prove it? and how are we to reconcile Faulkner's heralded influence on García Márquez with our knowledge that the Spanish translations of Faulkner available to the Colombian novelist were often inaccurate and inexpert?

Even the more creative critical undertakings of this type, such as Hugh Kenner's THE POUND ERA, may have their problems. Joyce, it seems to me, is far more central to the era than is Pound. Although he aided few writers (Svevo aside) and formulated no significant literary theories (Stephen's do not even function in ULYSSES), Joyce is a far better artist than Pound and a far more seminal figure; he is in no danger, as I suspect Pound is, of becoming an historical footnote. Even today, even among those (notably English) writers who reject his example, Joyce remains the exemplar of the Modernist Age, which might as accurately be labeled The Age of Joyce. Yet even such a book as, say, THE JOYCE ERA might be, would probably miss at least some of the point. The issue of influence, effect, seminality—what I call the Joyce aura—is far too complex for an approach such as this.

So where does this leave us? Devoid of theory, cut off from manuscript sources, seeking only a metaphor, we might do well to look at some writers and their reactions to Joyce. In such an effort as this, it is not Joyce per se—the critics' Joyce, perhaps—but the artists' Joyce, the Joyce to whom, against whom other novelists react, whom we must seek. Thus, in the generation just after ULYSSES, we have the obvious case of Samuel Beckett, his early debt to, repudiation of and yet continual involvement with Joyce: a relationship which, when explored more fully, may reveal as much about the master as about his one-time disciple.

The case of Vladimir Nabokov may be similarly revealing and similarly difficult to define. *A Portrait*, Nabokov tells us, he never much liked; the WAKE he despises ("a formless and dull mass of phony folklore"); ULYSSES he claims not to have read until the 1930's, "when I was definitely formed as a writer and immune to literary influence." (Whether this is true or not seems to me of little issue; it is the claim of non-influence that operates here.)   Yet Nabokov's definition of art (from the Afterword ot LOLITA) is strikingly Bloomian (Leopold, that is): "For me a work of fiction exists only insofar as it affords me what I shall bluntly call aesthetic bliss, that is, a sense of being somehow, somewhere, connected with other states of being where art (curiosity, tenderness, kindness, ecstasy) is the norm. There are not many such books."[1] ULYSSES, of course, is the most prominent of them.

It is not he language of LOLITA or the self-reflexivism of PALE FIRE or the myth and irony and wealth of metaphor which permeate his mature works that connect Nabokov to Joyce. Joyce's significance for Nabokov, I believe, as for Borges, is metaphoric, humanistic, a vision of the world and a means for the artist or perceiving and presenting that vision. When we finally do decipher the extent of Faulkner's debt to Joyce (the Blotner biography merely confuses the matter), we are likely to find, I suspect, a similar indebtedness. Indeed, we might easily argue that the entire second generation of Modernist novelists were formed by their reaction to Joyce. But my own special interest is with a later generation still, the so-called post-Modernists: what vision of Joyce, if any, do they have? to what extent can they be said to develop under his aura?

III.

This is obviously an issue which cannot be determined in so brief a time and space as this. It is the subject of a book, called MODERNIST SURVIVORS, on which I have been at work for the past several years. But a few general observations, both national and individual, can be offered and might be of some help. For the differences in reactions to Joyce have been both private and national.

In England, with the single significant exception of B. S. Johnson, who refers consistently and affirmatively to Joyce as the model upon whom other novelists must build, no contemporary English novelist or critic makes positive use of the Joycean example. C. P. Snow may be said to speak for them all: "Looking back," he wrote in 1953, "we see what an odd affair the 'experimental' novel was. To begin with, the 'experiment' stayed remarkably constant for thirty years. Miss Dorothy Richardson was a great pioneer, so were Virginia Woolf and Joyce: but between POINTED ROOFS in 1915 and its successors, largely American, in 1945, there was no significant development. In fact there could not be because this method, the essence of which was to represent brute experience through the moments of sensation, effectively cut out precisely those aspects of the novel where a living tradition can be handed down. Reflection had to be sacrificed; so did moral awareness; so did the investigatory intelligence. That was altogether too big a price to pay and hence the 'experimental' novel . . . died from starvation, because its intake of human stuff was too low."[2] In the name of "reflection," "moral awareness" and the "investigatory intelligence"—of Victorian omniscience, that is—and in opposition to that demon of "experiment"—a pejorative term when used by an English novelist or critic—the whole of the Modernist revolution is neatly excised from literary history. No Joyce or Woolf, no Kafka, no Proust after SWANN'S WAY, only the early Mann, no Faulkner, Beckett, Nabokov, Kazantzakis or Hemingway, nothing of this greatest of ages in the history of the novel remains in Snow's wonderfully neat and majestically stupid formulation. And it is only in degree that it differs from other English critical comment: F. R. Leavis, Snow's arch-enemy, agrees entirely; the novelists Kingsley Amis, John Wain and William Cooper, Snow's disciple, build their fictions upon this negative model and return to pre-Modernist modes; even more perceptive critics, such as John Bayley and Malcolm Bradbury, agree in essence that Modernism is dead, not to be revived, was perhaps from the start a still birth. As Bayley has said of ULYSSES, with no evident awareness of the self-contradiction, "Of all modern authors the closest to Shakespeare is certainly James Joyce, but for all its marvellous and intricate power to move us ULYSSES is leaden with its own art, sunk in its richness like a great plum-cake."[3] Joyce

is omitted almost completely from a study whose subtitle is
"Character in the Novel from Dickens to the Present Day,"[4]
and the most admired of English novelists of the day is that
throwback to Thackeray, Margaret Drabble.

The situation is rather different in France. In France,
the very diverse novelists of the so-called Nouveau Roman
react to Joyce in very diverse ways, but all of them do react
to him. Alain Robbe-Grillet, for example, explicitly uses
Joycean technique in order to deny, explicitly, the Joycean
vision. Michel Butor clearly feels that he has taken the Joycean
impulses of his novels as far as he can and that it is time now to
develop new impulses; but even his most recent work—radio
plays, scenarios for operas, ostensible travel books—are informed
by his awareness of and respect for Joyce and the Modernists.
As for Claude Simon, his best works are written demonstrably
out of reference to Joyce (and to Faulkner and Proust as well);
when he moves away from their example, his work demonstrably
suffers. Current French fiction is not notably Joycean, and—as
a result, I would claim—it is less successful than the French
fiction of a decade or so ago. But even these new works are
informed by the Joycean insistence that the novel must move
on in technique as it continues to relate to past values. Robbe-
Grillet, Butor, Simon and their compatriots will not lead us
decisively into the new, post-Joycean literary age, but at least
they are not foolishly regressing into the Victorian past.

Contemporary novelists of the United States have made
constructive use of the past—the specifically American past—as
a means of understanding the present predicament. And Joyce
has served—alongside the Rosenberg spy trial, the Salem witch
hunts, the colonial experience and the coming of the Atomic
Age—as a link to that past and a comment on its present
relevance. Robert Coover, in THE PUBLIC BURNING, uses
myth ironically, as we are told that Joyce first used it, as a means
of commenting on modern dimunition; and Coover's myth-
making, at once uniquely American and recalling Joyce, is
expansive, excessive, highly imaginative and idiosyncratic: in
the spirit of ULYSSES and FINNEGANS WAKE and responsive
to the givens of American history and American life. In THE
BOOK OF DANIEL, another mythic study of the Rosenberg
case, E. L. Doctorow suddenly quotes Joyce: "Mr. Leopold
Bloom ate with relish the inner organs of beast[s] and fowls"[5]:
the beginning of "Calypso" and the herald of Bloom's entry

into this fictional Dublin. The lines appear out of context and
are never returned to; they are Doctorow's acknowledgement
of Bloom's continuing presence and his announcement that
the humanistic values encapsulated in Bloom are of relevance
even today, even in the alleged post-Modernist period, in the
midst of our dimunition.

For John Barth, Joycean mythopoesis is even more
directly a means of putting us in touch with our past, historical
and literary. In LOST IN THE FUNHOUSE, the young artist
figure Ambrose cites his model: "The Irish author James Joyce,
in his unusual novel entitled ULYSSES, now available in this
country, uses the adjectives *snot-green* and *scrotum-tightening*
to describe the sea. Visual, auditory, tactile, olfactory,
gustatory."[6]   LOST IN THE FUNHOUSE is throughout an
up-to-date version of Joyce's PORTRAIT—more self-aware,
perhaps, since its author had read the master; more comic,
more mythic, more in the tone of ULYSSES and the WAKE;
an homage paid to Joyce by attempting, on one level at least,
to go beyond his example.

A very different Joycean model appears in Thomas
Pynchon's GRAVITY'S RAINBOW, which challenges the reader
(by explicit reference and indirect allusion, by paraphrase and
direct quote) to think of Joyce and his vision and then presents
us with a world in which so human-centered a vision can simply
not be maintained. When Pynchon's protagonist, scion of an
ancient American family, thinks of himself as "Last of his
line, and how far-fallen,"[7] we are led immediately to Bloom's
"Last [of] my race."[8]   Bloom's world-centered line, we know,
will go on, but Pynchon's Americans may well be at the end
of theirs. Pynchon understands very precisely that union of
theme and technique which characterizes the Joycean, Modernist
vision and tells us very precisely—in opposition to Doctorow
and perhaps to Barth—that in this world—post-not only World
War I, but also post-Auschwitz, Hiroshima, My Lai, Kampuchea,
Uganda and El Salvador—so potentially humanistic a vision
can no longer be maintained.

There may not be a single American vision of life in this
still mythic post—Modernist world, the so-called American
Century: our history remains unresolved, our attempts to escape
its impact (witness the aftermath of Vietnam) still part of our
constitution. But American novelists at least do not ignore or
deride their Modernist inheritance or convince themselves that

they have outgrown its example. Their work is uncertain perhaps, but most vigorous, and the Joycean model is at the heart of their experience.

In the United States, then, the Joycean example is honored but at times overturned; in France, it is left behind, replaced by a theory-ridden new novel; in England, it is assaulted as anathema, the root cause of all that is wrong with English fiction and English society. Only in Latin America is that example honored and made use of, an alien inheritance which functions alongside indigenous sources and thereby creates the most vital and challenging fiction in the world today.

I am speaking now not of those several novels which attempt to reproduce ULYSSES in Buenos Aires or Mexico City, nor even of those works in which Joyce or his novel appear directly (in Gustavo Sainz' OBSESIVOS DÍAS CIRCULARES, the narrator reads ULYSSES and uses it to shape his own fiction). I am referring rather to Carlos Fuentes' WHERE THE AIR IS CLEAR, with its echoes of DUBLINERS and A PORTRAIT OF THE ARTIST AS A YOUNG MAN, and to the same novelist's A CHANGE OF SKIN, which adopts Joycean narrative techniques, expands the Joycean vision and translates them to a Latin American setting and idiom. I am thinking also of THREE TRAPPED TIGERS, by the Cuban Guillermo Cabrera Infante, with its Joycean puns (the "megaesoteric J'aime Joys"), its Joycean names (two young ladies of the night named "Anna and Livia Pluralbelles"), its Joycean referrents ("the anniversary two weeks back the day when Bloom's moll sitting on the bog had let flow a long stream of unconsciousness which would become a milestone, a millstone . . . in literary history"),[9] its effort to comprehend the modern world through the metaphor of the Modernist Joyce. It is not simply the dual lessons of exile and language which link Cabrera Infante to Joyce: the pervasive feelings of rootlessness, our need to strike roots through language, by means of myth, as part of a literary and historical tradition—Joyce first expresses these needs. And by expressing them he becomes part of the solution. The inventiveness of Joyce, the humanity of Bloom, the perseverance—even heroism—which they share, the continuity which they offer to readers and novelists alike: this is the Modernist inheritance which such Latin American novelists as Fuentes and Cabrera Infante, Gabriel García Márquez and José Donoso, Mario Vargas Llosa and Antonia Callado graft to local idiom and native roots.

They demonstrate in the process that the old Joycean
vision and technique are still meaningful and revealing when
applied to a new world. This is the Joyce who serves Borges
as a savior, metaphor as much as man, representative both of
revolution and continuity, key to the old fictional world and
to the new and to the still developing, the figure around whom
all contemporary fiction—even that which rejects him—must
continue to evolve.

Notes

[1] Vladimir Nabokov, LOLITA (New York, 1959), p. 286.

[2] C. P. Snow, as cited in David Lodge, THE NOVELIST AT THE
CROSSROADS (Ithaca, New York, 1971), p. 18.

[3] John Bayley, THE CHARACTERS OF LOVE (New York, 1960),
p. 285.

[4] Patrick Swinden, UNOFFICIAL SELVES (New York, 1973).

[5] E. L. Doctorow, THE BOOK OF DANIEL (New York, 1979), p.
224.

[6] John Barth, LOST IN THE FUNHOUSE (New York, 1969), p. 71.

[7] Thomas Pynchon, GRAVITY'S RAINBOW (New York, 1973), p.
569.

[8] James Joyce, ULYSSES (New York, 1961), p. 285.

[9] Guillermo Cabrera Infante, THREE TRAPPED TIGERS, trans.
Donald Gardner and Suzanne Jill Levine (New York, 1978), pp. 232, 140,
150-1.

The Continuity of Joyce: Traces and Analogies in Later Foreign Writers

Ivo Vidan
Zagreb, Yugoslavia

No modern writer in English offers a greater challenge than Joyce to the comparativist scholar or, for that matter, to any researcher into the literary history of our time. The inner complexity of Joyce's work corresponds to the multiplicity of ways in which he has influenced the literature of the last sixty five years.

One could perhaps speak of Joyce's presence in three senses: a) direct influence; b) the mediation by authors who have been exposed to Joycean writing and who in turn affect other writers; c) a more or less general awareness of Joyce's work, of the artistic problems that he had to face, and of his means and artistic choices. In all three cases it is not conscious imitation that interests us, but the way in which Joyce appears to contribute to any author's grappling with the challenges of his own situation in the culture and the language to which he belongs.

In a review of Richard Yates's recent collection of short stories, *Dubliners* is invoked as a model for the American's own coping with the desperate and solitary citizens of his metropolis; and similarly relevant connections can be met every day in current literary criticism. Ambitious fictional works belonging to Northrop Frye's "encyclopaedic form,"[1] like Grass' *Der Butt*, which is in some respects closer to *Moby Dick* than to Joycean texture, are very likely the products of a climate in which *Finnegans Wake* is becoming the accepted norm of transgressing the linear handling of theme and narrative.

Joyce's central importance in modern letters appears most fully, however, when one considers the multifaceted nature of his own major work, *Ulysses*. The range of stylistic devices and of the perceptual and epistemological possibilities in the eighteen episodes, as well as the manifold significance of their coexistence as a totality, are unmatched in recent writing. It therefore comprises the weight of Joyce's international presence.

Roughly speaking, the techniques in *Ulysses* fall into two categories, and their influence follows the same division. The first branch covers ways representing subjectivity by several forms of stream of consciousness as well as by a narrative mode of introspection that at first glance appears to be objective. Generally speaking, Joyce's literary impact was first felt along these lines. It corresponds to the heritage of impressionism in the creation of personality and of modernist constructs, with a personal, though generally decipherable, symbolism legitimately emerging from the lyrical patterns composed of supposedly mental imagery.

The autotelic functioning of such patterns is often enhanced by an awareness of mythic correlatives. The imaginative patrimony of generic man functions within the individual work without relating it to a socially determined class of artefacts. But the mythic, in so far as it is anthropologically significant, breaks down the boundaries of the isolated text and lends it a modicum of objectivity that relates it to the mental universe inherited by our culture. Joyce's writing shares this awareness with the more traditional texture of Thomas Mann's works; in fact, its full significance is implied rather than stated, hence, much of its difficulty, as Wolfgang Iser has lucidly shown.[2]

The mythic aspect cuts through all the episodes, thus neutralizing the different narrative perspectives. And some of the techniques, especially those depending on quantification, on cataloguing, on accumulation, and on the collocation of different styles, expose a desire for mock objectivity and playfulness concerning the factual awareness of what happens in this world.

Some of these episodes (in particular "Aeolus," "Wandering Rocks," "Cyclops," and "Ithaca") seem to foreshadow more recent tendencies toward overcoming the hermeticism and the autonomous organization of subjectively symbolic constructs. They prefigure the randomness, improvisation, and inconsistent accumulation of effects, the trying out of narrative ploys—the laying bare of devices—that characterize the postmodern openness and aesthetic impurity of texts. Historically, we can thus clearly distinguish two types of Joycean impact. Joyce's influence on Virginia Woolf is not the same as that on Pynchon and Barth.

It should be true to say that the presence of Joyce in any national literature depends on what that literature requires at the particular moment in which its encounter with Joyce takes place. What happens on such occasions in cultures recognizably different from one another can be demonstrated with respect to the literature of France and of Yugoslavia in the 1950's and 1960's, i. e. at approximately the same period of time, but at different stages in the intrinsic development of literature in the two countries. France had already achieved a peak of sophistication, a vast repertoire of historically ascertainable styles, and easy commerce with intellectual abstraction. Yugoslavia's political and cultural independence were of only very recent standing, and the country was still striving towards urbanization and towards the acceptance of industrial rhythms and of more than just the merely cyclic movement of time. In the realm of ideas, there prevailed a simplistic understanding of the relationship between material premises and spiritual phenomena, the two being regarded as causally related in a mechanical manner.

In France, emphasis is still very commonly placed on the analysis of consciousness and its underlying motives, whether in terms of psychic mechanisms or in terms of the shaping powers in an individual's situation. Not Proust, however, but Joyce stands behind Nathalie Sarraute, and it is Joyce via Faulkner who is the source of the subjective constructs and the recurrence and interconnection of symbolic leit-motifs in the agonizing confessions and self-examinations of Claude Simon.

Yet at the same time the other objectivizing techniques of *Ulysses* have found their equivalents in some of the most original investigations into the possibilities of fictional forms. It is the catechism mould bequeathed by "Ithaca" that provides the narrative mode of Robert Pinget's *L'inquisitoire* (1962). This novel is written in the form of questions and answers. Hundreds of names and a topographically minutely imagined area appear in the questioning of an aged servant by some anonymous interrogators, without a continuous line being established, such as building up an argument or completing the history of a family, person, or criminal case. Superficial character sketches, conjectures about human relationships and hints at *faits divers* follow page after page, like an enormous stack of shuffled playing cards turned face up repeatedly without revealing any pattern. Critics have seen in this material an inventory comparable to Balzac's, but all the promising details, including the human features of the reluctant, sometimes comically testy servant, do not yield up a story, as they certainly would have done in Balzac.

In fact, as we progress through the text we seem to encounter an amorphous conglomeration of possibilities for stories that never get off the ground. In this respect, *L'inquisitoire* is an *anti-'Ithaca'*, because this penultimate chapter of *Ulysses* seems to be moving in the opposite direction. Here, numerous facts relevant to what has preceded in the book finally crystallize, and are spelled out explicitly; thus, they present a mock-elucidation of the puzzles and enigmas in the situation and the interpersonal relationships. We seem to be arriving somewhere ("Ithaca" is the central chapter of the "Homecoming" section), while the opposite is increasingly true of Pinget's *L'inquisitoire*. The French author creates a stylistic tension between the impersonal tone of the questions and the human content of the answers which the old frustrated servant produces from within his own horizon. Joyce's method in "Ithaca" is stylistically dehumanized on both the question and the answer side of the ledger. The episode's charm is all the more indirect, as it is hidden behind enumeration, strictly quantified descriptions, an impersonal exchange of questions and answers, an apparent lack of any subjective projection, a presentation strictly in terms of determinable facts. Ultimately, "Ithaca" anticipates Charlie Chaplin in the way in which it pretends to avoid both the comedy and the sympathy normally invoked, when a fictional character bumps against a cupboard:

> What suddenly arrested his ingress?

> The right temporal lobe of the hollow sphere of his cranium came into contact with a solid timber angle where, an infinitesimal but sensible fraction of a second later, a painful sensation was located in consequence of antecedent sensations transmitted and registered.[3]

Were it not for the comedy and for human pathos evoked by the incident in the very act of reading (when it is immediately translated into the nonscientific language of everyday experience), we might feel that we were in the antimetaphoric, non-symbolic world of Alain Robbe-Grillet's most radical theoretical statements.

in his essays collected under the title *Pour un Nouveau Roman* (Paris 1963), Robbe-Grillet attacks the humanist outlook, according to which literature should provide a "soul bridge" between men and things. He claims that there is no excuse for the anthropomorphic content of metaphorical language; as "the world neither signifies nor is absurd, it is simply *there*."[5]

Robbe-Grillet's best-known novels are instances of an apparent registration of surfaces that fall into patterns but do not try to colour the world they present with human emotionalism. In *La jalousie* (1957) "objective" description is used to present the elements of a highly melodramatic conjunction of events without any direct registration of feelings. There is no narrator, but only a point in space from which the scene is perceived, and it is only gradually that the reader realizes that apart from a woman and a man who frequently visits her, a third person is always present, the woman's jealous husband, whose field of perception is defined by the impersonal narrative voice that produces the text. This observer, hidden from the reader, watches both the couple sitting, talking, and gesturing, and the movements of the woman when she is alone. The observer's presence within the scene can be detected through the number of plates on the table, the number of chairs occupied on the veranda, etc.

Although the stream of consciousness technique as used by Faulkner, for instance, also creates imaginings, obsessive motifs, distorted reiterations in the memory of characters, such works as wholes are dominated by an all-embracing point of view, coordinating the parallel and contradictory utterances. In Robbe-Grillet, however, there is no principle by which to establish some order of reality or some authentic sequence for the events experienced or imagined. The recurrent motifs with variations and the submerged narrative focus can be found in his fiction before *La jalousie,* and are still present in his later works, e. g. *La maison de rendezvous.* Here, however, the thematic justification of *La jalousie* has yielded place to confusing ambiguities without a psychological or, indeed, any other kind of humanist alibi.

Robbe-Grillet works with a limited number of narrative elements. Objects, gestures, the position of the human body in space, and other details recur according to no clearly recognizable principle of organization. The recurrence of details in Robbe-Grillet can be compared to the presence of *leit-motifs* or to the repetition of sentences and words in the various episodes of *Ulysses*. In Robbe-Grillet, however, there are fewer of them; they recur more frequently and take up a far greater proportion of the text. Thus, the creative scope of the two writers is different, that of Robbe-Grillet being much narrower. The technique, if it originates in Joyce, has a different function, and the deliberate confusion of the reader, though part of the total effect, seems less important for Joyce.

The amount of detail in "Ithaca" is indeed overwhelming, and puts to shame the wealth of information provided by a nineteenth century realistic novel. It is not a closed field of elements that are being permutated, as in Beckett, who in this respect is a more immediate precursor of Robbe-Grillet. The technique, however, by which Joyce's world of objects and facts is conveyed, appears to be much closer to Robbe-Grillet than Beckett's is in so far as the cataloguing and enumeration appear to be precise and impersonal. In Robbe-Grillet they seem to amount to precise relationships in space, but anyone who has tried to draw a map of the island in *Le Voyeur* or the banana grove in *La jalousie* will have been confused by the hidden inconsistencies—just as one is when one tries to follow Joyce in his seemingly pedantic and painstakingly accurate computations.

In *Ulysses* the number of elements is unlimited. However seemingly impersonal the presentation, the very quantity and range are part of the Joycean exuberance. The very texture of "Ithaca," contrary to the meager story patterns of Robbe-Grillet, symbolizes life, and as a result human ubiquity—and human dignity. The Joycean mock-pretense of distancing himself from the human experience has apparently been taken over by Robbe-Grillet in complete seriousness. He puts man's manifestations on the same level as things, and he creates potential plots not through an interplay of human personalities, but through external collocations and formal relationships. His novels display more impersonality, more mechanical interconnection, coincidence, contingency, accidental detail, deliberately spoiling or contradicting the pattern.

The correlation between Robbe-Grillet's technique and a contemporary view of the world has been established by Lucien Goldmann in his essay on the *nouveau roman* in *Pour une sociologie du roman* (Paris 1964). He finds that there is a homology between the impersonal relationships in a Robbe-Grillet novel and the process in modern capitalist development that György Lukaćs has called reification. According to Goldmann, the market economy, dominated by what Marx called the "fetishism of comodity," makes characters disappear and objects acquire independence. This explains the passivity of the onlookers in *Le voyeur* and *La jalousie*, and the murder hidden as part of the order of things in *Les gommes*.

The manifoldness of *Ulysses* and the comedy produced by the very energy and variety of its protean inventiveness, transcend whatever manifestations of social passivity may be found in some aspects of Joyce's work. It is not surprising that in a young culture—or rather in one in which urbanization takes place later than in most other parts of Europe—*Ulysses* could stimulate the most imaginative attempts at a modern structuring of fiction and the creation of a rich urban verbal texture.

When in 1953, the novel *The Poem* (*Pesma*) by the Serbian poet Oskar Davičo appeared, it was considered an important event in Yugoslavia. For a literature in which story-telling has rarely distinguished itself by close knit plots and a concentrated dramatic sequence of events, *The Poem* is, as it were, a "well-made novel." It is a basically romantic assertion by the young revolutionary hero, and as such conforms to the expectations and demands of the politically inspired and sometimes institutionally enforced aesthetics prevalent in Yugoslavia since the end of the war. At the same time, the concept of the hero is profoundly opposed to the then existing norms of socialist realism. Davičo's richly metaphorical poetry has always been surrealist in inspiration (before the war Davičo belonged to the Belgrade surrealist group, the strongest in Europe after that of Paris) and opposed to all propaganda. His first novel gained political importance as another instance of Yugoslavian culture's cutting loose from Soviet guidelines. Today it seems symbolical that *The Poem* was published in the year of Stalin's death.

What has all this to do with Joyce? Nothing directly, except that aspects of *Ulysses* can be discovered in this, the first genuine Yugoslavian urban novel. In order to appreciate the peculiar character of the connection, it is necessary to give a fairly extensive summary of the story.

As in *Ulysses* the action of *The Poem* takes place in a big city, Belgrade, and lasts roughly 24 hours. The three main characters involved are two men, one middle-aged and the other young, and a woman. The relationship between the two men is to a certain extent that of a father and a son; and the boy's real father actually suspects the older man, Veković, to have been his wife's lover before the boy, Mića, was born. The woman, Anna, is a lighter, subtler, and more imaginative creature than Mrs. Bloom, but there is a parallel, too, because she is Vekovic's mistress and falls in love with Mića.

The pattern of relationships is, thus, very reminiscent of *Ulysses.* Unlike in *Ulysses*, however, they develop into something ethically determinable, and the story includes movement, pathos, catharsis, and meaningful transcendence. During the German occupation, which provides the background of the story, Mića is a serious single-minded member of the resistance:

> "The very hardships added up to life. Living in this way meant happiness, pride; being awake, while others drowsed . . . To be a fighter for the revolution was to be everything—footballer, explorer, trapper, philosopher— anything which in any given situation might serve the cause, and there was no doubt at all about it."[5]

The older man, Veković, is a famous poet, a member of the Academy, disgusted with living under the enemy. He plans to leave Belgrade and together with Mica, join the Partisans in the liberated territory. Once there, he finally wants to write the poem which he has borne in his mind for a long time. But a conflict arises between Mića and Veković. The old man loves the fullblooded life of the senses and—almost on the eve of his purifying departure to freedom—is not above entering into a casual sexual affair with a washerwoman right in the drying room of their apartmen building.

Mića, that ardent and selfless fighter for the happiness of man, is an ascetic who has never experienced full intimacy with a woman. To him, Veković's casual affair whick he witnesses by accident, seems an outrage to the liberation movement and an utter degradation of anyone connected with the cause:

> "The washerwoman and Veković were closely locked together, away from all the world, they no longer cared for what was happening in the world. They were at the peak of their pleasure now. How foul love-making was in its seeking of its glib delight, the play of it, its seeking of that moment outside of time and space! Love demanded two people's desertion from the field of battle. In this, the 1942-nd year of the calendar, love served the enemy. This was not a precise thought, framed in so many words, in Mića's mind. It was deep-set in his outraged feelings, that the thought came clear to him: Vekovic too was a deserter."

In spite of remonstrances from the other members of his resistance group, Mića tries to prevent Veković from joining them. So Veković, in order to prove his genuine allegiance, decides to commit himself publicly. He goes to the funeral of a retired general and makes a patriotic speech which provokes the Germans into arresting him. Mića has now realized his mistake, but after his group has decided upon a plan to rescue Veković the next morning, Mića himself is chased by German patrols. In the early hours after midnight he makes a narrow escape in a suburban street—by jumping into a garbage can. He is then saved by the composure and self-restraint of the woman in the neighbouring house. This turns out to be Anna, Veković's young mistress, who had seen Mića only once before and fallen in love with him. She had talked to Veković about him and called him Mayfly—that beautiful, lithe, quick creature which lives only for one day. And it is now, in the few hours before the action to rescue Veković, which he himself will not survive, that Mića for the first time encounters the reality and ecstasy of love. Daviço's passage on Mića's and Anna's experience are probably among the most poetical of all the suggestive descriptions of love-making in recent decades, and certainly more unrestrained than anything precedent, in Yugoslav fiction. Here, however, it is more pertinent to quote from the description of the lovers' rest:

> "Long since, all had grown utterly still, no barking of

dogs any more announced the movements of the night
patrols, there was no chatter of motorcycles, no long
feeler of ferociously white headlights.   But the street
outside never ceased to be, he knew the street was there,
he had not for one instant forgotten that street while he
smothered with kisses loins of such delicacy there might
have been no bone, with the fine washed-white steep
ridges of the edge of her pelvis, while he kissed the
controlled slimness of her waist, the softness of her
belly, sweet-scented and smooth, all soundless under-
ripples of life. He was very clear too where he would go
when he got Veković out and what he would do with
him when he got him to liberated territory.   He was
conscious too of his dearest comrades George and Peter
having been shot down last night, conscious of how
their death hurt him, consious of the smart, the torment
of it, but he now knew all this as a healthy man, preoccupied at the moment with something that overwhelmed him, knew that his heart was beating, his lungs
expanding, his kidneys cleansing his blood, knew all
this without giving a thought to what he knew or what
was coming to pass beside that knowledge."

The relationship between sex and environment—between
love and the garbage can, if one likes—is frequently and un-
sentimentally explored in *Ulysses*. It results in healthy, sobering
comedy, which puts all the aspects of life under lenses of equal
strength and brings them into mutual perspective. Here, however, Davičo has, with partial success, tried to explore a new
aspect of this relationship. He regards it as part of the wider
issue of war, moral responsibility and society. He does so
without disrespect for either and with a genuine apprehension
of the balance between the intimate and the public call upon
man.

Mića will leave Anna's house fortified by love. He will
go out and fight and die as a mature man who has realized
what fullness of life really means. Love-making has, in certain
sense, functioned as a kind of secular sacrament that prepares
him for death. There is a romantic dimension in this conception
of man, and it is utterly non-Joycean. We may call it tradi-
tionalist, and the authorial comments, the efforts at determining
what is conscious and what is unconscious in the development

of an attitude or a process of understanding belong to a pre-Joycean phase in fiction. And yet, one feels, can the pattern of relationship between the characters hardly be coincidental. The tight plot based on a Bloom-Stephen-Molly constellation with personalities changed, and turned activist, makes this novel a deliberate Anti-*Ulysses*. From a purely Joycean perspective, Davičo tries to put traditionalism into the service of a revolutionary awareness. But this relatively traditional procedure, and in particular the deft manipulation of the plot, was still a highly modern achievement in the Yugoslavian literature of the moment.

On the other hand, the purposeful pre-Joycean plotting is conjoined with a most valuable aspect of Joycean fiction, hardly present in Yugoslav writing before Davičo: the bold collocation of female anatomy and moral idealism, of the dynamism of sex and that of society. This "violent yoking together of disparate ideas" need not have found its way into Davičo's novel from Joyce; it had probably been prepared by his own surrealist poetry.

And yet, there are details in *The Poem* which cannot be nearer to anything than they are to *Ulysses*. Take Veković's walk to the cemetery, undertaken for a very non-Joycean purpose: the speech which will openly commit Veković against the Germans. It is worth comparing and contrasting with Bloom's contemplation at Paddy Dignam's funeral. Davičo's technique cannot really be described as consistent stream of consciousness, though some parts of this passage are—perhaps for the first time in Yugoslav fiction—fully functional and not merely experimental. The principle of association is consistently maintained, and it offers a number of strange contaminations and metaphors connecting the physical with the spiritual, the palpable with the abstract, the insensible with the human:

> "As he turned into St. Nicholas Street he suddenly scented the exasperating, soft, non-urban, country odour of the soil which despite that dirty, greasy light was breathing true spring only a stone's throw beyond those last three rows of small houses on the outskirts of the city. The outer edge of Belgrade. The outer edge of everything. After that came the open fields and the woods beyond. As if insistent too to have him aware

that he would never see liberated territory! The hurt
of that decision here wriggled free again, sounded his
consciousness.

   The outer edge of Belgrade and the last time for
him to be at the graveyard alive. This once. Then the
end. No, the end of the town. No, the end. Bluntly:
death.

   More in memory than reality filtered out a smell of
methylated spirit. From an uncorked bottle, thrown
out who knew when. And the odour of death beyond
that door which creaked. Not like last year. Without
sadness. Hardened."

And the passage that follows almost immediately reminds
one also of Stephen Dedalus's walk on the Dublin sound in the
'Proteus' episode of *Ulysses*.

   "Thin gravel ground underfoot groaned, softer still,
the damp clay groaned, the silence blew out the holy
lamps of sound. The jasmine had not even budded
yet. The dehydrated branches of winter and the trampled
leaves seemed even more dismal than the graves, wooden
crosses askew, already mouldering, under them the tiny
flickering flames. The white and red marbles and the
black granite might gleam, could this March day but
cease to be November and yield its non-existent light.
Despite which, indeed, the white marble above the hum-
mocks of soil challenged, smooth as a woman's body
in a twilight room."

This kind or prose is expressive in a way which exceeds
mere communication. In Yugoslavia it was loosely called
Modernism for a number of years and it did not always meet
with favourable acceptance, as it does not agree with the
established simple taste for straightforward realistic narrative.
Even now it is only gradually finding its way to readers who
are still engaged in the acquisition of the specifically urban
sensibility, the ease necessary to connect disparate levels of
experience and to absorb the sophisticated, noncyclical rhythms
of city life. *The Poem* has played an important role in accom-
modating readers comparatively inexperienced with the
exigencies of a modern text; it succeeded, because its theme

and story were "beyond suspicion." In this context, it is of
interest to examine how close—all differences considered—
Davičo's novel is to Joyce's.   If *The Poem* can be seen as a
kind of Anti-*Ulysses*, it is so certainly in a very different way
from that in which Pinget undercuts the "Ithaca" method,
or in which Robbe-Grillet makes apparent use of its tone and
technique within a very different world view.   *The Poem* uses
certain patterns of story and environment in *Ulysses* in order
to achieve a concentrated image of a big city drama of human
relationships.   Joycean, too, are the range of urban imagery
used in the sophisticated manner of the all-inclusive meta-
physical poetry, and the exploration of consciousness on the
basis of mental associations.   But the values that the work
enacts and proclaims are very different from anything that
Joyce ever asserted explicitly.   In this sense *The Poem* trans-
cends the level of moral significance that can be indirectly
gleaned from *Ulysses*.   Its hero's transformation, although
modern, his selflessness, although in the service of a twentieth
century public purpose (not just old-fashioned patriotism),
cannot conceal that Davičo's aesthetic intention was basically
traditional.   In matters of technique, the stimulus coming from
Ulysses occurs only in the presentation of consciousness.   The
objective encyclopaedic chapters, the pseudo-impersonality
of "Ithaca," are not relevant to this writer, of a culture which
at least in the early fifties did not yet conceive of man as loosing
himself in a plethora of self-standing artifacts.

A confident master of highly imaged verse, Davičo, when
venturing into prose, did not feel that the novel was supposed
to bear inspection as an independent linguistic entity, as a
written artefact, irrespective of its dramatic impact or its
humanist revolutionary message.   Some years later, the Croatian
novel *The Cyclops* (*Kiklop,* 1965) by Ranko Marinković, sur-
passed *The Poem* as a consciously textured totality, with a
much stronger emphasis on being self-consciously "scriptible"
(Barthes).

The relationship of *The Cyclops* to Joyce consists in a
general awareness of Joycean structuring rather than in an
appropriation of some specific technique, but the Joycean
parallels reside more fully in the use of imagery and verbal
echoes than on the story level.   Several aspects can be distinguished:

a) The title *The Cyclops* does not refer to the eponimous

episode in *Ulysses,* but following Joyce, tries to introduce a
relevant Homeric association; it does not refer to a particular
character in the novel, as Joyce's does, but bears a universal
meaning referring to the conditions of human existence:
cannibalism, aggressiveness, and the war (of 1941), which has
just begun when the novel ends.

b) This theme becomes apparent through a variety of
metonymic devices throughout the novel; yet in terms of
Joycean verbal links its basic reference is to *Hamlet,* the key
theme coming from two well-known passages:

> "—Your worm is your only emperor for diet. . . A man
> may fish with the worm that hath eat of a king, and eat
> of the fish that hath fed of that worm.
>
> —What dost thou mean by this?
>
> —Nothing but to show you how a king may go a progress
> through the guts of a beggar." (*Hamlet* IV/3)

And:

> "—Alexander died, Alexander was buried, Alexander
> returneth into dust; the dust is earth; of earth we make
> loam; and why of that loam whereto he was converted
> might they not stop a beer-barrel?" (*Hamlet* V/1)

Thus the *Hamlet* association does not, as in *Ulysses,* concern
all possible variations of the father-son relationship (although
that aspect also occurs in the Croatian novel). In *The Cyclops,*
Hamlet primarily refers to the general state of rotting, of organic
disintegration, and consumption, but also to a steady process
of metamorphosis, and, with reference to the above quotations,
it also establishes an umbilical link, connecting life and death,
and produces ties—spiritual ones—between generations.   The
basic Joycean concerns have structured the unity of *The Cyclops.*

c) As in *Ulysses,* the events and human relationships involved are not really organized into a self-explanatory plot.
The action is located in a big city, its main characters are
journalists and bohemians, more or less idle, meeting in bars
or restaurants, perambulating the streets in circular trajectories,
their contacts rarely reaching genuine interpersonal understand-

ing.

d) The environment, however, provides a splendid location for bickering, broaching intellectual problems, and starting abortive narratives.   Corresponding to the exposition of Stephen's Hamlet theory and the unfinished anecdote of the two midwifes in "Aeolus," in *The Cyclops* we have the story of the wreckage of the ship Menelaus and of its passengers, intermittently taken up and never brought to a climax.

e) The variety of unsuccessful attempts at communication among the characters has its concomitant in frequent punning (often serial, performing gradual word transformations), linguistic ingenuities, and a play with titles and literary references (by Shakespeare eleven plays alone are alluded to or quoted): *The Cyclops* is probably the most densely intertextual modern novel in Croatian.

f) The central relationship that emerges is one between a young and an old man, who had been potential friends for a long time and whose mutual sympathy finds its expression—and their friendship its consumation—after a drunken brawl late at night, in the tiny apartment of the older one.   As in *Ulysses,* they separate after urinating together, but contrary to what happens (or does not happen) in Joyce, this symbolic gesture ends in something definite: by urinating on an electric cable the old man gets himself electrocuted, thus performing one of the most bizzare suicides in fiction (matched perhaps only by Krook's death by spontaneous combustion in *Bleak House*). Echoes, allusions, distortions of Ulyssean moulds abound— together with reverberations from Dostoevsky: around midnight the two innocent men start a discussion on whether it is permitted to kill even the lowliest of creatures.

Both Davičo's *The Poem* and Marinković's *The Cyclops* are novels that are very much part of the intellectual moment of their *milieu* at the time of publication.   Trying to counter well established conventions, they both use patterning and linguistic foregrounding in a way infinitely superior to what preceeds them in their own traditions.   Both make use of Joyce's literary legacy.   In Davičo, this is fused with an awareness of modern French poetic techniques, in Marinković with a wide range of intellectual commonplace and literary experimentation. Neither of them exploits simply one of the characteristic Joycean styles, but use more comprehensive patterns of fictional organization—in particular, do they highly charge the linguistic potential beyond the limits of realistic story-telling. In a culture where folk poetry and the epic heroic tradition are still alive, this is a sign of rapid sophistication.

The Joycean assertion of the vitality of a language—beyond anything that prose language had performed before—has to be set against *The Cyclops'* catastrophic background. It is thanks to the virtuosity of its language that *The Cyclops* can be seen as a "comic apocalypse," as R. W. B. Lewis[6] called the American novels of the 1960's dealing with the comprehensive destructiveness of such historical situations as World War II. These novels, from *Catch-22* to *Gravity's Rainbow* and beyond display a similar kind of resourcefulness. Such analogues to *Ulysses* are part of a humanist tradition still in the ascendant. Based on recent global anxieties they transcend them by the scope of the imagination they display. On the other hand, the French novels inspired by aspects of *Ulysses,* cutting across whatever story line may seem to be emerging, and neutralizing the potentiality of character, achieve consistency and saturation in craftsmanship by following more specialized Joycean techniques.

The inspiration—in France or Yugoslavia—need be not exclusively that of Joyce, but an awareness of Joyce's practice is present in all the cases discussed: the effect aimed at is in some way the opposite to what Joyce achieves: either more open to human growth or more circular and involute in its complete achievement. The richness and variety of Joycean discourse can be put to a great range of uses—dependent on what task the fiction in a particular language needs to fulfill at a particular moment. In France and Yugoslavia these tasks are historically different at the same moment in time. But in both countries the most advanced and the most independent writing has felt the need to enlist Joyce in its own pursuit of new fictional correlates to the changing universe of their authors. This perhaps will still be Joyce's position in the years to come—a furthering influence on new original fiction in all the languages which have had communication with Joyce's work.

Notes

[1] Northrop Frye, *Anatomy of Criticism,* (Princeton, 1957).

[2] Cf. Wolfgang Iser, *The Implied Reader,* (Baltimore and London, 1974).

[3] *Ulysses*, Modern Library, (New York, 1946), p. 690.

[4] *For a New Novel,* (New York, 1965).

[5] Oskar Davico, *The Poem,* published by Lincolns Prager, London, 1959.

[6] Cf. R. W. B. Lewis, "Days of Wrath and Laughter" in *Trials of the Word,* (New Haven and London, 1966).

Russian Joyce

Aleksandar Flaker
Zagreb, Yugoslavia

1. *Is Tolstoy Joyce's predecessor?*

In his writings on Tolstoy, Shklovsky emphasized the importance of Tolstoy's first literary effort, a manuscript with the title *Povest' včerašnego dnja* (The History of Yesterday). This work, written in 1851, was considered by Shklovsky to have anticipated modern literature "by more than half a century." Tolstoy wrote this fragment in the form of an interior monologue, much like the stream of consciousness technique. It is characterized by the complexity of the conscious and subconscious layers of a protagonist who records the impressions of a single day.

> Exterior events are recorded as especially worthless, interior ones as important. The novel appears to be inverted: directed towards an interior reality.

And Shklovsky continues:

> The interior monologue contradicts the exterior monologue. If Tolstoy had finished his thing, we would have before us a book similar to the one Joyce was going to write many decades later.[1]

Tolstoy's fragment, however important it was for the beginning of his development as a writer, never became a literary fact of life during his lifetime. It was first published only in 1928, when it was included in the "Collected Works."

This was during a time in Russian literature when fragmentary works with a minimal degree of fictionality were recognized as literary texts and when interest in the relationship between consciousness and the unconscious was already present in Russia as well as Joyce's works. A publication of the "History of Yesterday" in 1851 would have been an anachronism. During realism's predominance, a work of this kind would have been considered a "step back" toward Sterne or Goethe's *The Sorrows of Young Werther*, i. e. the refutation of the established system of literary norms. But as often happens in literary history, certain works, anachronistic at the time of their conception, later are regarded as original forerunners.

Instead of claiming Russian priority here, as Shklovsky does, the question concerning the relationship between Russian literature and the modernist paradigm of Western culture, as represented by Joyce's *Ulysses*, should be put differently. It should concern the development of Russian prose toward the use of interior monologue. If we look at the problem in this way, we will encounter Tolstoy's initial experiment within the macrostructure of his novels, wherever his characters' internal and external levels of consciousness are placed in relationship to each other. The principle of representing a character's interior life can also be noticed in Tolstoy's contemporary Dostoyevsky. It is Dostoyevsky who would gain the special position of the first Russian author who based a fictional text almost entirely on interior monologue. *Krotkaja* ("The Tame One," 1876), the story of a lonely man at the dead body of his wife, is a work that contradicts realistic conventions by introducing a form which, according to Dostoyevsky's own account, comes near to being the "shorthand minutes" of a man's "conversing with himself," "with interruptions and inversions, in an interrupted form." In the subtitle ("The Fantastic Story") Dostoyevsky characterizes this form as supposedly fantastic, and he justifies its use by referring to—the romantic tradition of Victor Hugo. The realistic conventions, however, are still in force in this story. Dostoyevsky himself admits that minutes appear "somewhat rough, less worked out." Moreover, the interior monologue in the story is not yet stream of consciousness. The protagonist "talks either to himself or as though he were *addressing* himself to an invisible listener, a judge."[2]

In Garshin's novella *Četyre dnja* ("Four Days," 1882), the reader does not get the impression that a listener is being addressed. Instead, the interior monologue of a Russian soldier wounded on the Bulgarian front draws close to the stream of consciousness technique.   The realistic convention of "narration," however, is still present.   The narrative technique is justified at the end of the story when the narrator reveals that he has "retold" his experiences to be "noted down" by the doctors of the division's lazaret.[3]   Nevertheless, this story is still cited today, even in reference works,[4] as one of the first examples of interior monologue.   In fact, it was published before Dujardin's famous work *Les lauriers sont coupées* (1888).   The publication of Garshin's work in the eighteen eighties represents a first stage in the disintegration of Russian realism.

In Russia as well as in the rest of the world, however, Dostoyevsky's and Tolstoy's long novels gained in importance at the expense of the shorter text forms, which appeared merely as byproducts of the dominant novelistic models as defined in Western Europe by de Vogüé's book on the Russian novel, *Le roman russe* (1886).   This occurred in precisely the same decade, in which the very idea of stream of consciousness was developed and which was characterized, apart from an increased interest in Russian literature, by the names of Henry James and Henri Bergson.   After all, from the standpoint of the realistic norm, it was Tolstoy's "psychologizing" of character, even in *War and Peace,* which encountered resistance. A passage from one of Turgenev's letters should make this sufficiently clear:

> And with regard to Tolstoy's so-called psychology there
> is much that could be said; there is no real development
> in any of the characters . . . and there is the same old
> way of transmitting the vacillations and vibrations of
> one and the same feeling, situation and what he so merci-
> lessly puts into the mouths and consciousness of all
> his heroes.   I love, someone says, but actually I hate,
> etc., etc.   How sick and tired one is of these quasi-subtle
> reflections, of these thought processes, of the observation
> of his own feelings.[5]

We know now that Dostoyevsky and Tolstoy in this very way undermined realistic narrative conventions from within and anticipated the process we have characterized as "Joycean."

2. The "Inversion" of the Russian Novel

When interior monologue is in question, Russian literary scholarship generally cites Anna Karenina's state of mind shortly before she commits suicide. Her "speech" runs on without any apparent intervention on the part of the author, who, at the moment of her *punishment*, seems to leave her to herself. It is as though the punishment for the moral transgression were developing out of herself. However, we should not forget that the structure of *Anna Karenina* is governed by Tolstoy's moral and ethical axiology, an axiology also visible in Dostoyevsky's work, and even in Garshin's pacifist novella. But it was Chekhov who would first challenge the ethical axiology so characteristic of nineteenth century Russian fiction and who would one day be accused by the very same Tolstoy of placing the adulteress Anna Sergeevna *jenseits von Gut und Bose* in the short story "The Lady with the Dog" ("Dama as sobackoj," 1899). Chehkov, however, had not yet destroyed the axiological hierarchy on which the Russian novel was based. This rejection of the nineteenth century novel as the dominant model in Russian literature was left to writers of our century: Vasily Rozanov and Andrej Bely.

The intrinsic conflict not only with the novelistic tradition but with the entire cultural hierarchy of nineteenth century Russia apparently gives rise to the texts of the journalist, philosopher of religion, and writer Rozanov. His texts, Shklovsky has shown,[6] effect the inversion of the Russian novel, turning it upside down, by a way of organization that is clearly *literary*, without conforming to the traditional idea of literature. "Solitaria" (*Uedinennoe*, 1911), "Fallen Leaves" (*Opavšie list'ja*, 1913/15), and "Apocalypse of Our Times" (*Apokalipsis našego vremeni*, 1917/18), are texts which, even today, cause generic problems so that they have been rated both as aphorisms, and as the creation of "the first and greatest, the most persistent inventor and accomplisher of interior monologue in Russian literature."[7] One thing is certain: the antihierarchic principle of the modern world and its presentation in literature finds consistent expression in Rozanov's literary collages. There, authentic fragments, pictorial and graphic, are pasted together on a genealogical level as well as on a linguistic level, covering the language of robbers and policemen, of clerks and news agencies, and backing the progress of mass media, especially newspapers, which increasingly transform the ethical values of Russian literature. It was not by accident that Gorky, while reading Rozanov, underlined the following statement in the book *Literary Exiles (Literaturnye izgnanniki,* 1913):

> Form: and *I am formless.* Order and system: and I am *unsystematic and even disorderly.* Duty: and *in my deepest heart each duty appeared to me to be comic, and with each 'duty' I wanted, in my deepest heart, to commit a 'joke,' a 'vaudeville' (except for a tragic duty).* Each moment, at each turn, my 'teacher' repudiated me, 'I' repudiated my teacher.[8]

Reading Rozanov in 1927 and 1930, D. H. Lawrence at first associated him with the tradition of Dostoyevsky, considering him to have caught "Russianitis," but he appreciated his "attack on Christianity," to which Rozanov opposed "original pagan vision, phallic vision."[9] Then Lawrence recognizes some fundamental elements of the structure of *Fallen Leaves*:

> The *Fallen Leaves* are just fragments of thought jotted down anywhere and anyhow. As to the importance of the where and how, perhaps it *is* important to keep throwing the reader out into the world, by means of the: At night: At work: In the tram: In the w.c.—which is sometimes printed after the reflections. Perhaps, to avoid any appearance of systematisation, or even of philosophic abstraction, these little *addenda* are useful. Anyhow, it is Russian, and deliberate, done with intention of keeping the reader—or Rozanov himself—in contact with the *moment*, the actual time and place. Rozanov says that with *Solitaria* he introduced new *tone* into literature, the tone of manuscript, a manuscript being unique and personal, coming from the individual alone direct to the reader. And the secret (bordering on madness) that I am talking to myself: so constantly and attentively and *passionately,* that apart from this I practically hear nothing—this is the secret of his newness, and of his book.[10]

The other "decanonizer" of the Russian novel, Andrey Bely, has already been compared to Joyce. One of the first comparisons was made by the author of grotesque short stories and dystopian novels, the connoisseur of English life and literature, the author of essays on H. G. Wells, O'Henry, and R. B. Sheridan—Evgeny Zamyatin. In his essay *Andrey Bely,* published in his Paris exile as early as 1936, Zamyatin's comparison is primarily concerned with the linguistic level. Writing about the impossibility of translating Bely's books, Zamyatin remarks that he doubts whether they are "written in Russian" at all:

> Bely's syntax is so unusual, his wording is full of neologisms. The language of his books is Bely's language in the same sense as the language of *Ulysses* is not English but Joyce's language.[11]

Zamyatin discusses two novels: *Peterburg* (1916) and *Kotik Letayev* (1917/18), but he returns to the Joyce comparison, when he talks about texts of the Soviet period:

> But Bely's tireless search for new forms, now mostly concerned with the lexis, are carried on to these latest novels: he remained 'Russian Joyce' to the end.[12]

From then on, the Bely-Joyce comparison remained a commonplace in Russian studies outside Russia; as was the case with Zamyatin, this originated from a wish to make readers who were familiar with Joyce's works acquainted with this "untranslatable" writer as well. We will also come upon this comparison in popular surveys of Russian literature, in which Bely's achievement is seen in his parallel development of a "polyphonic prose with neologisms, world-of-nebulae coinages, interior monologue (or stream of consciousness) and mythlike structure of plots."[13] And a German critic of Bely's texts draws special attention to *Kotik Letayev,* "in which the presentation of consciousness (*Bewußtseinsdarstellung*) in the Russian novel leads to the direction which James Joyce has shown to the English novel: the presentation of a 'streaming' consciousness as a concrete and at the same time suprarealistic (mythic) reality."[14]

In spite of all this insistence on a Bely-Joyce parallel, some authors prefer to associate Joyce's name with the poet-futurist Chlebnikov,[15] whose linguistic experiments were the farthest-

reaching in Russian poetry, and Holthusen cites Joyce's name—
together with Döblin's—in connection with Boris Pilnyak, a
postrevolutionary Russian prose writer who took over many
of Bely's stylistic devices.[16]   After all, Pilnyak's novel *The
Naked Year* (1921) is already contemporary to *Ulysses*, but
also to T. S. Eliot's poem *The Waste Land.* In short, thanks
to the multiplicity of these parallels, we have entered the circle
of the European avant-garde.

Bely's *Petersburg* has recently been compared to Joyce's
Ulysses by Lena Szilárd, a Hungarian scholar. In her analysis
she considers the psychoanalytic level (patricide motives) as
well as the mythical level of the two texts, their fundamental
complexity and their common principle of construction—a
circular movement—with which the apocalyptic vision of both
writers is connected. Other points of comparison are the relation
to Nietzsche's philosophy, and, finally, the use of language.
Regardless of the fact that Bely's novel is retold in the author's
name—with obvious Sternian overtones—while in *Ulysses* there
is no apparent narrator, both novels realize—in the language—
the "author's autonomous power over the world he himself
creates, as its demiurge." Both Bely and Joyce practice a "free
interplay of themes and styles known in the national literary
tradition, arbitrarily mixing them with bookish (literary, philosophical) and oral, spoken forms, abounding in lexic creativity."
Both writers, Szilárd concludes, "inverted the relations" within
the genre. If Bely, "in the framework of several Petersburg days
(half of the novel takes place in 24 hours, from the winding of
a bomb until its explosion), tried to elucidate the épopée of
Russian consciousness," Joyce set off the same way:

> Joyce's fundamental innovation is not the transposition
> of stream of consciousness, master of which he thought
> to be Tolstoy, but the inversion of relations: a single
> day of Dublin life is a tribute to tradition; the real novel's
> cronotop is—the odyssey of a consciousness which in-
> cludes in itself the totality of the spiritual experience—
> according to Joyce's idea—of average man (in this sense,
> not only Bloom is Odysseus, but also Stephen, and
> even Molly with sixty pages of interior monologue).[17]

Let us add: structural inversions are one of the fundamental
characteristics of the constitution of avant-garde structures,

and by the term "inverting the relations" they could be brought closer to each other, but their essence cannot be defined. Besides, it is only in *Kotik Letayev* that—except for some moments of "autobiographicality"—Bely makes the reconstruction of consciousness the dominant principle. Here, a relation between personal consciousness and cosmos is established, and the fundamental complexity of mythical allusions determines the structure up to the point that Steiner's anthroposophy becomes an obstacle in interpreting the novel as a "pure" pattern of the stream of consciousness novel. Such a "pure" pattern as Joyce's paradigm was not reached in Russian literature; it was hindered by its revolutionary functionalization.

3. *"Ulysses" as a Model for the Film of the Future*

The article on James Joyce in the 1930 *Literary Encyclopedia* (vol. 3, edited by Lunacharsky) reflects the Soviet attitude to this "master of international modernism," a response which is characterized by a very small number of translations (*Dubliners* was partly translated in 1927, and some chapters from *Ulysses* in the anthology *Novinki Zapada* in 1925). There is an emphasis on the destructive nature of Joyce's work and the lack of a positive social function of a text on "street-sweepers and grave-diggers of petty burgeoisie" that "paves the way for future literature, but fails to offer an alternative to the world it destroys." The author of the article compares Joyce to Bely as well as to Spengler and Proust, and explains his linguistic devices in terms of Russian avant-garde (*Zaum'*) and, most strikingly, by musical terms ("polyphone,"[18] "symphonic disentaglement") as well as by "cinetechnical" ones:

> All of *Ulysses* disintegrates into separate and often *complex cadres* of entangled perceptions and experiences. Their *montage* results in *focussing* of the perception of many characters *on one object*, in arbitrary mental jumps, *flashbacks* motivated by acts of remembrance and the like.[19]

Two years before this article on Joyce, a contribution by Sergei Eisenstein, the famous director of avant-garde films, had appcarcd in a markedly sectarian journal of "proletarian writers."   In his exhaustive answer to an inquiry about the relation between "cinema" and literature, the author of the film *Battleship Potemkin* (1925)—approved by a government commission formed by Lunacharsky as well as by the painter Malevich and the theatre director Meyerhold[20]—emphasized Joyce's great importance for the art of film. The director, who read Zola before shooting his films, who acknowledged cinematic qualities in Serafimovich's novel, who regarded Babel's texts as a "chrestomathy of the new cinematic imagery," and who among the contemporary writers showed a special liking for Sofia Fedorchenko—today an almost forgotten Russian writer—, appreciated *Ulysses*, "the most interesting phenomenon in the West," for its *methodological* value for both film and literature.   While his high regard for Fedorchenko's *People in War* (1917-1927), a montage of the fragments of soldier's conversations, lies within the trend of Russian avant-garde toward authenticity (*Novyj LEF* energetically presented "literature of facts" in those days!), he esteems Joyce as the first messenger of the "cinematography that is to be."   In Joyce, Eisenstein finds that "deanecdotization" and neglect for plot, those "physiological qualities of the detail" in close-up and the "entirely intellectual effect" which he himself had already realized in *Battleship Potemkin*—the one film he does not mention among those before which he read Zola! If we remember Eisenstein's sequences with wormy meat at the beginning of the film on 1905, and if we relate them to the "physiological complexes" of Joyce's novel, we can clearly see the affinity.   An excellent connoisseur of Russian as well as world literature, Eisenstein—at the end of the passage dedicated to Joyce (and Fedorchenko)—comes to the following conclusion:

> The *rest* of literature appears to me, in regard to its use for film, to be *only*, although this is certainly enough, an inexhaustible fund, an archive of *material*.[21]

Still in 1928, Eisenstein travelled to the West.   In Paris he met James Joyce, who, although almost blind, wanted to see parts of *Battleship* and *October*, and "showed great interest for [Eisenstein's] plans for 'interior cinemolologue' with far greater, unforeseeable possibilities as compared to literary 'interior monologue'."[22]

Eisenstein's recollection of his encounter with Joyce was

published in a text that he prepared after his lectures for the journal *Proletarskoe kino* in 1932. He had just returned from America, where he had been working on the (unaccepted) shooting of Dreiser's *American Tragedy,* which he considered as a realization of "interior cinemonologue." In this text, Eisenstein emphasizes once again that it is only film that can produce a "notion of total processes in the mind of an excited man." In this respect even literature is helpless and has to confine itself to "the primitive rhetoric of Dreiser's description of Clyde's interior stammering"[23] just as the theatre does not go beyond "the pseudo-classical tirades of O'Neill's heroes uttering secondary monologues 'apart'—'something they think' about, and informing the audience of what they talk about ('Strange Interlude')." However, according to Eisenstein, there is a kind of literature "that has stepped over the limits of orthodox restrictions," and only such—i.e. avant-garde—literature can reproduce the movement of human thoughts:

> Within the crude framework of literary confinements it has been fully realized in the immortal 'interior monologue' of the insurance canvasser Leopold Bloom in James Joyce's marvellous *Ulysses.*

Eisenstein also briefly mentions Joyce's literary predecessors, establishing a line which leads from the German romanticists and Gérard de Nerval to Dujardin, and then to the "absolute literary perfection" of interior monologue "as a specific constructive procedure" in the works of Joyce and Valéry Larbaud, his French follower.[24] Then follows an enthusiastic remembrance of his own work, obviously on montaged sketches he had prepared for *American Tragedy,* a real apology of interior monologue in both film and literature. There, we can find:

> ... sonority, formless or soundlike ...
> ... beats of intellectually formulated words ...
> ... passionate silly speech, only with nouns or verbs;
> at a moment with exclamation marks, with zig-zag of
> abstract [originally: non-objective] shapes ...
> ... polyphony of sounds ...
> ... polyphony of images ...
> ... diversity of rhythms ...
> ... fever of inner arguings

and its contrast:

> stonelike mask of the face

and later on:

> How attractive it is to listen to one's own mental move-
> ments, especially when in affection, to catch oneself in
> a process of seeing? what? of listening?
>   How to distinguish talking 'into onself' from taling
> 'out of oneself.' What is the difference between inner
> and outer syntax of language . . .

And, in the end, Eisenstein's far-reaching conclusion:

> And how obvious it is that the material for the sound-
> film is not *dialogue* at all.
> *The only material for soundfilm is, of course, mono-*
> *logue.*[25]

However, as we know, Eisenstein was not allowed to "step
over the limits of the orthodox restrictions"—neither in America
nor in his own country in the thirties. Joyce's pattern, transposed to the film strip, was subversive in its essence for both
environments. Only Orson Welles in *Citizen Kane* or Fellini in
8 1/2 would approach Eisenstein's ideal.

That Eisenstein remained faithful to *Ulysses* to the very
end is proved by a text published in 1940. For his thesis about
the ways in which literature can overcome its own confinements,
Eisenstein gives two examples: Rodin's Balzac sculpture and
Joyce's literary texts:

> Here, as nowhere else, literature reaches almost physio-
> logical palpability in everything he writes about. In
> addition to the whole arsenal of literary devices, there
> is a compositional arrangement that I would call 'supra-
> lyrical.' For if lyrics can reproduce on the level of im-
> agery the most intimate movements of an inner logic of
> our feelings, then Joyce even imitates the very physiology
> of the formation of our thoughts.

> The effects are only sporadically impressive, as they must

> pay for the total collapse of the very foundations of
> literary writing; they pay for the thorough *disintegration*
> of the *literary method* as such and for turning the text
> into 'abracadabra' for the ordinary reader.[26]

What follows is a criticism of "left art," i.e. avant-garde art in general. The criticism is reasonable, but in accord with the norms that dominated Soviet literature and art. Not before long Eisenstein would accept his last big order: *Ivan the Terrible*!

4. *Joyce's Expulsion*

In his text "Proudness" ("Gordost' ") Eisenstein calls *Ulysses* "the most heroic literary attempt" to represent human totality. This very statement is an act of heroism: it was written in 1940, when Eisenstein was assigned to direct Wagner's opera, in the year when the rejected Meyerhold was dying, and when the despised Bulgakov was writing "The Last Days" (*Poslednie dni*, later: *Pushkin*), the story of a conflict between artist and despotism.

The account with Joyce had already been settled before: at the Congress of Writers in 1934. The address dedicated to "contemporary world literature" and delivered by Karl Radek, was entitled "James Joyce or Socialist Realism?" Although Joyce was little known to the Russian reader—only a year ago the expressive dramatist Vishnevsky had complained of the general ignorance of the Irish author's works (with reference to Eisenstein und Meyerhold) as well as of Céline and Musil (with reference to Lunacharsky) in an article "Knowing the West" ("Znat' Zapad," 1933)—it was him who became the negative paradigm within the axiology of literary values that was being created under the sign of the normative poetics of Socialist realism.[27] To Radek Joyce was a literary model that should not be followed by Soviet and "revolutionary" writers. In his official speech at the Congress he started off with what was *not* present in *Ulysses*: the work deals with the Ireland of 1916[!], but the Irish insurrection of the same year is *neglected*; Joyce's method might be appropriate to Bloom, but it is *not* appropriate to the symbolic figure of world capitalism—Sir Henry Deterding; Joyce distracts from the effort of building Magnitogorsk and Kuznetskstroy and introduces writers to the backwaters of average man.[28]

Radek's report invited some criticism. Vishnevsky once again defended the acquaintance with Joyce—and Proust—, Nikulin insisted on the necessity of translating Joyce, Dos Passos and Céline (previously "Lefist"), avant-gardist Tretyakov opposed to Radek's "diagnosis in the dark"—considering the fact that Joyce had not been translated—, and the prominent *Pravda* journalist and columnist Michail Koltsov, while defending Radek, supported the idea that Soviet readers should form their own opinion about Joyce. A series of critical comments followed. Annabel Williams Ellis objected to the ignorance of the progressive English literature as shown in Radek's report and pointed out that in *Ulysses* "there exists a broader social background than comrade Radek assumes."[29] Even Wieland Herzfelde, the brother of the former dadaist and creator of photo-montage, John Hartfield, energetically opposed to Radek's evaluation of *Ulysses* as a "heap of dung, crawling with worms, photographed by a cinema apparatus through a microscope." The German delegate and editor of the Malik-Verlag, who had already experienced Fascist attitude toward art and had moved to Prague as early as 1934, pledged for bringing closer literature and scientific methods, for experiment in literature and for stylistic "apprenticeship to Joyce." He pointed out that one could not deny social functions to Joyce's work:

> I think that the inverted and disfigured picture Joyce created of man (who in fact does not exist as such) is not guilty of snobbish, artificial creation, but is a reflection of James Joyce's social point of view.[30]

The last word at the Congress, however, was granted to the official speaker, who freed the Organization Committee—and, consequently the Party—from responsibility for his personal opinions about certain "literary values." But he sharply reacted to Herzfelde's intervention as "dangerous" for proletarian literature and even regarded Joyce's orientation toward human inner life as a "reactionary" tendency. As to the proposed "apprenticeship" to Joyce, he concluded: "I don't write novels, but if I did I think I would learn how to write them from Tolstoy and Balzac, not from Joyce."[31]

This was not Radek's polemic wit. It should be remembered that the top ranking of Tolstoy and Balzac in world literature had been established in the thirties by György Lukàcs, who philosophically and with the knowledge of European literature supported a hierarchical and normative system within which there was no place for Joyce. Joyce's Stephen Dedalus from "Author's Youth," to which Eisenstein—with obvious Freudian slip—convoluted *A Portrait of the Artist as a Young Man*,[32] was exiled from the country in which he had just appeared—because of his rejection to serve his home, his home-country, and his church.

In his concluding speech Radek also had to answer to another foreigner, Jean-Richard Bloch. In fact, Bloch did not mention Joyce, but he pointed out the artistic significance of the "sexual question," energetically defending the principles of avant-garde as branded by Joyce's name:

> On the field of technique as well as on other fields, art originates from oppositions and becomes conscious of itself reacting against dominant tendencies of public taste and its aspiration to lightness.
>
> Whatever the character of society, there are and always will be artists who will use circular forms of language, and there will be those who will try new forms.[33]

With respect to educational functions of literature and art, and correspondingly to their accessibility to the masses ("lightness!"), experimentation with new forms was persecuted in the literature of the thirties and forties, while the literary "oppositions" to the normative system hiding behind the "public taste" were treated as political.

To conclude this discussion of "Russian Joyce" let us return for a moment to the question of the Russian novel. In the late twenties, the poet Osip Mandelshtam forecasted "The End of the Novel" ("Konec romana") in a collection of essays *On Poetry* (1928). By the Ovidian title of his poetic collection *Tristia* (1922) he had already indicated his "interior exile" within the postrevolutionary Russian literature. Mandelshtam could also be compared to Joyce by his "plotless" prose, coming close to the standpoint of the author's *alter ego* Parok, a common Russian plebeian intellectual of Jewish origin, who, in contrast to Leopold Bloom, was made to watch and feel "The Roar of time," as Mandelshtam's first prose book was entitled (*Šum vremeni*, 1925). In *The Egyptian Stamp* (*Egipetskaja marka*, 1928), Parnok presents, in fact, "the state of consciousness" of a man who, keeping himself apart, watches the historical process of destruction of the "old," prerevolutionary Petersburg Russian culture.[34]   He differs from Bloom and Joyce's other characters primarily by his historiosophicality, and is close to them by his amorphousness.

This is a parallel yet to be developed, but we would like to conclude with a quotation from Mandelshtam's short essay "The State and the Rhythm" ("Gosudarstvo i ritm"), dedicated to Dalcrose's system of rhythmical gymnastics as it was practiced in Hellerau near Vienna, and which was making advances to Russia. The essay, published in Kharkov in 1920, begins thus:

> While organizing a society, raising it out of the chaos and into the harmony of organic life, we are prone to forget that personality must primarily be organized. Amorphous, formless man, unorganized personality is the greatest enemy to society.[35]

"Russian Joyce" succumbed to this thesis, and even Mandelshtam succumbed to it, Mandelshtam who was not saved by the weapons of the exiled—of Stephen Dedalus from the "Author's Portrait:" *"silence, exile, and cunning"* (*Portrait*, 247).

Notes

[1] Transl. from V. Šklovskij, *Povesti o proze* 2, (Moscow, 1966), pp. 271-272.

[2] Italics A. F.; also see author's introduction to this story in F. M. Dostoevski, *Sobranie sočinenij* 10, (Moscow, 1958), pp. 377-378.

[3] V. Garšin, *Pervaja knižka rasskazov*, (S. Peterburg, 3, 1888), p. 22.

[4] See, for example, G. von Wilpert, *Sachwörterbuch der Literatur*, (Stuttgart, 21959), p. 258.

[5] Letter to P. V. Annenkov (Feb. 14th, 1868), quoted from: *Tolstoy*,

The Critical Heritage, ed. A. V. Knowles, (London, 1978), p. 181.

[6] See V. Šklovskij, *O teorii prozy*, (Moscow 1929), p. 232-238.

[7] H. Stammler, "Wesensmerkmale und Stil des proteischen Menschen," in: V. Rozanov, *Izbrannoe*, (Munich, 1970), p. xxv.

[8] "Pis'ma A. M. Gor'kogo k V. V. Rozanovu i ego pomety na knige Rozanova" ed. by L. N. Jokar, in: *Kontekst*, (Moscow, 1978), p. 313.

[9] D. H. Lawrence, *Selected Literary Criticism* ed. A. Beal, (London, 1961), p. 247—For the information concerning Lawrence's review of Rozanov's texts I must thank M. Beker.

[10] Ibid., p. 250.—About Rozanov's texts see also: A. Flaker, "Rozanovljeva destrukcija književnosti," *Umjetnost riječi* xix, 1975, 2-4, pp. 151-160.

[11] E. Zamjatin, *Lica*, (New York, 1955), p. 76.

[12] Ibid., p. 80.

[13] M. Slonim, *From Chekhov to the Revolution*, (New York, 1962), p. 194.

[14] J. Holthusen, *Russische Literatur im 20. Jahrhundert*, (Munich, 1978), p. 48.

[15] R. Poggioli, *The Poets of Russia*, (Cambridge, Mass., 1960), pp. 157, 263.

[16] Holthusen, op. cit., p. 148.—Soviet researcher P. Palievskij in *Puti realizma*, (Moscow, 1974), p. 75, stresses Pilnyak's anticipation not only in relation to Joyce but also in relation to Gertrude Stein's texts.—Holthusen, one should add, compares Andrey Bely's texts with those by M. Krleža: "Weltmodelle moderner slavischer Dichter: Andrej Belyj und Miroslav Krleža" in: *Innsbrucker Beiträge zur Kulturwissenschaft. Slavica Aenipontana* 2, (Innsbruck, 1978), pp. 3-18.

[17] L. Szilárd, "Andrej Belyj i Džems Džojs," in: *Studia Slavica Hungarica* xxv, 1979, pp. 407-417.—See also: "O strukture Vtoroj simfonii Andreja Belogo," in: *Studia Slavica Hungarica* xiii, 1967, p. 314.—Szilárd's study also cites other papers in which Bely is compared to Joyce.

[18] The term "polyphony" in relation to literature was introduced in Russian literary theory by Baxtin in *Problemy tvorčestva Dostoevskogo*, 1929.

[19] I. Kaskin, "Džojs Džems" in: *Literaturnaja enciklopedija* 3, 1930, p. 250. Italics A. F.

[20] See V. Šklovskij, Ejzenštejn, (Moscow, 1976), p. 117.

[21] "Literatura i kino", 1928, in: S. Ejzenštejn, *Izbrannye proizvedenija v šesti tomah* 5, (Moscow, 1963), p. 526. Italics A. F.

[22] "Odolžajtes'!" 1932, in: op. cit. 2, (Moscow, 1964, p. 77.—Joyce's biographer records the following about Eisenstein's meeting with Joyce: "Eisenstein described a visit to Joyce as 'a ghost experience,' because the

room in which they met was so dark that both seemed shadows. They stood and talked about *Ulysses*, and afterwards Eisenstein remarked to a friend, 'A great man! This fellow really *does* what all of you *wanted* to do, because you feel it but he knows it.' " (R. Ellmann, *James Joyce*, New York, London, Toronto, 1965), pp. 666, 811. Citing Eisenstein, Ellmann refers to Hans Richter's letter from 1958. A year before the meeting in 1927, Richter had planned shooting a non-objective (abstract) film with Kazimir Malevich!

[23] Eisenstein referred to Dreiser with irony; in his answer to the inquiry in 1928 he remarks that he had to read him shortly before they met in Moscow in 1927, while he did not have to do this for Joyce: "In any case, however strange it would appear, Joyce's writing was known to me." (Op. cit., 5, p. 526).

[24] Larbaud was almost unknown in Russia in those days. According to T. G. Khatisova's information in *Kratkaja literaturnaja enciklopedija* 4, 1967, p. 34, only one of his short stories was translated into Russian in *Literaturnaja gazeta* in 1925. Eisenstein probably connects Larbaud's name to Joyce because the French writer was preparing his translation of *Ulysses* (published in 1929) just during Eisenstein's stay in Paris. See Ellmann, op. cit., p. 614.

[25] Ejzenštejn, op. cit. 2, pp. 77-79.

[26] "Gordost' " (1940), op. cit., p. 90.

[27] For a review of the discussion on Joyce at the Congress see G. Struve, *Soviet Russian Literature 1917-1950*, (Oklahoma, 1951), pp. 252-259; V. Strada, "Introduzione," in: *Rivoluzione e letteratura*, (Bari, 1967), p. lxii (including an Italian translation of Radek's speech).

[28] See: *Pervyj vsesojuznyj s'ezd sovetskih pisatelej. Stenografičeskij otčet*, (Moscow, 1934), pp. 315-316.

[29] Ibid., p. 334.

[30] Ibid., p. 361—For the contributions of other German participants at the Congress (J. Becher, W. Bredel, F. Wolf, E. Toller, and a message by H. Mann) see: *Zur Tradition der sozialistischen Literatur in Deutschland*, (Berlin GDR, 1962).

[31] Ibid., p. 373.

[32] Ejzenštejn, op. cit. 5, p. 526.

[33] J. R. Bloch, *Moscou-Paris*, (Paris, 1947), p. 120.

[34] See N. Berkovskij, "O proze Mandel'štama," 1929. The article is exhaustively quoted in: O. Mandel'štam, *Sobranie sočinenij* ii, (New York, 1971), pp. 557-558.

[35] O. Mandel'štam, op. cit. iii, (New York, 1969), p. 123.

A Portrait of the Artist as a Caricaturist: Picasso, Joyce and Britten

Peter Egri
Budapest, Hungary

A caricature is a comic re-creation of a model done in the spirit of intellectual recreation. The re-shaping of the original implies the element of its relativization through a critical sense of incongruous contrast between the actual and the desirable, the disharmonious and the harmonious, the apparent and the real, the real and the true, the irrational and the rational, the ephemeral and the essential, the relative and the absolute. Such characteristic procedures of caricature as ironical exaggeration and sarcastic distortion serve the purpose of increasing and intensifying the contrast.

Although there exist almost as many varieties of caricature as there are examples, three major categories may be instrumental in determining the special brand of caricature Picasso, Joyce and Britten most excelled in. The three types may be conveniently termed occasional, trend and universal caricatures.

An occasional caricature is an incidental gibe at a chance phenomenon. Its humorous banter does not cut deep, its target is usually light, slight and small, and it may even involve the general acceptance of a person or thing some trait of whose is ironically relativized. Its gentle teasing or sharper mockery have been known and experienced both in life and art from ancient to modern times. An illustrated joke of a humorous magazine or the exaggerated imitation of the ticking of the metronome in the second movement of Beethoven's *Symphony No. 8* are characteristic examples.

For all his acute sense of the tragically grim discord and discordance of contemporary social relations, Picasso seems to have been interested in occasional caricature throughout his creative career. At the age of 12, he "edited" a humorous paper for fun, and a number of his later graphic works can be taken as grotesque expressions of his sarcastic wit, examples or approximations of occasional caricature: *Travesty of Manet's Olympia* (1901), *Guillaume Apollinaire* (1905), *Igor Stravinsky* (1920), *The Toad* (1949), *Female Composition* (1950), *Balzac* (1952), *The Reclining Model* (1954), *Old Man and Young Woman with Masks* (1954), *Don Quixote* (1955), *Portrait of D. H. Kahnweiler* (1957), *A Double Face* (1959), *Faun and Goat* (1959), *Spectators* (1961), etc.

These works are comparable in style with Joyce's humorous or satirical poems such as "O Jimmie Joyce you are my darling," "Dear, I am asking a favour," "O, there are two brothers, the Fays," "The Holy Office," "Gas from a Burner," "There is a young gallant named Sax," "There's a monarch who knows no repose," "A Goldschmidt swam in a Kriegsverein," "There's a George of the Georges named David," "Dooleysprudence," "Rouen is the rainiest place getting," or "A Portrait of the Artist as an Ancient Mariner."[1]

The parallel between Picasso's and Joyce's occasional caricatures is not restricted to a comical theme, a humourous treatment and an adopted genre but it also extends to the manner the artist moulded the material: in these pieces both Picasso and Joyce adhere, as a rule, to traditional forms even when otherwise and in other works they have already developed their avant-garde techniques.[2] (With Joyce a natural exception is the free verse pattern of "Rouen is the rainiest place getting/ Inside all impermiables, wetting . . .", which is a parody of T. S. Eliot's *The Waste Land*; and with Picasso the imaginative pictorial idiom of the dry point print entitled *Female Composition,* which is an ingenious combination of a lissom blossom, a reclining woman, and a cross-eyed old man with a moustache.) Incidentally, Joyce himself drew a caricature of Leopold Bloom in Myron C. Nutting's studio in the 1920's.

Another class of caricature is trend-based in the sense that it reflects an opposition in social trends and artistic attitudes. The historical soil for the creation of. this kind of caricature was characterized by Marx in his *Critique of Hegel's 'Philosophy of Right'.* Describing in 1844 the comic historical anachronism of the German *ancien régime* which could not help hiding its real nature under the appearance of an alien nature, he wrote:

> The modern *ancien régime* is nothing but the humbug
> of a world order whose real heroes are dead. History
> is thorough, and passes through many phases when it
> conveys and old form to the grave. The final phase
> of a world-historical form is its comedy. The Greek
> Gods, already once mortally wounded, tragically,
> in Aeschylus' *Prometheus Bound,* had to die once
> more, comically, in the dialogues of Lucian. Why
> does history proceed in this way? So that mankind
> will separate itself happily from its past.[3]

A trend caricature calls into doubt the justification of a
social and artistic trend, relativizes its very basis, and presupposes the artist's social and moral commitment to a cause,
a trend. Its vigorous wit is especially sharp in cases where well-
marked trends and stances clash within or between social
systems. Periods of change with their conflicting aspirations
are especially favourable for trend caricatures. Shakespeare's
Falstaff in *Henry IV* and *The Merry Wives of Windsor,* Cer-
vantes' *Don Quixote,* Swift's *Gulliver's Travels,* Fielding's
Joseph Andrews, Hogarth's series (*The Harlot's Progress,
The Rake's Progress, Marriage à la Mode, An Election*), Sterne's
Tristram Shandy, Mozart's Osmin in *The Elopement from the
Harem,* Daumier's satirical lithographs, Shaw's *The Dark Lady
of the Sonnets* and *Cymbeline Refinished,* or some of the
scenes in Picasso's series *The Dreams and Lies of Franco* are
varied and typical examples.

A universal caricature differs from an occasional and
trend-based one both in quantity and in quality. Its target
is not just an incidental trait of a complex phenomenon as in
an occasional caricature; nor merely some social-artistic trend
relativized and devalued from the viewpoint of another specific
social-artistic trend as in a trend caricature. The irony of a
universal caricature is directed against a vast field of social
life and its cultural manifestations, not infrequently against
a human plight or sometimes against *the* human predicament.
In the latter case, which is an extreme possibility, nothing is
found absolute in the ironically illuminated sphere but the
very principle of relativity.

The quality of representation, expression and moulding
is determined by a radical separation between the customary
appearance of reality and the system of values which the artist

may also experience relative, or may be in search of, or may possess, assert and vindicate. Immediate reality has no truth any more, and truth has no immediate reality as yet.

The experience of technological advance and alienation, of two world wars, revolutions and counter-revolutions, fascism and anti-fascism, socialism and sectarianism have left behind a sense of historical relativism. Freud's psychoanalysis has relativized the opposition between the conscious and unconscious spheres of the human soul. Bergson's philosophy has conceived of the difference between subjective and objective time as relative. Planc's Quantum Theory, Einstein's Theory of Relativity, Rutherford's discovery of the atomic nucleus, Bohr's theory of the complementarity of apparently contradictory statements, Heisenberg's Uncertainty Principle obliterating the dividing lines between the potential and the actual have relativized the cosmology of classical physics, increased the impression of disorientation and the need for reorientation.[4] All these factors as well as the mutual incompatibility and incongruence between what the isolated artist and the general public appreciate and depreciate have contributed to creating the cultural climate for the universal type of caricature Picasso, Joyce and Britten are individually different but equally characteristic exponents of.

II

Picasso's procedure is very apparent in the relationship between Courbet's oil painting, *Young Ladies of the Banks of the Seine* (Les Demoiselles des Bords de la Seine, 1856) and Picasso's 1950 Cubist variation on the theme, painted on plywood. The line of Picasso's continuous descent from Courbet's artistic endeavours has not infrequently been stressed and, I feel, sometimes overstressed. Apollinaire in *Les Peintres cubistes* expresses unambiguously the view that Courbet is the father of the new painters.[5] John Berger elaborates on the idea: "No painter before Courbet was ever able to emphasize so uncompromisingly the density and weight of what he was painting. You can see it in the way he painted an apple or a wave, or in the way he painted the heavy langour and the creased dresses of the two girls lying by the Seine."[6] Finding the equivalent of the physical sensation of the material objects portrayed (weight, temperature, texture, the force of gravity), Courbet betrayed an interest in objects which the Cubists in their own way responded to. Assessing the double inheritance Coubet and Cézanne had bequeathed to Picasso, Berger remarks: "Before Cézanne, every painting was to some extent like a view seen through a window. Courbet had tried to open the window and climb out. Cézanne broke the glass. The room became part of the landscape, the viewer part of the view."[7] Courbet changed the material density of the view; Cézanne modified and multiplied the viewpoint.

Pierre Cabanne establishes especially close links between Courbet's and Picasso's versions of *Young Ladies of the Banks of the Seine.* He points out how much Picasso admired Courbet's daring achievement of standing up against official academic conventions and representing his figures without any kind of stiffness, in contemporary costumes and in a natural plein air setting. Pierre Cabanne admits, of course, that the sensuous aspect of Courbet's representation disappears in Picasso's picture, but attributes the phenomenon to the fact that Picasso is not satisfied with the expression of a mere episode of life, but wishes to eternalize all moments of rest, calm and joy apprehending totality rather than a single anecdote. His primary concern is essence rather than appearance. This is Picasso's way of accentuating the impression of serenity, relaxation under the shadow of trees by the bank of the river.[8]

The Picasso I have seen, I must confess, is a totally different picture. It is not the increased expression of the essence of all moments of rest, calm and joy, but an essential rejection of rest and calm and an ironical refutation of serenity and relaxation. In the relationship of Courbet's and Picasso's pictures the dominant and determining element is not continuity but discontinuity. Picasso's re-creation of the girls' recreation is a caricature. The more minutely Picasso adheres to the details of Courbet's painting, the more radically he relativizes and ironizes the basic assumptions of its artistic universe. This is apparent in the themes, attitudes, structures and colours the two painters have adopted.

Picasso's painting is a variation on Courbet's theme, but the variation is so bold that is has, in fact, modified the original theme. Let it suffice to point out the aesthetic consequence of the fact that Picasso has thoroughly shortened the vertical dimension of Courbet's picture[9] and thus eliminated the sky,

G. Courbet, "Les Demoiselles des Bords de la Seine,"
Le Petit Palais, Paris.

P. Picasso, "Les Demoiselles des Bords de la Seine,"
Öffentliche Kunstsammlung, Basel.

the clouds, the opposite bank, the view over the river and most of the foliage of the trees. In doing so, he has made it rather obvious that his subject is not a refreshing relaxation in nature but rather an ironic reversal of the idea, experience and mood. A caricature does not need a vista.

The two painters' attitudes to their themes are diagonally opposed. Courbet's is characterized by sympathy and empathy, Picasso's by irony and alienation. A comparison of the girls' faces in the two paintings betrays the difference of stance with which they have been modelled. Courbet is far from idealizing the girls; they "are caught off their guard in this retreat, one sleep-relaxed in her fattening charms, the other looking out at the world with tired eyes that have lost all illusions."[10] They are for sale for the rich. Their dresses are more refined than their faces. The sleeping brunette's features are some-what coarse, the blonde resting on one elbow is contemplating the world with hurt, hopeless and helpless bitterness. "We feel the hardening of her face, its pathos, its mixture of desperation and calm acceptance."[11] The hard lines of their faces, however, are shown as the imprints of their hard lives; and the way in which the foliage shelters and nature embraces them indicates the artist's compassion. The point of the charge is directed against society which acknowledged the assault by a critical attack against Courbet.

Picasso—following a Cubist practice dating back to the 20's —doubles the faces of both girls, turns the two profiles against one another, confronts them sharply in geometrically stylized lines, builds them together in a unified construction, stiffens the faces into masks, and underlines animal qualities. The eyes even of Courbet's sleeping girl are wide open in Picasso's re-interpreting caricaturistic reversal, and her upper and lower profiles penetrate one another in such a clasp of a kiss as if Picasso meant to caricature both the girl's sweetly self-indulgent amorous expression and the attitudes of Courbet's Lesbian nudes.[12] The idyllic aspect of Courbet's *Demoiselles* is radically rejected by Picasso's transposition.[13]

This opposition of attitudes asserts itself in the principles of composition as well. Courbet's plastic figures become flattened-out and clashing geometrical planes arranged in accordance with Cubist strategy. The continuity of surfaces is broken into conflicting compartments. The natural perspective of a single view is replaced by the scientific simultaneity of a multiple view. The opposition between here and there, behind and before, now, earlier and later, mind and body, body and dress, dress and grass, human and non-human, living and dead, subject and object is relativized into a rich, restless and decorative tapestry-like pattern in which fingers have the shapes of leaves, fringes of luminous waves are personified into living figures; and geometrical patterns and sections, cells and compartments, illuminated and dark areas alternate and multiply in the spatial rhythm of an imposed order. The ornamental tendency inherent in Picasso's version of the *Demoiselles* is aptly characterized by Wilhelm Boeck's and Jaime Sabartés' *Picasso:*

> The figures seem largely dissolved into coloured line and surface ornament, so that only isolated features —heads, hands, shoes—are recognizable. The other realistic elements are enveloped in a mysterious veil of forms; their significance is systematically denied, as Islamic art had done for a thousand years. The affinity between Andalusian and Moslem art—demonstrable also in Picasso's earlier periods—is seldom disclosed as clearly as it is in this painting. The mysterious transformation of nature in *Demoiselles* springs from the same roots as the Spaniard's passion for *peinture écrite,* an expressive pictorial script without representational content.[14]

Even if this is no more than a tendency, and the representational quality of Picasso's painting cannot be denied, the direction of the stream is unmistakable.

The predominance of line in this caricature and in caricatures in general is not fortuitous: even in everyday life lines and outlines mark, separate and determine visual phenomena. In a caricature, visual demarcation develops into intellectual discrimination and critical judgment so indispensable for the fixation of a contrast of comic incongruence. This explains why caricatures are so often drawn, and even if they are painted, the picture is usually patterned by the organizing force of the line. While however, in an occasional caricature lines, as a rule, underline, even through exaggeration and distortion, some visible features of the phenomenon, in a universal caricature they frequently disintegrate and reorganize the sight.[15]

The colouring of Courbet's and Picasso's paintings is also markedly different. Courbet's natural, local colours are superseded by a rich, dense and decorative colour-scheme. The impression of feminine nakedness, the modelling power of various shades of flesh-coloured brownish and pinkish yellows, so obvious in the girls' faces, arms, necks and décolletages, are lost; instead a ghastly bright white is used, which forms a pattern and is rhythmically repeated on the curving and angular planes and decorative patches of the sleeping girl's fingers, hands, arms, left profile, dress, breast and feet, as well as on her companion's wing-like hat, horse-like face (right profile),[16] schematized bouquet, bent foot, the slit-like lines of the water, and even the head, arm and part of the belly of the cricket-like figure Picasso reads into the girls' bag and also uses as the personified equivalent of a patch of bright water seen through the leaves.

The gently breathing blue expanse of water, heightened by pearly reflexes and reinforced by the blue vista of the sky in the Courbet is replaced by a configuration of toned-down yellows, lending the water the texture of timber, and also cropping up on the contour of the musing girl's left face and wrist, on the sleeping girl's left profile as well as on the belly, back and legs of the cricket-like figure and its counterpart at the upper right corner of the Picasso. The blue of the Seine and the sky, however, returns in the colour of the dress and right profile of Picasso's sleeping girl. The greyish light blue heightened and refined by touches of transparent white in the dress of Courbet's girl becomes a definitely darker, enamel-like, sharp mid-blue in Picasso's painting. In Courbet's original, the dreaming girl's dress is pliant, in Picasso's translation it is brittle. In the Courbet the contiguous coloured surfaces (of white and yellowish gray bordered by brownish red) are mild, soft and tender, and caress, as it were, the girl; in the Picasso the corresponding blues, blacks and whites are in a discordant counterpoint, create a strong contrast, and visibly contribute to the breaking up of the figure into a geometrical arabesque, the inner rhythm of which reintegrates the disintegrated elements into a decorative composition. The same applies to the yellow- and black-striped glowing red dress of the musing girl, who in Courbet wears a vieux-rose dress; or to the contrasted white and brown profiles of Picasso's girl, the colour of whose shaded brown face sounds a deep-toned visual rhyme with the various browns of the boat, the tree trunks, some Negro masks or the faces of some of the *Demoiselles d'Avignon.*

Even nature is unnatural in the Picasso. By substantially reducing the height of Courbet's picture, the sheltering green foliage of the three trees has been essentially removed with a part of the remaining stripe painted brown.[17] Besides, the green of the grass has been made so intense, and the fallen green leaves, set against a black background (or stylized black ground), have been shaped so sharp, pointed and blade-like that the impression of idyllic relaxation and refreshment in nature, so characteristc of Courbet's version, is obviously and deliberately dispelled.

Thus the colour-scheme of Picasso's painting functions in the same way as its structural pattern does: both ironically relativize, dismember and reasemble the original model with the result that a peaceful human scene is transformed into a geometrically conceived and restlessly vibrating decorative pattern, in which subjective, human qualities are subordinated to objective, factual properties. The human being with his subjective fancies becomes a fanciful frieze.

Are Courbet's demoiselles mere commodities, objects of pleasure? So Picasso makes them part of a reified, "objective" network. Are they distorted human beings? So Picasso distorts their very physical appearance. Do they wish to return to nature? So Picasso endows them with animal characteristics. Are they pleasingly colourful and enticingly decorative? So Picasso reduces them to a level where they are hardly more than motifs of a many-coloured, ornamental pattern which by arranging actualities also creates and keeps a distance from immediacy.

The irony of such a distortion, reduction, transformation and reintegration implies and involves the unreserved expression of the total predicament of human alienation which is a state of existence or form of activity deprived of the properties of human values. This is why it results in a universal type of caricature.

The pattern itself is paradoxically ambiguous; it is a destroyer and a preserver of values: it distintegrates through re-integration, recomposes through decomposition, rejects through assertion, and affirms through denial.

Picasso resorted to this kind of caricature quite frequently in his mature period as is attested by his *Women at the*

Fountain, after Poussin's Eliezer and Rebecca (1921), *Bacchanal, after Poussin's The Triumph of Pan* (1944),[18] *David and Bathsheba, after Cranach the Elder* (1947-8), *Venus and Cupid, after Cranach the Elder* (1949), *Portrait of a Painter, after El Greco* (1950), *The Face of Peace, after Courbet's Lady with Gull* (1950), the series *Women of Algiers, after Delacroix* (1954-5), *Bust of a Woman, after Cranach the Younger* (1958), or the two witty sequences *Las Meninas, after Velázouez* (1957-8), and *The Luncheon on the Grass, after Manet* (1962).[19]

The depiction of acrobats, animals, social, psychological and sexual outcasts, the atmospheric use of symbolic blue and rose colouring, the methods of analytic and synthetic Cubism, the adoption of a decorative network and the creation of universal caricatures are but various aspects and degrees (thematic and formal articulations) of a concentrated and converging endeavour to find an appropriate medium through which Picasso's experience of the modern world can be conveyed and patterned.

III

By the time of World War I, James Joyce's view of the world had also been characterized by the experience of relativity. His contemporaries' accounts of him and the findings of critics and literary historians all bear out his disorientation and scepticism. In a conversation with Padraic Colum, Joyce said: "It would be a great impertinence for me to think that I could tell the world what to believe."[20] Shortly after the outbreak of the war, he declared:

> My political faith can be expressed in a word: Monarchies, constitutional or unconstitutional, disgust me. Kings are mountebanks. Republics are slippers for everyone's feet. Temporal power is gone and good riddance. What else is left? Can we hope for monarchy by divine right? Do you believe in the Sun of the Future?[21]

To Georges Borach, Joyce admitted to being against every state, because "The state is concentric, man is eccentric."[22]

Joyce's concept of the universal loss of values led to his particular brand of universal caricature. *Ulysses*, seen from this

point of view, is an ingenious eccentric's sense of the senseless-
ness of the human condition. The network of symbolic cross-
references between Homer's *Odyssey* and Joyce's *Ulysses* is a
constant source of caricature. Awakening to their new, humdrum, petty bourgeois lives are the hero Odysseus in the spine-
less Bloom, the devoted family man Telemachus in Dedalus
who breaks away from home, the faithful Penelope in the
multiple adulteress Molly, the enchanting Nausicaa in the
excitable little Gerty MacDowell who displays her charms, and
the bewitching Circe in the brothel-keeper Bella Cohen.[23]

The point, however, is that this kind of caricature is
double-edged. On the one hand, in Joyce's Homeric parallels
every aspect of the ideals of the harmonic, heroic world in
the *Odyssey* appears outdated and comical. On the other
hand, the *Odyssey,* thanks to its symbolic and structural
contribution to the microcosm of *Ulysses,* is a heroic version
of a petty world whose triviality it makes more prominent
and so more ridiculous. The corresponding figures render
themselves mutually ridiculous. This double incongruity,
however, does not ultimately express any particular unambiguous value judgment.[24] Ideals are relative, irony is
universal.

A dual irony inherent both in the treatment of a Classical
framework and of its contemporary application is also typical
of much of Picasso's work, such as his *Bathers* (1921), *Women
at the Fountain after Poussin's Eliezer and Rebecca* (1921),
Model and Surrealist Sculpture (1933), *Bacchanal, after Poussin's
The Trimph of Pan* (1944), *Antibes* (1946), *Triptych* (1946),
Combat of Centaurs (1946), *Two Stories: The Centaur Picador,
The Twilight of a Faun* (1947), *The Judgment of Paris* (1951),
Faun and Goat (1959), *Homage to Bacchus* (1960), or *Three
Masked Figures and Sphinx* (1965). A similarly Janus-faced
irony can be observed in the relationship of the pattern applied
and the thing or person patterned in his witty *Student with a
Pipe* (1913), *The Violin* (1913), *Harlequin* (1915), *Reclining
Woman* (1915), *The Three Musicians* (1921), *Seated Bather*
(1929), *Monument: Woman's Head* (1929), *Girls with a Toy
Boat* (1937), *Meanad* (1946), *Nursing Mother* (1952), *The
Coiffure* (1954), *Las Menians, after Velázquez* (1957-8), and
even in Juan Gris' Cubist *Portrait of Picasso* (1911-2).[25]

Joyce's caricaturistic achievement in *Ulysses* reaches its
climax in the pastiches and parodies of episode 14 ("The Oxen

of the Sun").[26]   A case in point is the passage describing the birth of Mrs. (Mina) Purefoy's child in the style of Charles Dickens.[27] "Meanwhile the skill and patience of the physician had brought about a happy *accouchement*." The skill of the physician, Dr. Dixon, was that of a junior surgeon; his patience was certainly in proportion to his professional skill: Mrs. Purefoy had been in labour for days, and the student doctor shared his time between his patient and his drinking pals. Nonetheless, the very first sentence of Joyce's caricature radiates the mood of Dickensian propriety, and by the choice of the italicized French term *"accouchement"* it precludes any possibility of even a linguistic impropriety—in true Victorian fashion. "It had been a weary weary while both for patient and doctor—just as it had been "a weary weary while" for Doady to endure the period of Dora's fatal illness in Chapter LIII of *David Copperfield*.[28] "All that surgical skill could do." or, to put it more correctly, all that a bibulous doctor's skill could do in 1904 "was done and the brave woman had manfully helped. She had. She had fought the good fight and now she was very very happy." The semantic incongruity of the brave *woman*'s *man*ful help is a satirical exposition and exposure of mild Dickensian humour (of the "I am so glad, yet so sorry" brand) in the form of a Joycean paradox. The cumulative effect of the insistence of "She had" shows ironically how anxious Dickens is to make a point. Moreover, since "She had" does not only repeat the message of the previous sentence, but inevitably also makes the first two words of the following sentence ("*She had* fought the good fight") a literal repetition, it creates the mocking impression that Dickens is stammering. It is all the more funny because what he is straining for with the repetition is only the somewhat ponderous statement of a commonplace ("She had *fought the good fight*") which is only accentuated by the stereotype of yet another repetition: "and now she was very very happy." Dickens' Dora, too, was "very happy, very," and wanted "very, very much" to see Agnes. The narrator in *David Copperfield* often states commonplaces: "I . . . feel the truth that trifles make the sum of life." He also has an inclination to use set phrases such as "the sea of my remembrance" or "that rain of tears."

In the next sentence of Joyce's parody happiness, gratitude and even the husband soon assume universal proportions:

> Those who have passed on, who have gone before, are
> happy too as they gaze down and smile upon the touching
> scene. Reverently look at her as she reclines there with
> the motherlight in her eyes, that longing hunger for
> baby fingers (a pretty sight it is to see), in the first bloom
> of her new motherhood, breathing a silent prayer of
> thanksgiving to One above, the Universal Husband.

The self-congratulating epithet of "the *touching* scene," the
humorous quality of the author patting his own shoulder in
the superfluously verbose comment of "a pretty sight it is
to see" (ridiculing Dickensian claims like "I have bethought
me of all that gracious and compassionate history"), the somewhat garrulous doubling of the clause expressing departure,
the earlier coupling of "weary weary" and "very very" as well
as the moving sweetness of the maternal scene justify Stuart
Gilbert's observation: "There is a pretty-pretty picture of the
mother and babe, as Dickens might have written it."[29] The
sham riddle of "One above" immediately solved in "the Universal Husband" also has a veritable Dickensian touch.

By way of a characteristically intimate and homely
association, the image of the omnipresent Universal Husband
is shifted into the figure of the actual husband, the conscien-
tious if aging second accountant of the Ulster bank, now
lamentably absent:

> And as her loving eyes behold her babe she wishes only
> one blessing more, to have her dear Doady there with her
> to share her joy, to lay in his arms that smite of God's
> clay, the fruit of their lawful embraces. He is older now
> (you and I may whisper it) and a trifle stooped in the
> shoulders yet in the whirligig of years a grave dignity
> has come to the conscientious second accountant of
> the Ulster bank, College Green branch. O Doady, loved
> one of old, faithful lifemate now, it will never be again,
> that faroff time of the roses! With the old shake of her
> pretty head she recalls those days. God, how beautiful
> now across the mist of years!

Theodore Purefoy repeatedly called in his Dickensian petname
Doady, the Victorian emphasis on, and the Joycean assurance
of, the lawful embraces of the faithful lifemate, the sentimental

clichés of "that mite of God's clay," "the whirligig of years,"
"the mist of years," Mina's emotional reminiscences of "that
faroff time of the roses," and her rhetorically balanced, touched
antithesis figuring Doady, "loved one of old, faithful lifemate
now," also recalling the attitude, style and the very subtitle
("Another Retrospect") of Chapter LIII of *David Copperfield,*
all combine in "a burlesque of Dickensian sentiment."[30]   The
burlesque is all the more effective since sublime and sentimental qualifications are contrasted with minutely practical
and technical details: Mr. Theodore Purefoy's "grave dignity"
is the property of Mina's beloved Doady, i.e. the *second*
accountant of the Ulster bank, *College Green branch*.   In this
way, the lower middle class character of the family idyll is
brought home.   It is even further strengthened by the evidence
of snobbery attested by the names of some of the nine Purefoy
children: "darling little Bobsy (called after our famous hero of
the South African war, lord Bobs of Waterford and Candahar)"
and Mortimer Edward, i.e. young hopeful, the new-born baby
to be named "after the influential third cousin of Mr. Purefoy
in the Treasury Remembrancer's office, Dublin Castle."   J. S.
Atherton rightly sees in this a parody of "Dicken's combination
of humour with social criticism."[31]

The Dickensian flavour of Joyce's witty imitation is increased by the use of *telling detail* ("that longing hunger for
baby fingers,"[32] "the old shake" of Mina's "pretty head"
with which she recalls old days, or "the true Purefoy nose"
of the baby), *tableau-like scenes* rounding off details in a
graphically portrayed Hegelian objective totality (mother and
child in a concrete setting), an *anthropomorphic representation*
(objects mediate human relations, even Time is humanized
and personified into jovial and benign father Cronion), and
a *synthesizing quality* (the passage gives a comically contracted
but even so a memorably self-contained picture of the past,
present and future of the Purefoy family).[33]

Joyce finishes his Dickens caricature assuming the attitude
of the omniscient Victorian novelist who, after involving his
audience in a confidential conspiracy ("you and I may whisper
it"), finally even addresses his own heroine and hero:

> No, let no sigh break from that bosom, dear gentle Mina.
> And Doady, knock the ashes from your pipe, the seasoned
> briar you still fancy when the curfew rings for you (may it

> be the distant day!) and dout the light whereby you read
> in the Sacred Book for the oil too has run low and so with
> a tranquil heart to bed, to rest. He knows and will call in
> His own good time. You too have fought the good fight
> and played loyally your man's part. Sir, to you my hand.
> Well done, thou good and faithful servant!

Thus at the pious coda[34] and harmonious culmination of his ingenious mockery, Joyce shows Dickens not only pathetically moving but also genuinely moved. . .

It may be worth noting that Chapter LIII of *David Copperfield* also ends with the imminent death of Dora and the actual decease of Jip, her faithful dog, whose growing old is no less focused by Dickens than Doady Purefoy's is by Joyce. The parodistic parallel between the aging dog and the aging husband seems later to be reinforced by Theodore Purefoy being urged with ironical appreciation to "Toil on, labour like a very bandog."[35]

Joyce's attitude to Diekens is comparable to Picasso's relation to Courbet.

1) Both Joyce and Picasso follow their original models with meticulous care. Picasso traces Courbet's *Young Ladies of the Banks of the Seine* from point to point, from detail to detail; even the shoes of the demoiselles are repainted with considerable and, for some, surprising attention. Joyce also imitates the characteristic traits of Dickens' manner of writing in complete factual and stylistic accuracy.

2) Imitation in both cases is a comic reinterpretation through playful mockery and witty exaggeration done in the spirit of a universal caricature.

3) The target of the irony both in Picasso's caricature of Courbet and in Joyce's parody of Dickens is not simply a particular work or life-work but the method of nineteenth-century realism in general. Hence the ironical relativization of the creation of types, of the representation of the particular and the general in a life-like, graphic unity, and of the artist's and author's dual ability of identification and criticism.

4) Neither Picasso's comic reinterpretation of Courbet, nor Joyce's ironical re-creation of Dickens stands in isolation. Picasso's caricatures of Cranach the Elder, Cranach the Younger, El Greco, Velázquez, Poussin, Delacroix and Manet are matched by Joyce's parodies of ancient incantations, Latinized mediaeval

English prose, Old English alliterative style, *Everyman*, Mande-
ville, Malory, Browne, Bunyan, Pepys, Evelyn, Defoe, Swift,
Addison, Steele, Sterne, Goldsmith, Burke, Gibbon, Walpole,
Lamb, de Quincey, Landor, Ruskin, Carlyle, and vulgar modern
slang.

From the end of the nineteenth century artistic caricature
has been much more than a mere mockery. The fact that the
artist is willing and able to adopt and adapt the most diverse
forms and to turn them, as it were, inside out also expresses the
relativization of forms, norms and social experiences. Besides
the testimony of Picasso and Joyce, the pastiches of Proust on
Balzac, Flaubert, Sainte-Beuve, Gautier, Faguet, Régnier,
Michelet, Renan and Saint Simon; or the literary caricatures
of Karinthy on novelists like Defoe, Dickens, Zola, Verne,
Wilde, Wells, Lewis, on dramatists like Shakespeare, Rostand,
Ibsen, Shaw, Pirandello and O'Neill as well as on a number
of Hungarian poets, novelists and playwrights also attest to a
sense of relativity and a quest for values.[36]

A similar tendency is manifested in Picasso's and Joyce's
stylistic versatility: their ability to use a number of stylistic
trends not only in succession but also in the same period or—in
the case of *Ulysses*—even in the same work. The simultaneous
presence and alternation in *Ulysses* of Naturalism, Impressionism,
Symbolism, Expressionism, Surrealism and even a linguistic
equivalent of Cubism have the consequence that a given
utterence in a particular stylistic trend often appears, as it were,
in quotation marks expressing the relativistic changeability of
the underlying attitude. Can one unconditionally admire the
impressionistic colour of the sea if it is both "bluesilver" and
"snotgreen?"[37]

5) Another corollary of parodistic and stylistic many-
sidedness is multiple perspective. Courbet still uses a single
perspective in depicting his *Young Ladies of the Banks of the
Seine;* the view unfolds as it is seen from the position of the
painter. The emphasis on the reliability of his individual
observation results in a unified vision, as had been the case
since the Renaissance. With Cézanne the absolute trustworthi-
ness of a single viewpoint becomes relativized. Picasso in his
reinterpretation of Courbet's *Young Ladies* applies a multiple
perspective, as the spreading out on one plane of the four profiles
of the two girls indicates. The feminine becomes contrasted
with the female, the face with the mask. The lateral view of a

huge shoe is of an equal importance with the side view of a large face.

Similarly, Dickens (and Balzac or Mark Twain) still view the world with the single sight of the omniscient author. With Henry James or Marcel Proust the novelists's unified vision becomes weakened and the protagonists' specific angles gain in importance. Joyce in *Ulysses* adopts a multiple perspective. In his Dickens-caricature he ridicules the narrator's omniscience. In Mrs. Purefoy's eyes Doady possesses grave dignity, has fought the good fight, and played loyally his man's part. In the revelling students' view, he is "the remarkablest progenitor" who did "charge to cover like the transpontine bison."[38] Mrs. Purefoy herself becomes from a meek mother a copulating cow. The idyllic turns vulgar. Different perspectives, even contradictory aspects are flattened out and levelled on the plane of universal caricature.

6) Picasso's geometrical schemes are matched by Joyce's structural patterns.[39] As early as 1923, T. S. Eliot recognized the importance of a highly patterned organization in *Ulysses*. With the clairvoyance and congeniality of the author of *The Waste Land,* he even pointed out the basis of compositional scaffolding in the artist's view of the world:

> I hold this book to be the most important expression the present age has found; it is a book to which we are all indebted, and from which none of us can escape. . . . In using the myth, in manipulating a continuous parallel between contemporaneity and antiquity, Mr. Joyce is pursuing a method which others must pursue after him. They will not be imitators, any more than the scientist who uses the discoveries of an Einstein in pursuing his own, independent, further investigations. It is simply a way of controlling, of ordering, of giving a shape and a significance to the immense panorama of futility and anarchy which is contemporary history. . . . Instead of narrative method, we may now use the mythical method. It is . . . a step toward making the modern world possible for art . . . And only those who have won their own discipline in secret and without aid, in a world which offers very little assistance to that end, can be of any use in furthering this advance.[40]

Joyce, as well as Picasso, certainly belong to this category. The way in which Joyce put the pattern to comic application and caricaturistic use in The Oxen of the Sun episode of *Ulysses* appears clearly in his letter written to Frank Budgen on 13 March, 1920:

> Am working hard at *Oxen of the Sun,* the idea being the crime committed against fecundity by sterilizing the act of coition. Scene: Lying-in-hospital. Technique: a ninepart episode without divisions introduced by a Sallustian-Tacitean prelude (the unfertilized ovum), then by way of earliest English alliterative and mono-syllabic and Anglo-Saxon . . . then by way of Mande-ville . . . then Malory's *Morte d'Arthur* . . . then a passage solemn, as of Milton, Taylor, Hooker, followed by a Latin-gossipy bit, style of Burton/Browne, then a passage Bunyanesque . . . After a diary-style bit Pepys-Evelyn . . . and so on through Defoe-Swift and Steele-Addison-Sterne and Landor-Pater-Newman until it ends in a frightful jumble of pidgen-English, nigger English, Cock-ney, Irish, Bowery slang and broken doggerel. This procession is also linked back at each part subtly with some foregoing episode of the day and, besides this, with the natural stages of development in the embryo and the periods of faunal evolution in general. The double-thudding Anglo-Saxon motive recurs from time to time . . . to give the sense of the hoofs of oxen. Bloom is the spermatozoon, the hospital the womb, the nurse the ovum, Stephen the embryo.[41]

All these schemes have been thoroughly elaborated, have a comic application, and the stylistic parodies are brilliant. Nevertheless, this kind of patterning is no less external to the human scene (the birth of Mrs. Purefoy's child) than Picasso's ornamental design is in his comic re-creation of Courbet's *Demoiselles.*

Even the most innocent-looking elements of Joyce's parody on Dickens (itself part of a scheme) are made parts of a multiple pattern. When Mrs. Purefoy imagines that along with her newborn baby all her nine children surround her bedside, the enumeration of Charley, Mary Alice, Frederick Albert, Mamy, Budgy (Victoria Frances), Tom, Violet Constance Louisa, darling little Bobsy and Mortimer Edward sets the scene for an intimate Dickensian family reunion.

The number nine, however, also has a great many structural connotations. The nine months of embryonic development and the appropriate nine biological stages are carefully thrown into relief.[42] The episode consists of nine parts. Its introductory section displays a nine-unit division. "The three paragraphs, each with a threefold repetition, form a verbal equivalent for Homer's island of Trinacria, literally, 'Three headlands' or, as it is described in Lamb's *Adventures of Ulysses*, 'having three promontories jutting into the sea.' "[43] "By its ninefold pattern," Harry Blamires adds, "this opening constitutes one more Angelus-like annunciation."[44] When in her letter of June 30, 1920, Harriet Shaw Weaver suggests that *The Oxen of the Sun* episode might also have been called *Hades* because its reading is like being taken the rounds of hell, Joyce seems to be interested in the idea to the point of interpreting it: "Do you mean that the *Oxen of the Sun* episode resembles *Hades* because the nine circles of development (enclosed between the headpiece and tailpiece of opposite chaos) seem to you to be peopled by extinct beings?"[45] Let us add to this that—with Dr. Dixon having left the assembled drinkers—there happen to be nine ribald revellers in the company when the child is born. It is no less noteworthy that when the nurse, an old acquaintance of Mr. Bloom, opens the door of the Lying-in Hospital in Holles Street, Dublin, to admit Mr. Bloom, we can read the remark: "On her stow he ere was living with dear wife and lovesome daughter that then over land and seafloor nine year had long outwandered."[46] Theme and treatment are both intellectually, even speculatively interrelated and ingeniously, even cosmically incongruous.

The factual network of all these references constitutes a Constructivist scheme which rearranges the Dickensian family idyll with no less thoroughgoing irony than Picasso's cubistically conceived decorative design does Courbet's natural idyll. Determinism is heavy; caricature is universal.[47]

IV

Benjamin Britten's many-faceted oeuvre is also characterized by a marked bent for the humorous, the witty, and sometimes even the caricaturistic.

An infant prodigy at the age of five, and a prolific composer throughout his life, he created a long sequence of works in which the humorous sparks of his occasional wit flash. The first of his *Three Two-part Songs* (1932) is ingeniously grotesque. The last movement of his string quartet *Alla Quartetto Seriose* first played in 1933 is a musical joke (*Alla Burlesca*). His symphonic cycle *Our Hunting Fathers* (1936) preserved the satirical touches of Auden's text. So did his sequence of five songs *On This Island* (1937) and his *Three Cabaret Songs* (1938) setting Auden's poems to music. *The Seven Ages of Men* (1938) and *Old Spain* (1938), Britten's incidental music to Montagu Slater's one-acters in verse were presented as a puppet show in London. His *Canadian Carnival* (1939) offers light and merry symphonic entertainment matching the theme of the orchestral composition. His *Introduction and Rondo alla Burlesca* (1940) suggests the tone and intention of the piece in its very title. In the cantata *Rejoice in the Lamb* (1943) the Lord is glorified by all nations and creatures—with a pet cat and a mouse included. Part II, No. 3 of his *Spring Symphony* (1949) intones ironical inflections.[48] In the biblical opera *Noye's Fludde* (1957) Noah's wife is a thoroughly comical figure; the slap she gives Noah leads to the outbreak of a storm, and the sounds of the raindrops are rendered by cups hit with wooden spoons. *Cantata Academica—Carmen Basiliense* (1959) is liberally sprinkled with humorous touches. *The Golden Vanity* (1966) is a funny vaudeville. At the merry beginning of Britten's serious operatic parable, *The Burning Fiery Furnace* (1966) two singers and a minstrel entertain the public in a joking spirit.

With its social satire and genuine mockery, Britten's version of *The Beggar's Opera* (1948) is a musical manifestation of a trend caricature, worthy of the spirit of its model, John Gay's musical play of 1728.

The most refined expressions of Britten's comic vein and humorous wit are his approximations or uses of the category of universal caricature: *The Young Person's Guide to the Orchestra* subtitled *Variations and Fugue on a Theme of Purcell* (1946), the comic opera *Albert Herring* (1947) and the parodistic *opera buffa* section of *A Midsummer Night's Dream* (1960).

Originally written for the educational film *Instruments of the Orchestra*, Britten's *The Young Person's Guide to the*

Orchestra is an autonomous and ingenious composition. Among compounds "of vaudeville, musical midway, and didactic consideration known as the 'children's concert,' "[49] Britten's work is of absolute musical value in its own right; it is most effective even without Eric Crozier's inserted commentaries presenting the whole, the sections and the instruments of the orchestra. Its independence and coherence are created by a playfully ironical mood realized in a four-part structure.

The first structural unit contains six thematic statements. Theme A presents Purcell's eloquent and animated tune from *Abdelazer, or The Moor's Revenge* (1695) sounded by the entire orchestra. Themes B, C, D, and E re-state the original melody as played by the four main sections, the woodwind, the brass, the string and the percussion groups. The re-statements are also reinterpretations: when Purcell's sonorous tunes and harmonious chords are replaced by, and reduced to, the bursting beats of the timpani, the bass drum, the tambourine, the side drum, the cymbal and the triangle, the resulting skeletal effect is weirdly grotesque. Theme F brings back Purcell's original melody by the whole orchestra.

The second structural unit offers thirteen variations (A-M) focusing individual instruments of the four main orchestral sections in the order of the woodwind, the strings, the brass and the percussion. In this analytical block of the composition ironic touches are achieved in a number of ways.

Each variation highlights a specific technical property of a particular musical instrument and at the same time constitutes an independent phase in the total musical process. The two aspects are inseparably interrelated and even reinforced by a thirteen-fold occurrence. The artistic outcome is the impression of automatism imposed on life: Bergson's definition of the comic.[50] The repeated structural configurations in Picasso's remodelling of Courbet's *Young Ladies,* and the process of birth articulated in the technically elaborate parodistic stages of the development of English prose in *Ulysses* also possess these two facets.

Most of the variations tend to convey wittily and exaggerate humorously some human qualities none of which are congruous with the mood of Purcell's theme which they vary. The flutes are impish, the oboes brooding, the violins over-zealous in executing their character variations *alla polacca,* the harp is gracefully vain and occasionally self-complacent, and the trombones, as Imogen Holst aptly observes, "extract every ounce of enjoyment from the flavour of parody in the sustained *marcato* of their pompous progress."[51] Even the words of the score mark the intention of personification: the harp is called the strings' "cousin," the piccolo the flute's "shrill little brother" and the double-basses are characterized as "the grandfathers of the String family, with heavy, grumbling voices;" the oboes "have a gentle, plaintive quality" and the clarinets "are very agile."[52]

The degree of instrumental personification not infrequently reaches the level of the imitation of singing. The phenomenon goes far beyond the singable quality of any beautiful tune. Not only the violins sing with enthusiasm, the violas with feeling, and the cellos "with splendid richness and warmth,"[53] but also the clarinets sing with a far-fetched, swaying gaiety, the bassoons with a grimly pompous, martially morose and belatedly hurt desire, the double-basses with a clumsy, awkward yearning, and even the timpani, yes, the timpani make an honourable, if unsuccessful effort, to sing, being repeatedly and parodistically encouraged by the preparatory insistence and urging accompaniment of the violins and violas which might very well introduce a grand operatic aria by Verdi or Rossini. (The aria character of an orchestral piece is also very obvious in the fourth variant of Britten's early *Variations on a Theme of Frank Pridge* (1937). Composed "with a wonderful sense of parody," this *Aria Italiana* is "snide Rossini.")[54] The song-like quality of these instrumental parts amounts to a playfully parodistic vocalization of the orchestra. The broader significance of the phenomenon is finely illuminated by Thomas Mann. In *Doctor Faustus*, characterizing his Schoenbergian composer-protagonist's oratorio "Apocalypsis cum figuris," Mann remarks: "Chorus and orchestra are here not clearly separated from each other as symbols of the human and the material world; they merge into each other, the chorus is 'instrumentalized,' the orchestra, as it were, 'vocalized,' to that degree and to that end that the boundary between man and thing seems shifted. . ."[55] Such a shift, a reflection of, or a reaction against, reification and alienation, is also typical of Picasso's and Joyce's creative procedures in which subjectivity is reified and objectivity is subjectivized.

Britten's *Purcell Variations* are also characterized by an exceptionally strong visual quality which in its turn also becomes one of the sources of merry comedy. Its film version, the *Instruments of the Orchestra* "oddly contrives to mirror the *visual* aspect of each instrument as well as its technical personality. How appropriate, for instance, is the matching of the mighty double-basses with their elephantine phrases ...,"[56] William Mann notes. Let it be added that the "elephantine phrases of the double-basses evoke the image of something mighty and clumsy even without seeing the huge instruments Similarly, the threefold cracking of the whip projects the picture of a violent dismissal by its very sound. It is little wonder that the work has attracted choreographers more than once, or that Britten's attention so often turned to the genre of the opera.

The third structural unit constitutes a swift and merry pandemonium through a thirteen-entry, enormous fugue bringing back all the instruments one by one in the order of their solo variations (A-M).

The fourth unit raises further hell by combining the fugue with Purcell's original theme. Sounded by the brazen blare of the horns, trumpets and trombones, and supported by the tuba and the double-basses, the Purcell theme with its grand, magnificent *maestoso* augmentation, solemn, metrically balanced slow procession, and deep, mighty register is melodious and harmonious tradition incarnate. Played by the rest of the orchestra, and punctured by the urchin-like whistle of the piccolo, the insolent shrieks of the flutes, and the merry mockery of the violins, Britten's fugue with its glowing and glaring construction,[57] *allegro molto* cavalcade, rhythmically labyrinthine syncopation and whirling, sparkling high register is impish, impertinent and impious innovation incarnate.

The total impact of this ingenious culmination is the kind of double-edged irony which also characterizes the relationship between Courbet's *Young Ladies of the Banks of the Seine* and Picasso's parodistic reinterpretation of the picture; or Chapter LIII of Dicken's *David Copperfield* and Joyce's parody of the Dickensian vein in *Ulysses*. In all three cases, a mutual relativization and ironization takes place in the pattern of universal caricature.[58]

Notes

[1] For the dating and discussion of these poems see Richard Ellmann, *James Joyce* (New York: Oxford University Press, 1959), pp. 31, 158, 167, 171, 346-9, 408, 409, 432, 433, 436-8, 583, 667. Fine and funny occasional caricatures on Joyce and Bloom can be found in Hugh Kenner's *The Stoic Comedians: Flaubert, Joyce and Beckett* (Berkeley, Los Angeles, London: University of Calidornia Press, 1974), pp. 33, 51, 61.

[2] A comparison of Picasso's traditionally conceived 1957 lithograph, Portrait of *D. H. Kahnweiler* (his dealer) with the 1910 Cubist painting, *Portrait of Monsieur Kahnweiler* clearly shows this.

[3] Karl Marx, *Critique of Hegel's 'Philosophy of Right'.* Translated from the German by Annette Jolin and Joseph O'Malley (Cambridge: Cambridge University Press, 1970), p. 134.

[4] Cf. John Berger, *The Success and Failure of Picasso* (Harmondsworth: Penguin Books, 1965), pp. 66-67, 69.

[5] Quoted in agreement and interpreted ingeniously in John Berger's *The Success and Failure of Picasso*, pp. 52-5. Cf. Pierre Daix, *Picasso* (London: Thames and Hudson, 1965), p. 85: "Apollinaire, Gleizes and Metzinger were all in agreement that 'Courbet is the father of the new painters'."

[6] Berger, p. 52.

[7] Ibid., p. 55.

[8] Pierre Cabanne, *Le siècle de Picasso* (Paris: Éditions Denoël, 1975), Vol. II, pp. 192-3.

[9] The size of Courbet's painting is 168 x 202 cms; that of Picasso's picture is 100.5 x 201 cms.

[10] Cf. Jack Lindsay, *Gustave Courbet: His Life and Art* (Somerset: Adams and Dart, 1973), p. 148.

[11] Ibid.

[12] Cf. Gustave Courbet's *Women Asleep* (1862) remodelled in 1955 by Bernard Buffet emphasizing age, crudeness and geometry.

[13] Cf. Franz Meyer, "Les Demoiselles des bords de la Seine," nach Courbet in Agathe Straumann—Klaus Hess (eds.), *Picasso*, aus dem Museum of Modern Art, New York, and Schweizer Sammlungen (Basel: Kunstmuseum Basel, 1976), p. 150.

[14] Wilhelm Boeck—Jaime Sabartés, *Picasso* (London: Thames and

Hudson, 1961), p. 301. Cf. E. de Lorey, "Picasso et l'orient musulman," *Gazette des Beaux-Arts*, LXXIV, 2 (1932), 299-314.

[15] A comparison of Picasso's *Travesty of Manet's Olympia* (1901) with his series *The Luncheon on the Grass, after Manet* (1962) shows such a difference between the styles of an occasional and a universal caricature.

[16] The figure of the horse is one of the recurring symbolic leitmotifs of Picasso's oeuvre, usually standing for a victim and often associated with women.

[17] Cf. Sir Roland Penrose and Dr. John Golding (eds.) *Picasso 1881-1973* (London: Paul Elek Ltd., 1973), p. 215.

[18] Executed between August 24-9, in the days of the battle and liberation of Paris, this picture, while it retains the duality of the pattern, emphasizes the element of pleasure.

[19] For different approaches to, and treatments of, these reinterpretations also compare: Frank Elgar—Robert Maillard, *Picasso* (München, Zürich: Droemersche Verlagsanstalt, 1956), p. 258. J. Sabartés, *Les Ménines* (Paris: Cercle d'Art, 1958). Frank Elgar, *Picasso*, translated from the French by Francis Scarfe (New York: Frederick A. Praeger, Publishers, 1960), p. 244. Michael Ayrton, "Einführung" to *Bild und Abbild* edited by K. E. Maison (München, Zürich: Droemersche Verlagsanstalt, 1960), p. 29, cf. p. 200. Pablo Picasso, *Les Dejeuners*, texte de Douglas Cooper (Paris: Editions Cercle d'Art, 1962). John Berger, *The Success and Failure of Picasso* (Harmondsworth: Penguin Books, 1965), pp. 96-8, 180-6. Pierre Daix, *Picasso* (London: Thames and Hudson, 1965), pp. 203-4. Jean Sutherland Boggs, "The Last Thirty Years" in Sir Roland Penrose and Dr. John Golding (eds.), *Picasso 1881-1973* (London: Paul Elek, Ltd., 1973), pp. 221, 225-6, 229. Naturally, not any kind of an imitative reinterpretation can be considered caricaturistic. Both beauty and horror exclude caricature, since the ridiculous—as already Aristotle observed—"is a certain error, and turpitude unattended with pain, and not destructive." Aristotle, *The Poetic*. Translated by Theodore Buckley, Barrett H. Clark (ed.) *European Theories of the Drama* (New York: Crown Publishers, 1965), p. 8. For this reason, at variance with John Berger's view (*The Success and Failure of Picasso*, pp. 94-5), I do not consider Picasso's 1918 portrait of *Madame Wildenstein* even a gentle caricature of Ingres' 1828 *Drawing*. Picasso's version is too beautiful to have anything to do with turpitude and a comic contrast deriving from it. On the other hand, Francis Bacon's 1953 reinterpretation of Velázquez's 1648-50 portrait of *Pope Innocent X*, though it is plunged in distorted turpitude, is too tormented with horrifying pain to be ridiculous or to allow anything like a comic distance on the part of the spectator.

[20] Padraic Colum, "A Portrait of James Joyce," *New Republic* LXVI

(May 13, 1931), 346-8.

[21] Quoted in Richard Ellmann, *James Joyce* (New York: Oxford University Press, 1959), p. 394.

[22] Georges Borach, "Conversations with James Joyce," translated by Joseph Prescott, *College English* XV (March 1954), 325-7.

[23] Cf. Marvin Magalaner and Richard M. Kain, *Joyce: The Man, The Work, The Reputation* (New York: New York University Press, 1956), pp. 271-3.

[24] Cf. David Daiches, *The Novel and the Modern World* (Chicago: The University of Chicago Press, 1939), p. 135.

[25] For some (rather meager) biographical connections between Picasso and Joyce, see Richard Ellmann, *James Joyce*, pp. 606, 627. For enlightening references to the Picasso-Joyce relationship compare: Lawrence K. Emery, "The Ulysses of Mr. James Joyce," *The Klaxon* (Winter 1923-4). Gertrude Stein, *The Autobiography of Alice B. Toklas* (New York: Harcourt, Brace, 1933), p. 260. Joseph Frank, "Spatial Form in Modern Literature," *The Sewanee Review* LIII (1945), 221-40, 433-56, 643-53. Cf. L. Moholy-Nagy, *Vision in Motion* (Chicago: Theobald, 1947), pp. 341-52. Claus Pack, "Analogies: Joyce, Picasso, Klee," *Romàn*, No. 3 (June, 1951), 264-8.

[26] Cf. M. Klein, "The Oxen of the Sun," *Here and Now* (Toronto) I, (January 1949), 28-48.

[27] James Joyce, *Ulysses* (London: The Bodley Head, 1963), pp. 550-2. Subsequent quotations from the Dickens caricature will refer to these pages.

[28] All Dickensian quotations in the analysis of Joyce's parody on Dickens are taken from Chapter LIII of *David Copperfield*. The connection between this chapter and Joyce's passage is referred to in Matthew Hodgart, *James Joyce* (London: Routledge and Kegan Paul, 1978), p. 112.

[29] Stuart Gilbert, *James Joyce's Ulysses* (Harmondsworth: Penguin Books, 1963), p. 266.

[30] Harry Blamires, *The Bloomsday Book* (London: Methuen, 1966), p. 163. Anthony Burgess calls the passage "a glorification of Purefoy the father . . . in the manner of Dickens": *Joysprick: An Introduction to the Language of James Joyce* (London: Andre Deutsch, 1973), p. 120. Cf. pp. 59-61. Appositional phrases like "loved one of old, faithful lifemate now" marking characteristic features somewhat circumstantially are also typical of Balzac's style and are ridiculed in Proust's pastiche of Balzac. Cf. Marcel Proust, *Pastiches et Mélanges* (Paris: Gallimard, 1919), pp. 11-2.

[31] J. S. Atherton, "The Oxen of the Sun" in Clive Hart and David Hayman (eds.), *James Joyce's Ulysses: Critical Essays* (Berkeley, Los Angeles, London: University of California Press, 1974), p. 332.

[32] These "baby fingers" of the Dickens parody are presumably not

unrelated to those "little fingers twining round" Doady's "hand!" in the Dickensian original, especially in view of the fact that they belonged to Dora, Doady's "child-wife."

[33] Similar qualities are ironically adumbrated in "Kopperffy David," a caricature on Dicken's *David Copperfield* in *Így írtok ti* (This is the Way You Write, Budapest: Athenaeum, 1921, II, pp. 84-6) by the Hungarian humourist Frigyes Karinthy. Karinthy, however, also emphasizes Dickens's habit of repeating certain characteristic traits of his figures, his interest in the grotesquely eccentric, and his being a British author, a feature which another British author like Joyce is less susceptible to, even if he is Irish.

[34] For Joyce's biblical parodies, see Ruth Bauerle, "A Sober Drunken Speech: Stephen's Parodies in 'The Oxen of the Sun'." *James Joyce Quarterly* V (Fall 1967), 40-5.

[35] James Joyce, *Ulysses*, p. 554. For Dickensian tones, overtones, touches and references in Joyce's "The Dead" and *Finnegans Wake*, see Matthew Hodgart's *James Joyce*, pp. 54, 140, 150, 157, 176, 177.

[36] The above remarks do not attempt to identify Joyce's, Picasso's, Proust's and Karinthy's attitudes. Joyce's stance resembled Proust's when Joyce was writing *A Portrait of the Artist as a Young Man*; Karinthy's parodies are half-way between a trend and a universal caricature. Nevertheless, the role of relativity constitutes a significant parallel. Cf. László Kardos, *Frigyes Karinthy* (Budapest: Anonymus, 1946), pp. 21-7.

[37] James Joyce, *Ulysses*, p. 45.

[38] Ibid., pp. 554-5.

[39] The phenomenon is not, of course, necessarily comic, but in Picasso's and Joyce's universal caricatures it becomes a means to convey a comic vision.

[40] T. S. Eliot, "Ulysses, Order and Myth," *The Dial* LXXV (November 1923), 480-3.

[41] Stuart Gilbert and Richard Ellmann (eds.), *Letters of James Joyce* (New York: The Viking Press, 1966) I, pp. 139-40. Although in the final text Joyce effected some changes, the letter shows clearly the basic structure of the episode.

[42] For Joyce's chart, see J. S. Atherton, "The Oxen of the Sun," *James Joyce's Ulysses*, p. 338.

[43] Ibid., p. 314.

[44] Harry Blamires, *The Bloomsday Book*, p. 153.

[45] James Joyce's letter to Harriet Shaw Weaver, August 16, 1920. *Letters* I, p. 16.

[46] James Joyce, *Ulysses*, p. 503.

[47] The fact that both Picasso and Joyce created works belonging to

the category of universal caricature, does not, of course, mean that the two artists are in every respect alike. Picasso's social commitment made it possible for him to do trend caricatures and non-ironical representational works as well. The difference is also manifested in Joyce's light and Picasso's serious treatment of the Minotaur myth in *Ulysses* (p. 538) and in pictures like *Young Girl with Minotaur* (1934-5) or *Minotauromachy* (1935), respectively. *Guernica* (1937) is unimaginable without Picasso's anti-fascism, *Dove* (1949) without his involvement in the peace movement, *Massacre in Korea* (1951) without his leftist humanism. Nevertheless, his stance and method do show significant convergences with those of Joyce. The Joycean view of history has its partial parallel with at least a period of Picasso's ideas of the same. "History," Stephen Dedalus said, "is a nightmare from which I am trying to awake." (*Ulysses*, p. 42) "There ought to be an absolute dictatorship of painters," Picasso observed, "a dictatorship of one painter—to suppress all who have betrayed us, to suppress . . . history. . . . But common sense always gets away with it. Above all let's have a revolution against that!" "They should put out the eyes of painters, as they do to goldfinches to make them sing better." (Quoted in John Berger's *The Success and Failure of Picasso*, p. 32. For Picasso's later position, see Berger, p. 177).

[48] Cf. Donald Mitchell, "The Musical Atmosphere" in Donald Mitchell and Hans Keller (eds.), *Benjamin Britten*, a Commentary on his work from a group of specialists (London: Rockliff Publishing Corporation, 1952), pp. 12-3.

[49] Arthur Cohn, *Twentieth-Century Music in Western Europe* (New York: Da Capo Press, 1972), p. 57.

[50] Henri Bergson, *Le Rire* (Paris: Ancienne Librairie Germer Ballière, 1900), pp. 30, 33.

[51] Imogen Holst, "Britten and the Young" in Donald Mitchell and Hans Keller (eds.), *Benjamin Britten*, p. 278.

[52] Benjamin Britten, *The Young Person's Guide to the Orchestra, Variations and Fugue on a Theme of Purcell*, Op. 34 (London: Boosey and Hawkes, n. d.), pp. 11, 17, 31; 20, 21.

[53] Ibid., p. 29. Cf. Peter Evans, *The Music of Benjamin Britten* (London: Dent, 1984), p. 301.

[54] Arthur Cohn, *Twentieth-Century Music In Western Europe*, p. 58. Cf. Donald Mitchell, "The Musical Atmosphere," Donald Mitchell and Hans Keller (eds.), *Benjamin Britten*, pp. 11-2. In his orchestral suites *Soirées Musicales* (1936) and *Matinées Musicales* (1941) Britten orchestrated melodies by Rossini. In his *Soirées Musicales* "except for orchestration, the Rossini originals are fundamentally untouched. Both the Swiss movement ('Tirolese') and the Spanish evocation ('Bolero') take on humorous twists . . ." (A. Cohn, p. 57).

[55]Thomas Mann, *Doctor Faustus,* Translated by H. T. Lowe-Porter, (London: Secker and Warburg, 1949), p. 375. While in Britten's *Les Illuminations for Tenor or Soprano Solo and String Orchestra* (1939), "the orchestra of strings becomes an instrumental chorus" (A. Cohn, p. 64), in his *Hymn to St. Cecilia* (1942) "especially appealing are the varied colors of the voices, to a degree imitative of instrumental timbres, plus a scherzo section that is as close to light string instrument style as a chorus can achieve." (A. Cohn, p. 66).

[56]William Mann, "The Incidental Music" in Donald Mitchell and Hans Keller (eds.), *Benjamin Britten*, p. 300.

[57]Among the various patterns he used in *Ulysses,* Joyce also adopted the organizing form and force of the fugue: the technique of episode 11 (Sirens) is *fuga per canonem.*

[58]A typological convergence is, of course, no strict identity. Britten's innovations are not so radical as Picasso's or Joyce's, or for that matter, as Schoenberg's, Berg's and Webern's. He does make use of the twelve-note system in works like *The Turn of the Screw* (1954) or partly in *A Midsummer Night's Dream* (1960), but his ties with popular and traditional music are not severed. Therefore in his universal caricatures he not infrequently tends to retain the traditional plasticity of moulding from the outside, while he ironizes it from the inside. In this his *Purcell Variations* resemble Prokofiev's *Classical Symphony* or Stravinsky's *Pulcinella.* "Parody," Donald Mitchell observes, "is one of Britten's major gifts," but his parodies show the ambiguity of emotional association and disassociation in a similar way to the attitude of a child who makes fun of his parents by imitation. (Donald Mitchell, "The Musical Atmosphere" in Donald Mitchell and Hans Keller, eds., *Benjamin Britten,* p. 11). Britten's Purcell realizations (with *Dido and Aeneas* included) bear witness to his understanding and appreciation of his great predecessor.

The outer elaboration and inner ironization of traditional forms are also conspicuous in Britten's comic opera *Albert Herring* (1947). The source of the comic effect is not simply the theme of the opera (Maupassant's short story "Le Rosier de Madame Husson" adapted by Eric Crozier) or its characterization, but also the ironization, through exaggeration and incongruity, of the generic form itself. The opera displays sola aria, duet, trio, quartet, even nonet, indeed all the paraphernalia of the traditional opera in such a far-fetched manner that the effect is uproariously comical. In Act II, Scene 1, ensemble recitatives are contrapuntally interwoven. When Sid, the butcher's assistant pours rum into Albert's lemonade, the latter's awakening erotic interest is rendered by a parodistic quotation of the potion chord from Wagner's *Tristan.* Caricature is coupled with self-caricature: when Police Superintendent Budd is talking about rape, a motif is heard from Britten's opera *The Rape of*

Lucretia (1946). Simple words (like "We paid three and six" in Act III)
are rendered by an elaborate musical structure. Cf. Hans Keller, *The Rape
of Lucretia, Albert Herring* (London: Boosey and Hawkes, 1947), pp. 21,
27, 28, 32. Eric Walter White, *Benjamin Britten: His Life and Operas*
(London: Faber and Faber, 1948, Part II, Ch. 4). Donald Mitchell, "The
Musical Atmosphere" in Donald Mitchell and Hans Keller, *Benjamin
Britten*, pp. 24, 34-5, 46-7. Norman Del Mar, "Albert Herring," Ibid.,
pp. 148, 150, 156, 160, 161. Lennox Berkeley, "The Light Music," Ibid.,
p. 291. Eric Crozier, "Albert Herring—Arbeit am Libretto" in Dr. Heinrich
Lindlar, ed., *Musik der Zeit: Benjamin Britten, Das Oppernwerk* (Bonn:
Verlag Boosey and Hawkes, 1955), pp. 43-5.

In Britten's opera *A Midsummer Night's Dream*, the fairies sing
in an impressionistically veiled dissonant style; the lovers in repeated, merry
solo-phrases and recicatives snatched from each other's lips; and the
artisans in the finale in the strictly harmonic, parodied and itemized idiom
of Donizetti, Rossini and Verdi. Cf. Hugh Wood, "English Contemporary
Music" in Howard Hartog (ed.), *European Music in the Twentieth Century*
(Harmonsworth: Penguin Books, 1957), p. 159.

While Classical and Romantic variations/Beethoven's *Seven Variations
on a Theme from Mozart's The Magic Flute*, Brahms's *Variations on a
Theme by Haydn*, Tchaikovsky's *Variations on a Rococo Theme* or Elgar's
Enigma Variations/usually have three main structural units/theme, character
variations, and theme resumed, enhanced and "owned"/, the witty set of
Britten's *Purcell Variations* possesses the above four sections/theme,
character variations, fugue and fugue plus theme restated, increased and
"disowned"/: here the attitude of emotional identification is replaced by
the stance of ironical disassociation, comic alienation.

Joyce and Joyceans: A Critical View on the Problem of Institutionalization

Gottlieb Gaiser
Konstanz, F. R. G.

I

The volume in hand has been compiled from papers presented during a three-week Joyce course at the Inter-University Centre of Postgraduate Studies in Dubrovnik (May 1981)—an outstanding academic and a great social event. Sixteen resource persons and twenty-two students from eleven countries had assembled—many of them at their own expense—to discuss Joyce's works. Not many writers have been honoured by special conferences outside the regular university courses. But with Joyce, there is nothing extraordinary about it. Every year, a considerable number of similar events take place. In 1981, a five day symposium was also held in Albuquerque, New Mexico, a four day event in Pittsburgh, Pennslyvania, and a number of meetings on a smaller scale, like those organized by the James Joyce Societies of New York and Washington, D. C.

Most participants at such conferences are acquainted with one another, as their common field of research offers enough opportunities to keep contact—friends through Joyce. Geographical distance becomes irrelevant at least every two or three years, when an International James Joyce Symposium takes place: almost all Joyce specialists attend these big events in Trieste, Paris, Zürich, or Dublin. The symposia do not only provide a competent forum for discussion and a survey of current research work, but are also the scene of numerous cultural and social events, some of which cannot hide a touch of irrationality. When in 1982 the VIII International James Joyce Symposium will be held in Dublin—the James Joyce Foundation expects it to be "the largest gathering of Joyce scholars, critics, students, and readers ever assembled"[1]—, it will traditionally include the date on which the fictional events of *Ulysses* take place (fictionally "took place" in 1904), and which no Joycean will ever forget: June 16—Bloomsday. There will be a walking tour in Bloom's footsteps, to the demolished site of Number Seven Eccles Street and to the Ormond Hotel, to that part of Dublin where "Nighttown" had been and to Davy Byrnes'. The day will be concluded with an extravagant dinner that might well be spoiled by "Kidneys à la Bloom" served after the dessert. Even in the years between the symposia, Bloomsday will be commemorated and celebrated in more or less official meetings or in private circles, with genuine Irish whiskey, preferably JJ & Son, and Fendant de Sion. Such traces of ritual may reveal a certain resemblance of Joyce criticism to a fan-club, but they also indicate a strong in-group consciousness that has even found its way into language. "Joycean," as most Joyce specialists choose to call themselves, was not listed in the 1961 edition of the *Oxford English Dictionary* (comprising the English vocabulary up to 1933), but has now been entered in the current *Supplement*, both as an adjective ("Of, pertaining to, or characteristic of the Irish writer James Joyce (1882-1941), or his work") and as a noun to label an "admirer or follower of Joyce."[2] While philosophical schools are conventionally named after their founder, this practice at least is unusual in literary criticism.

Joyce's position in the topography of literature is indeed remarkable in many respects. Despite a comparatively small body of writing, his high rank in literary history is undisputed. His lasting influence on literary production is acknowledged in all sorts of encyclopedias as well as by contemporary novelists. The number of scholarly works on Joyce is piling up on the shelves of university libraries, by far surpassing the reading capacity even of a specialist. Robert Deming's 1977 *Bibliography of James Joyce Studies* lists no fewer than 5885 items, while the 1964 edition had only 1434 entries.[3] And the "Joyce industry"[4] keeps producing without any sign of a recession. 1982, the year of the centenary of Joyce's birthday, is expected to be a peak year with special issues of periodicals, and dozens of new books. Even in the years with less favourable market conditions there is a regular platform for the publication of material and articles on Joyce and his works; presently, the Joyce community has three periodicals at their disposal: the *James Joyce Quarterly,* the *James Joyce Broadsheet,* and *A Wake Newslitter.* Joyce does indeed "keep the university professors busy."[5]

But at the same time, he remains "caviare to the general," as Sisley Huddleston had predicted in one of the earliest reviews of *Ulysses.*[6] Sales rates seem to contradict this view, for at least *Ulysses* is selling extremely well: in 1972, fifty years after its first publication, Random House had sold 880,000 copies, and Penguin had sold 300,000 of the paperback edition after only four years.[7] Here, a bonus is at work which is characteristic of a certain category of longsellers: *Ulysses* has become a modern classic. Once a book has been established in the literary canon, its material existence is secured, for generations of students will have to buy it because it is included in their reading lists. However, the high percentage of students who started to read *Ulysses* but failed to finish it should be an indicator of the book's fate with a general reading public. The fact that such negative experiences do not affect Joyce's firm position in the literary hierarchy in turn, exposes the authoritative character of the canon. It owes its existence to a self-defined cultural elite consisting of creative writers and members of university departments. So Joyce's "after-life" continues mainly in artistic and academic circles, and, even here, it is practically restricted to a single work, the title of which is used almost interchangeably with its author's name: *Ulysses.*[8] References to *Ulysses* no longer have to be justified, for integration in the literary canon presupposes a consensus concerning its evaluation. At the same time, the pre-canonical stages of reception are faded out; the central problems of the past are remembered only as marginal notes, mocked at as errors of an age that had not been ripe for *Ulysses.* One is tempted to nod in approval. And yet—

When *Ulysses* was published in 1922, literature was already on its way to modernity. Such eminent writers as Proust, Gide, Kafka, and Bely, Pirandello, Pound, Eliot, Valéry, and Rilke had already changed the character of literature. In the wake of Symbolism and Naturalism, the literary scene Imagism, Dadaism, Futurism in its initial phase, etc. In their avant-garde movements: Expressionism, Cubism, Vorticism, Imagism, Dadaism, Futurism, in its initial phase, etc. In their manifestos, these isms professed more or less antitraditional and esoteric programmes, their artistic productions were highly experimental, in many respects more radical than *Ulysses*, both in form and in content. But still they were only experiments on a small scale; Joyce was the man to incorporate such bits and pieces in an ambitious project, into an avant-garde *book.* So Joyce did have recourse to an appropriate level of "material," to use Adorno's wording; *Ulysses* was, in fact, "due," at least artistically.

Joyce's contemporaries apparently had not caught up with the development within the field of literature and failed to do justice to the achievement of *Ulysses*. Its initial difficulties and subsequent ban, however, cannot be accounted for merely by reference to cognitive problems of its audience. Such an argument would foster the illusion that literary history is moving along purely aesthetic lines, with literary quality as the only criterion of evaluation. This "intrinsic fallacy"[9] suppresses the pragmatic dimension of literature, which is not just a gratuitous frame but a formative influence. Canonization, in particular, may be shown to be the result not only of selection based on literary principles, but also of authority, personal interests, and social strategies. The political schema of power and suppression, as Pierre Bourdieu points out,[10] also enters the field of "symbolic goods," turning nonconformity into an attempt to overthrow the existing hierarchy. Literary history, rewritten after the ultimate success of the Modernist revolution, tends to disregard such struggles for dominance, keeping up the notion of literary immanence and the myth of continuity. A reconsideration of the decades between the publication of *Ulysses* and its institutional acceptance, however, will provide sufficient evidence to shatter the belief in literary evolution on purely aesthetic grounds.

II

The avant-garde movements completed a development towards esotericism that had started with the dissociation of a literary elite from the bourgeois public at the beginning of the nineteenth century (mind the seeming continuity of literary history!). But, at the same time, the avant-garde revolted against the established cultural elite and their pretensions to legitimacy. The perpetuation of the antagonism to a general reading public, on the one hand, and the rejection of the dominant literary tradition, on the other, left the avant-garde artist in a self-chosen state of isolation and alienation. Communication was consequently restricted to other intellectuals sharing similar attitudes. This constellation naturally favoured the formation of coherent groups, a number of which became centres of artistic movements. As avant-garde literature neither was nor wanted to be accepted by the established media, in-group organs were founded to evade the gate-keeper function of traditional periodicals. The progressive literary scene "took place" in a multitude of strictly non-commercial "little magazines" and "little reviews" with very low circulations, fairly undisturbed by dominant standards of control.

This short sketch of the situation of avant-garde literature in the early twenties reveals striking parallels to Thomas S. Kuhn's periods of scientific revolutions.[11] Such a period, which interrupts the cumulative progress of "normal science," is marked by the emergence of a new paradigm that proves to be incompatible with the established one, and, consequently, is rejected by the—essentially conservative—scientific community. Only if a number of specialists, disregarding the effective mechanisms of control, apply the innovatory paradigm in their research and succeed in producing convincing results, are there prospects of eventual legitimacy. Innovation stands or falls with the social basis supporting it. After an initial stage of consolidation within the paradigm group, therefore, strategies are developed both to recruit disciples and to solicit institutional security. These pragmatic steps toward directing the process of institutionalization are taken with an ultimate goal in mind: the predominance in an area of research. An innovatory paradigm that attains this goal loses its former revolutionary character and introduces a new period of "normal science."[12]

The avant-garde with their doctrine of innovation certainly represented a revolutionary paradigm within the field of literature. The creation of their own channels of communication and publication both provided a basis for inner consolidation and secured their artistic independence. But outstanding literary achievements were scarce; *Ulysses* was one.

Although Joyce was not committed to any of the avant-garde movements, his work is intimately connected with them and is clearly written in their spirit. So it is no accident that more than half of *Ulysses* first appeared in the *Little Review, a Magazine of the Arts—Making no Compromise with*

The Public Taste. But even the readers of this organ of progressive art were divided on the evaluation of a text that had
been announced as "a prose masterpiece."[13]   Such eminent
authors as Ezra Pound, who himself had promoted the
publication of Joyce's work, T. S. Eliot, or the young Hart
Crane were absolutely enthusiastic about the first chapters of
Ulysses, while others complained that writers like Joyce were
becoming "too clever even for coterie."[14]   The discussion
within the *intelligentsia* was interrupted by a non-literary,
but authoritative verdict that forced the editors of the *Little
Review* to stop the serial publication of *Ulysses* after 23 in-
stalments (1918-20), four of which had been confiscated by
the postal authorities: a New York court, to which the case
was taken by the Society for the Suppression of Vice, ruled
that *Ulysses* was obscene.

    After this verdict, the chances of finding an American
or English publisher for the completed work were reduced to
a minimum.   Once more, friends stepped in to help Joyce—and
the cause of the avant-garde.   Sylvia Beach, the owner of an
avant-garde bookshop in Paris, decided to become a publisher,
if only of one book.   When *Ulysses* was eventually published,
the 1,000 copies of the first edition were sold within a month.
Despite a campaign to promote this difficult and expensive
book written in a foreign language, the success was unexpected.
But the high praise by prominent poets and its ban in the United
States had roused the interest of a larger literary public as well
as that of pornography hunters.   While reports of satisfaction
with the latter are scarce, the former were less secretive about
their experiences with *Ulysses* and entered into a very lively
discussion.[15]

    With its *public*-ation as a book, *Ulysses*—at least po-
tentially—has left the hermetic circle to which it had been
confined by the *appear*-ance in an avant-garde magazine. Up
to this point, reactions had been limited to a narrow circle
of the initiated; the book, however, is principally accessible
to everybody.   The journalistic reception of *Ulysses* is therefore pre-structured by an insider-outsider dichotomy.   Avant-
garde critics, on the one hand, share the background and the
premises of progressive art and conceive of themselves as
members and advocates of a literary elite.   Traditional critics,
on the other hand, lack the initiation required for an understanding of the avant-garde.   Guided by established literary

values and the prevalent moral code, they are likely to judge an avant-garde work by the very standards which that work may be trying to abrogate.

The early reviews of *Ulysses* fully confirm this argument. Most of the reviews written by representatives of a bourgeois public even fall short of a literary evaluation: Joyce's work, officially branded as incompatible with the prevailing norms and values, is mainly excoriated on grounds of decency, morals, and religion. Where its artistic qualities are considered all the same, they are hardly ever appreciated, as they do not comply with such standards as "balance, rhythm, harmony, and reverence for simple majesty."[16] Joyce's bourgeois critics counter his challenge to both literary and social conventions by dismissing him as an artist. On a pragmatic level, the repudiation of *Ulysses* by exponents of the literary tradition must be rated as a measure to bar the aspiration of an innovatory paradigm toward legitimacy.[17]

Whereas the serial publication of *Ulysses* had been discussed controversially within the avant-garde, their book reviews displayed a high degree of concordance,[18] as they were also directed against the bourgeois attempts at suppressing progressive art as such. In their criticism, therefore, they defended Joyce against conservative attacks and, at the same time, tried to contribute to a more adequate understanding of the text. Joyce himself was actively engaged in soliciting favourable reviews from friends and critics. In a way, he even influenced the direction of the critical discussion. Just before *Ulysses* was published, Valéry Larbaud was allowed to use Joyce's schema of correspondences in order to hand on these—so far secret—informations. And when Joyce felt that the Homeric parallels had not been sufficiently appreciated by his reviewers, he induced T. S. Eliot to cover this deficiency.[19] It is not by chance that Larbaud, Eliot, and Pound were the authors of the three most important early essays on *Ulysses*. Creative writers themselves, most influential within the avant-garde, enthusiastic about *Ulysses*, and friends of Joyce, they tried to support what they regarded to be a grand work of literature as best they could. In turn, their own work was greatly influenced by Joyce, as were the literary productions of many young writers. Ford Madox Ford had predicted this development:

> Certain books change the world. This, success or failure,
> *Ulysses* does: for no novelist with serious aims can hence-
> forth set out upon a task of writing before he has at least
> formed his own private estimate as to the rightness or
> wrongness of the methods of the author of *Ulysses*. If
> it does not make an epoch—and it well may!—it will at
> least mark the ending of a period.[20]

While established authors were not willing to change their literary practice, a new generation of writers, in search of the most adequate mode of expression, followed the path paved by Joyce and the avant-garde, thus giving a comparatively broad social basis to the innovatory paradigm. Acceptance, however, was restricted to the field of literary production. The power to allot legitimacy and to revise the literary canon rested with the literary establishment: represented by the academic institutions and acknowledged by the bourgeois public.

For almost twenty years, Joyce was practically ignored by academic critics. During that time, it was again Joyce's friends and avant-garde intellectuals who, after the flood of reviews had ebbed, kept alive the sympathetic discussion of *Ulysses*. Joyce's academic presence seemed to be largely confined to his mention in histories of the novel, but seldom was their level of argumentation above that of bourgeois reviewers. Joyce's treatment by A. C. Ward, John Cunliffe, E. M. Forster, Herbert Read, or even Edwin Muir was hardly apt to repudiate Edmund Gosse's early verdict: "There are no English critics of weight or judgment who consider Mr. Joyce an author of any importance."[21] The situation began to change when, thanks to a sympathetic judge, the ban over *Ulysses* was lifted and the book could be published both in the USA (1934) and in England (1936). But it was only on occasion of Joyce's death that the first monograph written by an academic appeared:[22] Harry Levin's *James Joyce: A Critical Introduction* (Norfolk, 1941).

The long period between the publication of *Ulysses* and the beginning of its academic reception cannot only be accounted for by a self-imposed delay of a literary criticism that does not want to "compromise itself by unduly engaging in the fluctuating traffic of revaluation."[23] What Levin's words conceal so nicely is the connection between academic criticism and literary legitimacy, the tenacity with which an institution clings to the values and conventions it once has accepted.

Academic criticism stopped ignoring Joyce only after it was no longer able to account for a major part of contemporary literature, which was based on a different paradigm.

Levin's initiative certainly "helped to make Joyce 'respectable' within the academic community,"[24] but it took another six years before Richard Kain's *Fabulous Voyager* (Chicago, 1947) introduced a period of serious and productive critical work on Joyce, characterized by a flood of articles and books published in the fifties. The continuously expanding discussion of Joyce's works soon required a special forum. In this function, the *James Joyce Review*[25] was founded in 1957. Marvin Magalaner expressed the changed attitude of academic criticism in his preface to the second series of *Joyce Miscellanies* (1959): "most writers on Joyce today go at their tasks with quiet confidence. There is no longer a need for the extravagances of literary manifestoes—for loud proclaiming of the rightness and seriousness of their labours."[26]

Joyce scholarship had apparently reached the stage of respectability. And so had Joyce. After his acceptance by academic critics, he had finally been admitted to the most conservative of literary institutions: the literary canon as the codification of the established paradigm. *Ulysses* was no longer revolutionary; it had attained legitimacy. The need for justification had shifted from the adherents of Joyce to his adversaries, as Bernard Benstock states in an account of 1966:

> There can be little doubt that Joyce's position in the literary heavens as a star of the first magnitude is a fixed one, and the tone of recent books on Joyce indicates the solid degree of awareness on the part of contemporary critics that his 'genius' can be referred to without apology. Should they intend to attack, it is apparent that they must do so with the necessary precautions one takes against a well-entrenched adversary.[27]

To keep metaphors blooming: Joyce is now within the walls that had resisted his assaults for so long. The former rebel against literary tradition has turned into one of its staunchest representatives.

III

Joyce's acceptance by the academic community is both a milestone and an indication of a more comprehensive shift of paradigms. Literary criticism has adopted the heterogeneous concept of Modernism as their new paradigm, including the avant-garde principle of innovation. The superseded tradition, accordingly, did not only lose its predominance but also its validity in the contemporary context. Its former significance was relativized by a historical perspective, and thus sacrificed to the requirements of literary history and the continuity of a seemingly teleological development.

The belated institutionalization of Modernism primarily responded to changes in the field of literary production, as was shown in the previous section. But it had also been favoured by non-literary conditions. As universities began to lose their privileged character and became accessible to a broader public, the increasing number of students had to be met with a corresponding growth in academic capacity. Literature departments were no exception: more and more scholars were employed to teach within a fairly limited area of research. Reputation and status, however, proved to be dependent on the quality and the quantity of publications. And scholarly work was published only if it fulfilled the requirement of originality, introduced new aspects into research, or "contributed" to the alleged progress within a special field. As a consequence, the academic critic was constantly involved in a competitive struggle. In this situation, a kind of literature that deliberately precluded the plain reader and even refused to disclose an unequivocal meaning opened possibilities far beyond a mere expansion of research into areas that had been previously marginal or suppressed. Modernist literature not only exposed the illusoriness of the belief in definitive interpretation, but also provided a body of works that could function as a test case of scholarly discussions *ad infinitum*. Since the academic critic is obliged to be both productive and original, "he has a certain vested interest in devoting himself to works that are by nature complex and subject to elaborate decoding,"[28] as Malcolm Bradbury does not fail to mention. *Ulysses* certainly belongs to this category, *Finnegans Wake* marks its limits.

Once Modernism had been established as the working

paradigm, its revolutionary character became neutralized *via* codification.   Its potential qualities were re-discovered only recently, when post-structuralist philosophers like Jacques Lacan or post-modernist critics like Ihab Hassan started to apply modernist principles to literary criticism—notably of Joyce's works—, transposing the implications of a changed world-view into theoretical discourse.   This critical avant-garde, in turn, occupies an outsider position within the academic community, which rejects their practice on the same grounds as it advocates avant-garde criteria in the field of literary pro-duction.   This moment of inertia is inherent to all institutions, and characterizes their essentially conservative attitude toward paradigmatic change.   Revolutionary patterns are only likely to be institutionalized if they promise to re-establish the stability of an institution that had no longer been able to cope with its very subject matter or area of application.

In the case of Modernism, symbolic power had been allotted to a different concept of art, which has since served as a new standard of evaluation.   The dominant paradigm had changed, but the structures of legitimacy remained untouched. Innovation had become the measuring rod for twentieth century works of art, and it is still the valid criterion for judging con-temporary literature.   But what room is there left for innovation after Joyce and Beckett have drawn the lines of demarcation: can anything go beyond *Finnegans Wake* (1939), on the one hand, and *Imagination Dead Imagine* (1966), on the other? Most of this continuum has been exhausted by now, and literary production has consequently been moving away from innovation and experiments for more than two decades.   But present-day writers are still being judged on the basis of modernist (or post-modernist) criteria.   Is this the reason why literary critics—notably Joyceans—are constantly complaining about the present state of literature?   Certain parallels to Joyce's pre-canonical stages are evident; but now *Ulysses* represents the tradition which cannot do justice to a changed literary scene.   The institutionalization of the modernist principle of innovation has paradoxically turned innovation as such into a conservative concept.   The professedly progressive Joyceans, being eminent representatives of the established paradigm, are actually in danger of becoming dogmatic conservatives, who tend to judge contemporary works of literature according to standards of the past, while neglecting contemporary developments within the field of literary production.

Notes

[1] James Joyce Foundation Newsletter 37, (Sept. 1981), p. 1.

[2] A Supplement to the Oxford English Dictionary, ed. by R. W. Burchfield, vol. 2: H-N, (Oxford: Clarendon, 1976), p. 440, cols. 2 f. According to the professed criteria of the *OED*, "Joycean" has apparently developed into one of the "words that have formed the English vocabulary" (cf. *OED*, vol. 1, "Preface").

[3] See Robert H. Deming, *A Bibliography of James Joyce Studies*, Lawrence, Kans. (University of Kansas Libraries, 1964); (Bostton, Mass.: Hall, 1977), rev. & enl.

[4] Cf. Bernard Benstock, "The James Joyce Industry: an Assessment in the Sixties," *Southern Rev.* 2 (1966), pp. 210-28.

[5] Joyce, as related by Jacques Benoîst-Méchin, who wanted to see the *Ulysses* schema. Quoted in: Richard Ellmann, *James Joyce*, New York, etc., (Oxford University Press, 1959), p. 535.

[6] Rev. *Ulysses*, in: *Observer*, (5 March 1922), p. 4. Quoted in: Robert H. Deming (ed.), *James Joyce: The Critical Heritage*, 2 vols., (London: Routledge & Kegan Paul, 1970), p. 214.

[7] Cf. Thomas F. Staley (ed.), *Ulysses: Fifty Years*, (Bloomington and London: Indiana University Press, 1974), p. vii.

[8] Cf. Rosemarie Franke, "Die Rezeption des *Ulysses* im deutschen Sprachbereich: Übersetzung, Verbreitung und Kritik," in: Therese Fischer-Seidel (ed.), *James Joyces, Ulysses: Neuere deutsche Aufsatze*, (Frankfurt/M.: Suhrkamp, 1977), pp. 105-59. An examination of "Joyce"–articles in encyclopedia confirms her statement "daß der Name Joyce oftmals als Synonym fur den Werktitel [*Ulysses*] verstanden werden darf" (p. 113).

[9] A slightly belated attack against René Wellek and Austin Warren, *Theory of Literature*, (New York: Harcourt, Brace & World, 1949), and the New Critics.

[10] See Pierre Bourdieu, *Zur Soziologie der symbolischen Formen*, (Frankfurt/M.: Suhrkamp, 1970). Cf. also Jacques Dubois, *L'institution de la littérature*, (Brussels: Labor, 1979).

[11] See Thomas S. Kuhn, *The Structure of Scientific Revolutions*,

(Chicago: University of Chicago Press, 1962).

[12]Cf., in particular, Peter Weingart, "Wissenschaftlicher Wandel als Institutionalisierungsstrategie," in: Weingart (ed.), *Wissenschaftssoziologie II: Determinanten wissenschaftlicher Entwickliung*, (Frankfurt/M.: Athenaum Fischer, 1974), pp. 11-35.

[13]Margaret Anderson (ed. *Little Review*), quoted in: Forrest Read (ed.), *Pound/Joyce: The Letters of Ezra Pound to James Joyce, with Pound's Essays on Joyce*, (London: Faber & Faber, 1968), p. 130.

[14]Alfred R. Orage, "The Too Clever," in: *The New Age*, (6 June 1918). Quoted in: Marvin Magalaner and Richard M. Kain, *Joyce: The Man, The Work, The Reputation*, (New York: Collier, 1956), p. 173.

[15]In 1922, *Ulysses* was reviewed at least 58 times.

[16]S. P. B. Mais, "An Irish Rebel: And Some Flappers," *Daily Express* (London), 25 March 1922, n. pag. Quoted in: Deming (ed.), *Critical Heritage* (ref. n. 6), p. 191.

[17]A prime example of the collision between a new paradigm aspiring to legitimacy and the old paradigm defending its supremacy is provided by a later incident (1931). The B.B.C. had planned a programme on Joyce, a radio series of lectures on modern literature. But its transmission was barred by the protest of influential literary conservatives like Alfred Noyes and Douglas Jerrold. Their intrigue to keep avant-garde literature out of the mass media roused the indignation of many literary intellectuals (also outside the avant-garde), who demonstrated their solidarity with a manifesto against the suppression of the Joyce programme (among the signers: Eliot, Forster, Huxley, Shaw, Woolf; Blackwell, Cape, Longman). To a certain degree, they were successful. After a month's delay, Harold Nicolson's lecture was broadcast, but—he had been forbidden to mention *Ulysses*.

[18]John M. Murry's review in *Nation & Athenaeum* (22 April 1922), pp. 124 f., is an exception. To a politically and socially engaged avant-garde, *Ulysses* must have been a disappointment. "By the excess of his anarchy, Mr. Joyce makes himself socially harmless. There is not the faintest need to be concerned about his influence. He will have some, no doubt; but it will be canalized and concentrated. The head that is strong enough to read *Ulysses* will not be turned by it." Quoted in: Deming (ed.), *Critical Heritage* (ref. n. 6), p. 196.

[19]Cf. Ellmann, *Joyce* (ref. n. 5), p. 541. Eliot did so in his famous "*Ulysses*, Order and Myth," in: *Dial* 75/5, Nov. 1923, pp. 480-83. Joyce applied the same strategy after a severe attack by Wyndham Lewis, who, in *Time and Western Man* (London: Chatto & Windus, 1927), also reproached him for his formlessness. He asked his friend Stuart Gilbert to write a "study" on the painstaking organization of *Ulysses*, for which he

supplied most of the material himself. So Gilbert can proudly mention: "indeed there are several passages which I directly owe to him." (*James Joyce's Ulysses: A Study*, (London: Faber & Faber, 1930), (New York: Vintage, 1952), p. viii.

[20] Signed: Hueffer, "A Haughty and Proud Generation," in: *Yale Review* 35, Dec. 1922, pp. 538-48. Quoted in: Deming (ed.), *Critical Heritage* (ref. n. 6), p. 129.

[21] Letter to Louis Gillet, dated 7 June 1924. Quoted in: Gillet, *Stèle pour James Joyce*, (Marseilles: Sagittaire, 1941), p. 182.

[22] Myles Hanley's *Word Index to James Joyce's Ulysses* (Madison: University of Wisconsin Press) was published as early as 1937, but that book's genuine interest was to test a new method of indexing; its subject is rather incidental. Cf. Hanley's "Introduction," pp. 1 ff.

[23] Harry Levin, "Leech-Gathering," in: *TLS* 52, 26 July 1963, p. 565, col. 2.

[24] Thomas F. Staley, "James Joyce," p. 386, in: Richard J. Finneran (ed.), *Anglo-Irish Literature: A Review of Research*, (New York: Mod. Lang. Ass. of America, 1976), pp. 366-435.

[25] Due to financial difficulties, the *Review* had to be stopped in 1959, but it was replaced by the *James Joyce Quarterly* in 1963.

[26] Marvin Magalaner (ed.), *A James Joyce Miscellany: Second Series*, (Carbondale, Ill.: Southern Illinois University Press, 1959), p. xv.

[27] Benstock, "Joyce Industry" (ref. n. 4), p. 215.

[28] Malcolm Bradbury, *The Social Context of Modern English Literature*, (Oxford: Blackwell, 1971), p. 133.